MURDER IN THE MILE HIGH CITY

The First 100 Years

Murder in the Mile High City

The First 100 Years

Linda Wommack

with Linda Jones

CAXTON PRESS
Caldwell, Idaho
2016

ISBN 978-087004-603-2

Library of Congress Cataloging-in-Publication Data

Names: Wommack, Linda, 1958- author.
Title: Murder in the Mile High City : the first hundred years / by Linda Wommack ; with Linda Jones.
Description: Caldwell, Idaho : Caxton Press, [2016] | Includes bibliographical references and index.
Identifiers: LCCN 2016015103 | ISBN 9780870046032 (alk. paper)
Subjects: LCSH: Murder--Colorado--Denver--Case studies. | Crime--Colorado--Denver--Case studies.
Classification: LCC HV6534.D45 W66 2016 | DDC 364.152/30978883--dc23 LC record available at https://lccn.loc.gov/2016015103

Lithographed and bound in the United States of America

CAXTON PRESS
Caldwell, Idaho
193928

TABLE OF CONTENTS

ILLUSTRATIONS

ACKNOWLEDGMENTS

First and foremost, my heartfelt thanks to friend and colleague, Linda Jones. It was during one of our many visits that she suggested such a book and very graciously contributed her time, effort, work, and research to this project.

The accounts of the forty-two murders contained in this work have been greatly enhanced by newspapers articles, editorials and interviews. To assemble the historic photographs, I relied once again on the fabulous work of friend, Coi E. Drummond-Gerhig, Digital Image Collection Administrator for the Denver Public Library. This was a vital aspect to the content of the book, as photos of the crime scenes, victims, and murderers were essential for this book. The archives at the Denver Public Library Western History Department were instrumental in the extensive research of each of these murder accounts.

In the volumes written about various aspects of Denver's unique history, there is not a book devoted to the compilation of various murders in Denver's first hundred years. Not only does this work fill that void, it also offers an overview of the controversial death penalty through the decades.

I am indebted to the many museum curators and directors who gave so freely of their time, offering their knowledge and assistance in the research, as well as providing additional photos. My thanks to the museum and archives of the Colorado State Penitentiary, including the Colorado State Penitentiary Index 1871 - 1973. Other sources accessed were the Local History Center, Canon City Public Library; the Denver Police Museum; the Colorado History Center, the National Archives and Records Administration at the Denver Federal Center, and the Arapahoe County District Court Records.

For actual crime statistics and court records, I relied on the following sources: Denver County District Court Records, Colorado State Archives Correction Records, and the Colorado State Division of Vital Statistics.

A few in-depth works on the subject in general added to this book of Denver's murder history. Of particular note was Stephen J. Leonard's excellent book, *Lynching in Colorado*, as well as *Going to Meet*

A Man; Denver's Last Legal Public Execution, written by Professor William M. King of the University of Colorado. Dick Kreck's excellent works on specific Denver murders, including Anton Woode, Isabel Springer and the Smaldones, were invaluable in my research.

Special thanks go to those who believed in this project and gave freely of their time and advice. First on that list is my husband Frank, who tolerated the many late nights of research and writing, and helped to work out the research obstacles. My sincere thanks to my dear friend, Connie Clayton, who was instrumental in helping with the concept of the book and didn't let me stray too far. Connie diligently edited the manuscript with wit and humor, and became my support line on many levels.

To all of you, I am most appreciative for your interest and support.

Linda Wommack
January 25, 2015.

INTRODUCTION

Murder and Mystery. The two seem to go hand in hand. Why a person commits murder is a mystery. Conversely, there is often mystery surrounding murder.

Through mounds of research, over several years, Linda Jones and I found both in the accounts of Denver murders included in this book. *Murder in the Mile High City* contains forty-two accounts of murder and mystery during the first century of Denver's history.

In 1858, the year the city was founded, three murders occurred within the span of a month. Denver officials, in an attempt to establish some sort of local law and order, created The People's Court.

Yet murder in the "Mile High" city continued. John Stuffle was the first murderer to appear before The People's Court. His trial was short and justice was swift. He was hanged the day after the court pronounced the death sentence, on April 9, 1859; the first semi-legal hanging in Denver City.

There are many interesting historical threads throughout this narrative of "Mile High" murder.

A mysterious, well-dressed gambler, Charley Harrison, arrives in Denver City and soon rescues his love interest, Ada LaMont, who also has a mysterious past, from a possible attempt at murder. Harrison then becomes involved in the murder story of Jack O'Neill, who has the dubious distinction of being the first burial in the City Cemetery, also known as "O'Neill's Ranch." Harrison again figures into our narrative when he rescues William N. Byers, owner of the *Rocky Mountain News*, from a mob bent on doing harm to Byers for editorials he had written regarding the character of Charley Harrison.

A true murder mystery in Denver's early years is that of Captain Silas Soule on April 23, 1865. Just days after he testified to the atrocities committed by Colonel John M. Chivington at the massacre at Sand Creek, Soule was murdered in the streets of Denver. The suspected assassin, identified by eyewitnesses as Private Charles W. Squiers, had once been under Chivington's command. It was widely suspected that Squiers was an assassin paid by Chivington himself. Chivington, who resigned his military commission, thereby escaping any charges, goes on to figure in several Denver murder incidents. He served as Denver's undersheriff during the hanging of Andrew Green in 1886. As the Arapahoe County coroner, he presided over the autopsy of Daniel Arata, hanged by vigilantes in 1893.

Vigilante justice often took many forms in Denver's early days. Along with the many hangings, there was mob violence, gang violence and riots. In 1875, members of an Italian mob murdered three men and a young boy. Racial tensions, fueled by politics, led to Denver's darkest day when the Chinese Riot of 1880 occurred, resulting in murder.

Mob violence, crime and murder continued through the decades. The most well-known name fitting this description were the Smaldone brothers, who, during their shady career in the latter half of the century, may or may not have been involved in murder. That mystery continues to this day.

There are legends in Denver's law enforcement that also figure prominently throughout the narrative. David J. Cook, who formed the Rocky Mountain Detective Association, was often called upon to assist with murder cases in Denver and across the region. In 1869, Cook was elected sheriff of Arapahoe County. He would become instrumental in solving the mystery of the Italian mob murders in 1873, as well as bringing an end to the Chinese riots in 1880. Famed Denver detective Sam Howe solved many of the murders in Denver's red light district, including the 1884 arrests of Bell Warden and Mattie Lemmon, prostitutes, who also killed for pleasure. Howe, along with Cook, was also involved in the 1886 murder case of Andrew Green. Convicted of murder, Green's public hanging became a horrifying spectacle, as the young man's body hung in the air for an agonizing fifteen minutes and he slowly strangled to death. As a result, this was Denver's last legal public hanging.

Denver police officer Harry Ohle died in the line of duty by a bullet fired by "Little" Eddie Ives, who then put another bullet into his partner, Denver police officer Robert Evans. Evans was recovering, only to be murdered in his hospital bed by Farice King, a jealous woman bent on revenge. *The Denver Post* reported the story, stating, "the tangled skein one bullet started." True enough.

As it turned out, "Little" Eddie Ives, who indeed fired the bullet, was convicted of murder and sentenced to death by hanging. On January 10, 1930, Ives was hanged at the Colorado State Penitentiary with the same mechanical contraption known as the "twitch-up" method, used in the botched hanging of Andrew Green in 1886. Just as that hanging went horribly wrong, so did the hanging of Ives. During the execution, the rope jumped off the pulley and Ives flew up to the ceiling and dropped back down to the floor. Ives squirmed and thrashed on the floor and yelled, "You can't hang a man twice." The executioners thought otherwise and hanged him again. The double hanging would eventually lead to the state's abolishment of death by hanging. On March 31, 1933, Governor of Colorado Edwin C. Johnson signed into law the bill allowing for lethal gas to be used for execution.

While there were plenty of female murderers, none ever received the death penalty in Colorado's history. A few may even have escaped a prison sentence simply because of gender. This very well may have been the case for Gertrude Gibson Patterson. On trial for the murder of her husband in 1911, she was declared not guilty by a jury of twelve men. One writer of that era later opined: "Yet if Charles A. Patterson were a contortionist as well as a roller skater, he might possibly have planted one bullet in his back — scarcely four. Anyway...it was a famous affair, and Mrs. Patterson had the nicest legs that were ever planted in a defendant's booth, which helped her more in 1911 than it might today, now that we have women on juries." The Patterson murder trial captivated the citizens of Denver, many of whom disagreed with the not guilty verdict. A month later, Angelina Garramone was convicted of first degree murder. When the judge gave her a sentence of life in prison, she shouted: "Life! Life! They give me life — but they let Patterson go and she commit murder." As if that weren't enough for the citizens of Denver, what has become known as the most sensational trial of Denver's first century was also taking place. Isabel Springer's extramarital affairs caused jealousy and revenge which led to murder at the Brown Palace Hotel. The murder trial was local and national news for months.

The innocence of children also figures in this tale of Denver murders. Pearl O'Loughlin was convicted of first degree murder in the death of her ten-year-old stepdaughter, Leona. She was sent to the Colorado State Penitentiary to serve a life sentence for feeding her stepdaughter rice laced with crushed glass. The triple murder trial of Bernice Williams, in 1943, sent shock waves through Denver and across the nation. Although convicted of only one count of murder, her confession to killing all three of her babies made national news. Eleven-year-old Lester Gordon Brown, Jr., was enjoying an innocent day at the circus in 1958 when he was lured away by a circus worker, sexually assaulted and murdered. And then there is the story of Anton Woode who was only twelve years old when he entered the Colorado State Penitentiary at Canon City on August 8, 1893. Convicted of first degree murder, Woode was the youngest person ever in the history of the United States to be convicted of murder and sent to prison.

Readers may be familiar with the notable murder mysteries in the latter half of Denver's first century. The infamous "Spiderman Murder" personifies the mystery in murder. Convicted of murder in 1942, Theodore Coneys spent the rest of his life in prison where he died in 1967. In 1955, when John Gilbert Graham placed explosives in his mother's suitcase, prior to her airline flight, he not only became one of the most infamous killers in America history, his actions made him the first mass murderer by means of an airline. The United Airlines airplane exploded over the Colorado prairie, killing all on board, including Graham's mother. Sentenced to death, twenty-five year old Graham served one of the shortest prison terms. He was executed in the gas chamber at the Colorado State Penitentiary in January 1957.

Mystery and murder. Why would someone murder a priest at the altar of the church? Could it be a case of an alter ego and a secret life?

Murder in the Mile High City. It happened in the first century of Denver's history. It happens today. These are just a few of the mystery murders found in the archives of the city's first hundred years.

Denver Public Library, Western History Department

Denver street scene, 1865.

Part I

1858 - 1879

The area that would become the city of Denver was in the middle of the region known as "The Great American Desert." It would become the birthplace of the Colorado gold rush. Largely ignored by the Spaniards and Europeans, it was deemed worthless and hardly worth any effort to settle the land or challenge the Arapaho or Cheyenne Indians who often wintered near the river. Yet, with the discovery of gold, Denver's destiny was laid out.

Gold had been discovered at the confluence of the South Platte River and Cherry Creek in 1858 by William Greenberry Russell, creating mass migration the likes of which the Rocky Mountain region had never seen. William McKibben, a member of the Russell party, later recounted:

> *Our joy knew no bounds, we huzzaed, whooped and yelled at the prospect of being loaded with gold in a few months, and gave vent to any amount of hisses and groans for our apostate companions that were making all speed for home. We congratulated ourselves, sir, that we inaugurated a new era in the history of our beloved country.*[1]

In the midst of this frenzy, a town was created. Tent cities and eventually log cabins were erected on both sides of Cherry Creek. The town of Auraria lay on the west bank, while Denver City was laid out on the east side. By 1859, Denver City, named for the Kansas Territorial Governor, James W. Denver, became the primary stopover site to the riches held by the Rocky Mountains. General William Larimer of Leavenworth, Kansas, laid out the town of Denver City with a futuristic eye. Denver, "The Queen City," as she would come to be called, would soon encompass the land east of the Platte River,

1

nearer to Cherry Creek, with plenty of room for growth. Merchants and businessmen organized the bustling tent town into a sense of permanence. Businesses opened, homes were built and trees were cleared.

Governor Denver sent a group of men to Denver City to set up a formal government, including law enforcement. He asked three of his closest friends to fill the need. They were Hickory Rogers, Judge H. P. A. Smith and Edward Wynkoop.

By April 1859, William Newton Byers had printed his first edition of the *Rocky Mountain News*, and proudly editorialized the virtues of the growing city.

And so they came. Among the miners, the businessmen and the future politicians were the bummers, the gamblers, the prostitutes and the gunslingers. It was a lawless atmosphere of the West. One of the pioneers of Denver City, William Parsons, wrote of his arrival in 1858:

> *The gambler, horse-thief, and more accomplished desperado...the vice and hideous deformities incident to new countries grown suddenly populous will be seen in this the newest one of all.* [2]

Parsons would be proven right, as murder and mayhem rocked the early days of Denver.

* * *

Murder and The People's Court
Hang 'em High

By the time William Byers issued his first edition of the *Rocky Mountain News* on April 23, 1859, three murders had occurred in the new city.

With the discovery of gold in the Pikes Peak region of Kansas Territory, the government officials in Kansas were slow in establishing law enforcement due to the sudden influx of people to the area. In an effort to establish some sort of law and order, given the recent murders, the citizens of Denver City took action by assembling a People's Court. This was a common practice on the frontier. Desperate

The first *Rocky Mountain News* building was built in the dry bed of Cherry Creek. It was later washed away in a horrific flood.

Denver Public Library, Western History Department

Denver Public Library, Western History Dept. William N. Byers, owner and publisher of Denver's first newspaper, the *Rocky Mountain News.*

for some sort of law, a public meeting was held by both of the Cherry Creek settlements, Auraria and Denver City, on April 11, 1859, to address the issue of legal law enforcement. *The Rocky Mountain News* covered the outcome of the meeting in the first issue of the paper:

At a meeting of the citizens of Auraria and Denver City held at Wootton's Hall, on the evening of the 11th inst., a motion was carried and resolved. 'Resolved, That on account of our distance and from, and difficulty of communicating with the proper authorities, we the people who are the power here, authorize the late county officers-elect to enter at once upon the discharge of their respective duties, without waiting for their commissions from the Governor, after having given the proper bonds.[3]

Judge Seymour, selected to serve on the People's Court, agreed with this sentiment, as he had little use for the authority of Kansas officials. Believing in the citizens of Denver City, he said: "...we the people are the power here."

The People's Court of Denver City, and the entire Pikes Peak region for that matter, would serve in history to be the most complete record of such an assembly of territorial jurisdiction. And it wasn't always pretty.

The People's Court worked as needed. There were no salaries for the judges and no set court fees. Generally, the court worked with an open mind and presumably without prejudice. When in session, the People's Court worked under the laws of Kansas Territory and included a judge, a jury of twelve citizens, lawyers for both sides, and witness testimony. The court sessions were always held in public forums with invited citizen participation.

With the early settlement of the Rocky Mountain region due to the discovery of gold, it is no surprise that the first case of murder to be heard by the People's Court involved gold, greed and revenge.

A man by the name of Binegraff, his first name being lost to history, and his two sons arrived in the area of the Cherry Creek gold diggings in 1858. They had a small cattle ranch north of the city on Vasquez Fork, now known as Clear Creek, just east of present-day Arvada. A third son, Arthur, along with Binegraff's son-in-law, John Stuffle, left their home back East, to work on the new family enterprise.[4]

On the morning of April 6, 1859, Binegraff and his older son left the dugout cabin to round up stray cattle, leaving the younger son, Arthur, and Stuffle behind. Returning to the homestead that evening, the group found both Arthur and Stuffle missing. The next morning, with no sign of either party, a search was conducted by the Binegraff men. It wasn't long before the family discovered the body of Arthur behind a log, with a bullet in his head. The murder scene was near the juncture of Clear Creek and Ralston Creek, near today's 56th Avenue and Sheridan Boulevard.

Meanwhile, that very morning, a weary-worn John Stuffle arrived in Denver City, where he immediately made his way to "Uncle" Dick Wootton's saloon and proceeded to have a good time, paying with gold dust. Stuffle's strange appearance — witnesses would claim his clothing was blood-stained — as well as his behavior, aroused suspicion. When the Binegraff men arrived in town later that morning to report the murder, Stuffle was immediately arrested and confessed. He admitted he had accompanied Arthur Binegraff to the Rocky Mountain region for the express reason to kill him, although he did not elaborate as to the reason for such vengeance. He further stated the gold dust he had been spending all morning had been taken from the dead man's body.

Stuffle's admission made the first trial by the People's Court of Denver City an open and shut case.

Court convened that very afternoon with Judge Seymour W. Wagoner presiding. Stuffle was provided an attorney, and the prosecuting attorney was selected, as were twelve jurors. The trial was held at an outdoor venue. The trial was short and sweet and made even shorter by the defendant. When Stuffle took the stand, he again admitted to the murder and gave a motive that he wanted the gold dust in Binegraff's possession. (The gold dust Stuffle spent at Wootton's saloon amounted to ten dollars.) The jury took precious little time in returning a unanimous verdict of murder.

James Pierce, one of the founding fathers, later recalled:

> *The evidence was all heard in profound silence by the mass. I never witnessed a more orderly trial in any court in my life than this was. Of course we found him guilty of murder in the first degree.*[5]

Judge Wagoner now found himself in a precarious position. Wagoner, while elected locally as probate judge for the newly-created Arapahoe County in Kansas Territory, had not yet been approved by the Kansas authorities. This technicality was either lost on or did not concern the jury who decided the defendant's punishment as death. This caused a second dilemma for Judge Wagoner.

There was no jail to hold the convicted Stuffle. The jury and the crowd were unanimous in their solution to the dilemma; hang him. And so, the next day, April 9, 1859, the first semi-legal hanging in Denver City occurred.

A crowd of nearly a thousand citizens gathered around an old cottonwood tree in the area of McGaa and 10th streets to witness the hanging. Richens "Dick" Wootton himself described the scene:

> *Three men got into a two-horse wagon and were driven under a cottonwood tree on the bank of Cherry Creek. These three men were the prisoner, the executioner, and a minister. A rope was placed around the murderer's neck and thrown over a limb of the tree. Then the minister, a good Christian man, kneeled down in the wagon to offer up a prayer, and the executioner also got on his knees. The fellow was to be hanged didn't follow their example, but stood up, until the executioner poked him in the ribs, and asked him if he didn't know better than to act like a heathen. After prayer the wagon was driven out from under the tree, and the man who had murdered his friend, to get possession of a few dollar's worth of gold dust, was left*

dangling from the cottonwood limb until he was pronounced dead, and cut down.[6]

Denver City's first trial by the People's Court, by all accounts, was orderly and just in the minds of the citizens, with a convicted murderer sentenced to death. From the time of the murder, to the trial by the People's Court, to the hanging all events occurred in just forty-eight hours.

It was the hope and intention of the city officials that this would curb crime in Denver.

They couldn't have been more wrong.

The Gunfight
The holsters were slicker and the gunmen quicker

As with any frontier town, and Denver City of 1859 was no exception, gunplay often resulted in murder. In the early formation of the settlement, rivalry and competition between Denver City and Auraria crossed the boundary of Cherry Creek, resulting in murder between two one-time friends. It happened just one week after the first murder.

Peleg T. Bassett and John Scudder were long-time friends dating back to their work together as pilots on the Missouri River boats. For whatever their reasons, a new adventure, the chance of a gold strike, or capitalizing on business and land acquisitions, the two friends arrived in the settlement shortly after the announcement of the new gold rush. Bassett chose to locate on the Denver City side of the creek, while Scudder located on the Auraria side. With the two settlements in their own rivalry for commercial dominance, the two friends soon found themselves at odds. Scudder set up a business in land development and sent this letter back to friends in Missouri in January 1859:

> *We think we have got a good thing, and expect to get rich out of it. We have linked our fortunes with the Georgia group, who first opened the mines in this country in the spring of '58, and have laid out a city named Auraria. Every man is hard at work building cabins. We have a claim club whose business it is to see that all town sites and farming and timber claims are recorded.*

So far we have done well, and hope the county officers that will be elected in March will take up the business as we leave it. If so, there will be no trouble; if not, the bloody scenes and riots of Eastern Kansas will again be enacted, and many good men will fall in defense of their actual rights. Governor Denver sent out last fall a body of men with commissions sufficient to organize and carry on the business of the country. We look for a large immigration in the spring. Tell all who come to the country from St. Louis to look for the St. Louis ranch, which may be found on Ferry Street in front of which will be found a wagon box on end, which reads thus: 'Office of John Scudder, Recorder of Claims, Land Agent, Houses for Sale or Rent, Pine Lumber for Sale. Walk In...Office Hours when the door is open.[7]

Meanwhile, on January 4 1859, John Scudder, as well as Peleg Bassett, were asked to serve on a committee headed by General William Larimer to facilitate the negotiations of bringing the Pacific Railroad to Denver City. Scudder was a great promoter of the town and its future. In March, he fired off a series of letters to his prominent friends and business acquaintances, touting the virtues of the new Rocky Mountain settlement, and urging the St. Louis business community in particular to ship their goods to the new supply station of the Rocky Mountain West. Evidently his promotion of the new settlement impressed the locals as he was appointed the first treasurer of the Auraria Town Company.

On the Denver City side of the creek, Peleg Bassett had recently been named the first town recorder for Denver City. The rivalry between the two towns now became personal. It wasn't long before personal animosity resulted in violence.

In early April, the two had a heated argument over local government policy. A few days later, another argument ensued between the two over a personal mail issue. Name calling led to threats against each other. On the morning of April 16, 1859, Scudder learned of several remarks Bassett had made against his honor and his name. Being the Southern gentleman that he was, Scudder crossed the creek to call on Bassett at his cabin on the south side of Larimer Street, between Fourteenth and Fifteenth streets. Heated words were again exchanged and when Bassett finally admitted to the truth, he uttered a few expletives and grabbed a pick handle. Lunging at Scudder, who instinctively moved back, the argument turned violent. As Scudder recovered his footing, Bassett came at him again, whereupon Scudder pulled his gun and fired. Bassett fell backward, falling to the floor with a wound to his chest. The sound of the gunfire brought bystanders to the scene, including General William Larimer. Bassett was moved to comfortable quarters and a doctor was summoned.

Meanwhile, Scudder, feeling the shooting was self-defense, immediately turned himself in to Sheriff Edward "Ned" Wynkoop. That night, Peleg Bassett died from the effects of the gunshot wound.

Believing he would be exonerated at a public trial of The People's Court, Scudder must have been stunned when the advice from friends and attorneys, and even Sheriff Wynkoop, was to the contrary. It was the belief of these men that with the recent murder of Arthur Binegraff and subsequent hanging of John Stuffle the previous week, that the citizens would not tolerate another murder and may, in fact, discount the plea of self-defense. Thus, Scudder left the settlement before Bassett was laid to rest in the City Cemetery.

Scudder spent a year in Salt Lake City, where he found work with William H. Russell who was preparing the launch of the Pony Express. With his new job and advice from his employers, Scudder returned to Denver in the spring of 1860. Appealing to the city officials, he asked for a trial in his defense.

The People's Court accommodated and Charles A. Lawrence served as the judge over the proceedings. The trial began on April 18, 1860, exactly one year to the date after the death of Peleg Bassett. Prosecuting the case was W. P. McClure. The defense attorneys were Hiram P. Bennett, and the future mayor of Denver City, John C. Moore. The testimony presented by the defense council convinced the jury that Scudder's action were indeed self-defense and he was acquitted of murder by the People's Court. Scudder went on to have a productive career with the city of Denver.

A Woman's Love Scorned
Hell hath no fury . . .

Wagonloads of travelers and fortune seekers traveled west to Denver due to the promotion by William Byers and his *Rocky Mountain News*. Overland wagon trains took weeks, even months, to cross the windswept prairie west to the Rocky Mountains. It was during this overland journey that our first mysterious murder takes place.

It was the summer of 1859, in the dirt streets of Denver City, when a striking dark-haired beauty stepped out of her Conestoga wagon, and boldly announced to all within earshot:

> *As a God fearing woman, you see me for the last time. As of tomorrow, I start the first brothel in this settlement. In the future my name will be Ada LaMont. Any of you men in need of a little fun will always find the flaps of my tent open.*[8]

What could possibly cause a woman to utter such a statement upon arrival in a new city? It is a story of scorned love, mystery, murder and, in the end, tragedy. Yet, with that bold statement, Ada LaMont had a new attitude and a new profession: she became the undisputed first lady of Denver's tenderloin district.

Her story starts off like those of many early pioneers, now known in Colorado as the "59er's." A young seventeen-year-old from the Midwest, Ada married a promising young minister in a blessed union that all in attendance were sure would last the test of time. Two years later, the cry "Pikes Peak or Bust" roared across the land. Like thousands of Easterners heading west on little more than a hope and a prayer, the newlyweds packed a wagon and from St. Joseph, Missouri, they joined the Westward Migration.

Along the overland journey, somewhere on the sun-baked prairie of Kansas, a young minister mysteriously disappeared one evening. A search party was organized, yet found no trace of the man. Meanwhile, other members of the wagon train discovered a young woman of questionable background was also missing. When the search party returned empty-handed again, it was generally agreed that the two had willingly left the wagon train together. With the fear of an Indian attack, the wagon train resumed their journey the following day. As her wagon moved along on the westward journey, a silent, brooding

Denver Public Library, Western History Department
Charles Harrison, the dapper gambler.

Ada LaMont contemplated her life and her future.

The change in the young woman arriving in Denver was one of defiance and determination. With her sensational Denver debut, Ada kept her word, and guaranteed her success. Establishing her new enterprise in a tent at the outskirts of the infant city, roughly 1st and Ferry Streets, it was soon the most popular establishment of its kind. Nearly every single man in the settlement (and most of them were single,) visited her establishment on a regular basis. Her bagnio became known from St. Louis to San Francisco. Within a year business was thriving, so much that she was able to upgrade by opening the first parlor house in Denver.

Located north of the rivers' confluence and in the newest part of town, near F Street, the two-story building was first class. Ada served quality liquor, when she could get it, and her house and working girls were clean and well groomed. Due to her business acumen, Ada reigned supreme in Denver's tenderloin world for more than ten years.

Ada's beauty and popularity attracted the dashing and mysterious Charley Harrison. Harrison was a well-known gambler with his own dubious reputation, and the proprietor of the notorious Criterion Saloon. The two soon struck a relationship that turned romantic. The new couple of Denver's seedy side were often seen at public events. Ada's business flourished, and in her personal life she was finally happy again.

In July 1860, following a glorious 4th of July celebration, a horrific

11

rain storm poured on the city for three days, causing major flooding and damage to businesses in the downtown area. Members of the local volunteer militia, a motley crew at best, were called in to help with the clean-up efforts and control looting of businesses. One night, a small group of these men, in their cups as it were, boldly entered Ada's establishment demanding favors and helping themselves to the liquor, breaking the emptied bottles. Ada's pleas to the men fell on deaf drunken ears. As the destruction to Ada's place continued, suddenly the front door crashed open. Charley Harrison and a few of his friends rushed inside to Ada's aid. Harrison managed to subdue the drunkards in his quiet sober efforts, something his opponents lacked. Finally, with a few enticements, Harrison got the men to leave on their own, avoiding violence and bloodshed. Ada's hero had saved the day.

In December 1860, Harrison's reputation gained a few more points when he single-handedly saved the *Rocky Mountain News* publisher, William N. Byers, from a lynch mob. For the next year, Harrison continued his practice of protecting Ada and her business establishment. Rumors of payoffs to the local police were rampant.

By the spring of 1861, the romance had cooled somewhat. Rumors around the saloon circuit were that Harrison had another woman. Whatever the personal circumstances, for Harrison April 1861 was his turning point. The Civil War had broken out, and Harrison, being a Southern loyalist, used his saloon for their headquarters. The Civil War was a hot topic and one that was bound to cause trouble in any saloon. Harrison was actually charged with an act of rebellion and ordered to leave the Colorado Territory, which he did in the fall of 1861.

Following Harrison's departure, Ada's life took a sudden and fateful turn for the worse. An extremely odd set of circumstances caused a friend of Ada's to happen across a human skull on the eastern plains of Kansas, on a return trip from Kansas. The skull had a large hole in the back and a spent bullet lodged in the bone. Rotting clothing was found nearby which held a Bible, with the inscription written by Ada to her new minister husband. A remarkable find indeed. When presented with the news and the inscribed Bible, Ada went into seclusion. She began to drink. She lost interest in herself and her business. Eventually she left Denver for good.

A few years later, Ada went up to Georgetown during the midst of

Denver Public Library, Western History Department
The Criterion Hall, circa 1862, was located on Denver's Larimer Street.

a frenzied rash of ore wealth. It was a new discovery, this time silver, and Ada tried to establish herself again. Yet nothing halted Ada's downward spiral. She died in poverty in a single-room shack. Even her funeral was unattended.

The murder of Ada LaMont's husband was never solved, and remains a mystery in history to this day. For Ada, whatever she might have known, it may have been too much to endure.

Murder and the City Cemetery
Dead Man Walking

In his keen development of Denver City, General William Larimer included land for a cemetery. The site selected was a gently sloping hill two miles from the heart of Denver City. Close enough to the city, yet far enough away, allowing for future development, the Mount Prospect Cemetery, commonly referred to as the City Cemetery, was laid out in the spring of 1859. The majority of the first burials in the cemetery were the results of various violent activities, including murder, hangings and gunfights. Within a short year the cemetery would receive its most infamous Denver resident.

As in any frontier town, including Denver City of 1859, gambling was a way of life. Sometimes it became a raging fever, with violence frequently erupting over the poker tables in saloons along Cherry Creek to the very street named in General Larimer's honor.

Jack O'Neill was the first gambler with a reputation as such to arrive in Denver.[9] A long-time professional gambler from New York City, O'Neill had panache, the type of which sold in the dime novels of the era. A large man at over six feet tall and weighing more than two hundred pounds, O'Neill was a solid man in mind and stature. His dress, primarily black and white in color, stood out among the dust and mud of early Denver City.

With fewer than a dozen tents or crude log buildings erected when Jack arrived, he built the first wooden structure to house a saloon. A long narrow bar ran the length of one wall, while the rest of the building hosted a cluttered disarray of chairs and gambling tables. Oil lamps displayed a weak glow while their greasy smell combined with the tobacco smoke. O'Neill set up his living quarters, with his mistress Salt Lake Kate, next to his saloon. The saloon was soon the most popular along the dirt streets of Denver City, and O'Neill became a well-respected pioneer citizen of Denver City. So popular was his Capitol Saloon, and Jack O'Neill himself, it became known affectionately as "The House That Jack Built."

Meanwhile, another notable pioneer, Samuel M. Rooker, the first man to bring his family to the settlement, became a founding father of Auraria. He and his son, John, had systematically acquired many valuable land grants throughout both competing town sites, thereby hedging their bets for their future and fortune in real estate. In fact, John Rooker built the first lumber home on the Auraria side and received additional shares in the town company. While the Rooker family enjoyed their status among the higher society, young John began to stray from the strong family values. Spending more and more time in the saloons, he slipped into drinking heavily, gambling and spending time and money with the ladies of the evening.

On the evening of March 29, 1860, O'Neill chose to take in a night of gambling and libations at the nearby Western Saloon on Ferry Street, owned by the beloved pioneer, "Uncle" Dick Wootton.[10] O'Neill sat down to a full table of gamblers, with the games changing from high ball to low ball poker, as well as seven card stud and five card stud. Late into the night the gamblers had dwindled until only O'Neill and John Rooker remained in the game, with a large pot of money at stake.

The game was five card draw, and O'Neill had called Rooker's hand. Rooker announced "Two of a pair in picture cards." O'Neill replied with confidence, "Three jacks," and laid out his hand. In an instant, Rooker threw down his hand, four kings, and rose to collect the pot. Calmly, O'Neill told Rooker he hadn't called the hand correctly and the pot was his. O'Neill was right, Rooker called his hand as two pairs instead of four of a kind. An argument ensued and tempers flared while poker chips, gold pieces and gold dust flew through the air. Suddenly both men rose to their feet threatening the other. The patrons of the Western Saloon fell into silence as every man watched, stone-faced, while the two gamblers stared at one another in silence. Finally Rooker told O'Neill to arm himself, saying, "We will meet again." Word of the incident and forthcoming confrontation spread through the infant town, with heavy wagers placed on the outcome.

There was a history of animosity between the two men. A few weeks earlier, O'Neill and his mistress, Salt Lake Kate, attended the local horse race festivities with another couple, gambler Charley Harrison and Ada LaMont. Also in attendance was John Rooker, accompanied by a few of his gambling buddies. It wasn't long before Rooker and his cronies, fueled by liquor, caused a bit of a ruckus in the crowd by taunting an elderly gentleman. Irritated, O'Neill stepped through the crowd and confronted Rooker on behalf of the elderly gentleman. An inebriated Rooker reacted to O'Neill with threats laced with profanity. The ever self-confident O'Neill responded to the threats by suggesting the two settle the matter with bowie knives. Rooker backed off but he didn't forget the embarrassment.

Rooker was fuming with this second humiliation to his personal honor by Jack O'Neill. That night following a game of cards at the Western Saloon he planned his revenge well. He borrowed a fast horse from a friend and stabled it at the outskirts of town, where he paid a stable boy to bring the steed into town by mid-morning. He loaded his double-barreled shotgun and just before sunrise the following morning, Rooker made his way back to Wootton's Western Saloon. Knowing the saloon would not open until noon, Rooker quietly made his way in through the rear entrance. He positioned himself at the front of the saloon where he had a clear view of O'Neill's cabin at the northwest corner of Ferry and Wewatta streets. Around 10 a.m., O'Neill left his cabin. As O'Neill approached the saloon, Rooker shouted: "You sonofabitch, I got you now!" Rooker pulled both triggers of the shotgun. As O'Neill was hit with the buckshot, he managed to pull out his gun as he hit the ground. Rooker ran through the back of the saloon, jumped onto his borrowed horse and left town. O'Neill, with Kate by his side, died later that morning.

Jack O'Neill, dead at the hands of a cold-blooded murderer, was the most prominent person to die in Denver up to that time. His funeral, held the following day, a Saturday, was attended by his mistress Kate, Charley Harrison and Ada LaMont, as well as several prominent Denver citizens. Laid out in his finest dress clothes, his body was lowered to rest in the City Cemetery by mortician McGavron.

The following day John Rooker returned to town. Once again, the People's Court was assembled to judge the actions of Rooker. In an amazing event of early frontier justice, the court was organized by Samuel Rooker, the father of the accused. On Sunday morning, the people's court assembled in the Cibola Hall saloon and playhouse. Standing behind a table to address the court, the self-appointed judge, Samuel Rooker, first placed his revolvers on the table and then made his case. In a confident manner, smacking of arrogance, he explained his version of the circumstances leading up to his son's shooting of O'Neill. He further explained that the killing was justified, citing his son's Southern upbringing and the right to vengeance upon the humiliation of his honor. No one was given the opportunity to speak on behalf of the deceased. In such a manner, John Rooker was acquitted of murder.

This makeshift trial caused an outcry among the press, led by William Byers, editor of the *Rocky Mountain News*. In an editorial dated April 4, 1860, Byers demanded justice:

> *The act may have been perfectly justified; if so it is due to Rooker that it should be so declared to the world. If otherwise, then it is due to the public good, and necessary to the public safety that he answer for his rash act. Somebody knows the facts*

in the matter, and it is due to the public that they be developed. It is high time that the citizens of Denver should show enough interest in their own welfare to right public wrongs, and not leave it to every citizen to take vengeance in his own hands, even to the taking of human life.

Friends of Jack O'Neill, including that other notable gambler Charley Harrison and even future mayor John C. Moore, let their anger be known regarding O'Neill's murder with a public denouncement of the one-sided events at Cibola Hall, but nothing was done to bring the killer to justice.

A coward's attack ended a Colorado pioneer's life prematurely, yet Jack O'Neill gained an ironic immortality. The cemetery site was soon called "O'Neill's Ranch" by the locals in honor of their fallen citizen. The City Cemetery is now the fertile grounds of Cheesman Park.

The death of Jack O'Neill and the apathy of the community would fester to a slow boil, exploding with further murders in the early days of Denver City.

.

The Case of the Dapper Gambler
Know when to hold 'em and know when to fold 'em

On the frontier, and early Denver is no exception, a familiar figure was instantly recognized. Tall, immaculate in style and dress (usually in black), his eyes were the only clue to his profession. Steady of nerve and constantly observant, he was the frontier gambler. This stereotype lives on as a character of the Old West.

Colorado's legendary gambler, Charley Harrison, arrived in Denver City in 1859. Harrison became a legend in early Denver, yet during his brief stay his life was clouded in mystery.

Charley Harrison had honed his gambling skills in the hotels and gambling saloons of New York City before his journey west in 1849. Very little is known of his time in the West until his arrival in the Denver from Salt Lake City in the summer of 1859. Nevertheless, from the day that he rode into Denver City and opened a monte game at the Denver House, Harrison gained respect as an honest and fair dealer.

Well-built, attractive in person, meticulously groomed in black attire and sporting a well-trimmed silky beard, Harrison was approximately forty years of age in 1859. With his pearl-handled Colt revolvers strapped at the hip, Harrison stood in intriguing contrast to the roughs and "bummers" of the gambling element.

With such a favorable reputation, Harrison had no problem in acquiring a percentage of the house stakes at the Criterion Hall at Larimer and F streets, the finest gambling establishment in town.[11] A two-story framed building, the Criterion boasted the finest in entertainment, dining, liquor and gambling rooms. Harrison did so well at the Criterion that within a few month's time he bought into the establishment with the proprietor, Ed Jump. With Harrison's partnership, the Criterion reached a new level in Denver's gambling community. Harrison treated the gambling aspect of the establishment as he did the entire operation, that is to say; honest and above board. The typical cheating devices of gambling such as rigged faro boxes, loaded dice, rigged roulette wheels and marked cards were forbidden at the Criterion. Thus, with Harrison's improvements, the Criterion Hall enjoyed great popularity as a fair gambling establishment. William N. Byers, editor of the *Rocky Mountain News*, was a frequent customer and often ran ads for the Criterion in his paper. He and Harrison maintained a cordial relationship and, in fact, following the death of Jack O'Neill, the two worked together, leading the citizen's outrage in Denver City over the failure to file charges against O'Neill's killer.

These episodes are well documented in the news pages of the *Rocky Mountain News*; however, in July 1860, the outspoken editor of the paper, William N. Byers, and Charley Harrison would find themselves linked together as major figures in a controversy that would bring Denver City to the verge of anarchy.

On July 12, Harrison, while enjoying a casual conversation with friends, including a couple of local attorneys and a judge, left the table when an argument at a poker table caught his attention. Harrison approached the game to defuse the situation. The gamblers in the poker game included James Innis, Tom Hunt and Carl Woods, known gamblers with a shady reputation, and John Rooker, now back in town following his killing of Jack O'Neill, as well as Charles "Professor" Stark, an ex-slave who was known for his skill with a bowie knife.

Stark had been among the few who were able to buy their freedom from his master in Missouri. Working on Mississippi River boats, he was able to save money for his journey west, where he worked in Omaha, Nebraska, before his arrival in Denver City, where he found occasional work as a mule skinner and enjoyed card play.

This particular evening, Stark evidently took exception to the rules of the card game and exchanged heated words when Harrison approached the table. Harrison, in his reputable calm demeanor, attempted to rectify the situation and moved toward the bar. Rebuked, Stark bolted from his chair and sent another slew of angry words toward Harrison. Harrison didn't respond. Enraged, Stark moved toward Harrison and pulled out his bowie knife. Harrison shouted to him to put the knife down as the entire crowd watched in stunned silence. Stark lunged at Harrison who ducked, but Stark thrust his knife again. Harrison again ducked. Someone in the crowd shouted for Stark to put down the knife. Stark didn't heed the advice. When Stark came at him a third time, Harrison pulled his gun and fired, hitting Stark in the thigh. Stark still came toward Harrison who fired two more shots. Stark fell to the floor. The crowd gathered around and someone sent for a doctor. Stark lingered between life and death until July 21, 1860, when he finally succumbed to his wounds.

Following the death of Stark, an inquest was held by the People's Court, eventually clearing Charley Harrison of any murder charges by declaring the action was in self-defense. William Byers lamented the judicial process in his editorial of July 25:

> *From the facts learned since the shooting, we are led to believe the act was unprovoked, in short, cold-blooded murder. The man who has shot down an unarmed man, and then repeats his shots, while his victim writhes at his feet, until the charges of his pistol are exhausted-even if justified in the first act, is unfit to live in, and an unsafe member of a civilized community.*

The editorial hit an already shaky nerve given the evident crime element. However, Byers had not only underestimated the evolving business establishment of Larimer Street, he had no idea of Harrison's influence. The gambler and business owner had gained a well-earned reputation as an honest and fair business operator. In fact, he worked with the local law officials in ridding the city of the corrupt element of the gaming establishment, also gaining the respect and influence of the local politicians.

As soon as Byers' editorial hit the streets of Denver, the gambling elements of Larimer Street were in an uproar. Hell bent on lynching Byers, a mob soon formed. Tension was high in the city. Seymour W. Waggoner, a thirty year old probate judge and member of the first Territorial Constitutional Convention, understood the gravity of the situation. He immediately requested a meeting with Harrison where the two friends agreed that the editor's assertions were lacking in fact. The judge then requested that Harrison and Byers meet to discuss their differences. Harrison agreed.

Meanwhile, as the day turned to evening, the angry mob grew larger. As Harrison finally made an appearance, the crowd cheered. Amazement turned to disbelief as Harrison, along with Judge Waggoner, walked past the crowd and toward the office of the editor, Byers. The meeting lasted a few hours with the judge presenting evidence and witnesses to show the facts of the Stark shooting in direct contradiction to the statements made by Byers in his paper. Waggoner further argued that in an honest effort to placate the angry citizens, Byers should issue a public apology.

Harrison, the target of Byers' editorial, emerged from the meeting and immediately calmed the angry mob. For Byers' part, with the evidence presented, as well as the mounting pressure, he issued a printed press release that very evening, saying in part:

> *From two conversations with Judge Waggoner-we learn unmistakably that the first insult was given by Stark and that he was the first to draw arms and make an attack. We had before understood Stark was unarmed but such was not the case. He was armed with a bowie knife and made two or three lunges at Harrison before the latter fired...In justice to Mr. Harrison, we will say that the statement above, made by Judge Waggoner, presented quite another complexion to the unfortunate transaction on the 12th inst. We await the result of the investigation instituted today, hoping Mr. Harrison will be acquitted of all blame, and shall in our next, give a report of the same.*

While Harrison received a retraction from the editor, Byers never saw fit to print a follow-up of the investigation as he stated he would, which by the way, exonerated Harrison for a second time. However, the editor of Golden's *Western Mountaineer*, wrote: "Whatever the character and intent of Mr. Harrison (for the shooting of Stark), his recent conduct in connection with this matter seems to have been honorable and moral."

Again, Byers seemed to be out of touch with the mainstream population of Denver, and so the matter between the gambling establishment and the local media still simmered.

A few weeks later, a handful of members of the lower-class gambling mob, bummers as they were called, influenced with strong whiskey, invaded Byers' office with threats of death, upon which Byers was marched at gunpoint to the Criterion Saloon. Included in this vigilante group were Carl Woods, George Steele, James Innis and John Rooker, the same group of gamblers Harrison had dealt with on previous occasions. The alcohol induced plan of the mob was to try Byers in a saloon court for unjustly accusing their friend, Charley Harrison. However, upon their arrival at the Criterion, the self-imposed vigilantes were met by a surprised Harrison. Taking charge of the grave situation, Harrison told the mob to wait while he had a few words with Byers. Taking the editor inside the saloon, Harrison immediately took Byers through the kitchen and out the back door, leading him back to his office at the *News*. It was not long before the vigilantes discovered the ruse. The group followed the pair with leveled guns, but withheld their fire for fear of hitting Harrison.

Reaching Byers' office, Harrison advised Byers and his employees to arm themselves. Byers never forgot this act or the fact that Charley Harrison had saved his life, an act that enhanced Harrison's stature in Denver. By disavowing the lower gambling element of the city, business at the Criterion actually increased with a higher class of clientele. Yet Byers would continue to be critical of Harrison in his paper, if he felt the situation was warranted.

In November 1860, a nearby rancher named James Hill came to Denver on a Saturday morning and began a two-day binge of drinking and gambling. That night, while drinking at the Elephant Corral, Hill became involved in a bloody brawl that erupted on the street in front of the saloon. When one member of Hill's group, James Cockron, pulled his gun, sat on the chest of a fallen Andrew Goff and proceeded to pistol-whip the nearly unconscious fellow, the street brawl turned ugly. The loud commotion caused Charley Harrison and Sheriff Edward Wynkoop to leave their supper table at the saloon. Observing the brutality on the street, the two men interceded and broke up the fight. Cockron aimed his gun at Harrison, who quickly pulled his own revolver. Sheriff Wynkoop took charge of the situation, threatening charges if all parties did not disperse immediately. As the crowd backed away, Hill shouted expletives at Harrison and Wynkoop.

James Hill, a large burly man, continued his weekend drinking binge at the Criterion Saloon on Sunday evening. Among those in the lively crowd that evening was Harrison, now the owner of the establishment, who was entertaining Sheriff Wynkoop and other noted politicos. The merry crowd soon became disturbed by angry voices from the bar.

The bartender had refused Hill another drink, as Hill was visibly intoxicated. Hill responded with a rash of insults in quite colorful language. Both Harrison and Sheriff Wynkoop moved toward the bar and attempted to calm the situation, but to no avail. James Rice, who knew Hill, managed to take him aside and calm him down. Or so it seemed. It wasn't long before someone said something and Hill let loose with another eloquent string of profanity. Harrison continued to try to calm Hill with an offer to buy the man a drink and attempted a gesture toward a handshake, upon which Hill grabbed for his gun. Harrison instinctively grabbed Hill's gun while drawing his own Colt revolver. Harrison fired three shots at Hill, who then fell to the floor. Harrison seemed stunned as Wynkoop rushed to his side. Doctor William Bell, who had left the saloon following the first disturbance, rushed back when he heard the gunshots. He examined the fallen man, finding a bullet hole in his abdomen. Hill, barely alive, was taken to quieter quarters next door, where he died in the early morning hours of Monday, November 26, 1860.

That very day, Byers ran a news item masquerading as an editorial in the *Rocky Mountain News:*

We learn this morning that Mr. Andy Goff's life is despaired of. Mr. Cockron gave himself up this morning, and an investigation will be made as soon as the result of the wounded man's injuries are known. Out of this affair grew the quarrel, which a few hours later resulted in the shooting at the Criterion. How long,

*citizens of Denver, shall our Sabbaths be desecrated by such
scenes of violence and blood?*
Byers evidently did not know of the subsequent exchange of
violence between Cockron and Harrison, or the fact that while Cockron
was in custody by the time of the editorial, it was due to the second act
of violence Cockron perpetuated the previous evening.

In any case, the outrage over violence in the city was clear. With
news of the second incident, resulting in the death of Hill by Harrison's
gun, Hill's friends demanded action.

A warrant was issued, charging Harrison with murder. Harrison
refused to surrender to The People's Court. In a strange turn of
events for Harrison, he now found himself the subject of a lynch
mob. Marshal Asa Middaugh took charge of the crowd gathering in
front of the Criterion Saloon. Calming the crowd, he was able to gain
entrance to the saloon, where after a calm discussion, he presented
the warrant to Harrison. After further discussion, Harrison yielded to
the marshal with the words, "Self defense, Marshal, he drew first." As
the marshal led his prisoner outside, the crowd had divided into two
camps; either in support of Harrison, or justice for the death of James
Hill. As Harrison walked through the crowd, which by this time had
extended to F Street, he could not help but notice many associates
and customers of his who had turned on him, now siding with the
deceased rancher.

The Coroner's Jury, reaching a decision just two hours later, read
in part, "We the undersigned persons, summoned by the marshal of
Denver City to hold an inquest over the body of James Hill, deceased,
do hereby return the following verdict: The deceased came to his
death from the gunshot wound inflicted upon his person at the hand of
Charles Harrison." It was signed by W. H. Bennett, S. S. Curtis, M. A.
Hinds, J. J. Mead, W. W. Smead, and George Trowbridge.

The People's Court was called into session that afternoon and a
jury selected. With a trial date set for the following week, the citizens
of Denver City settled in for a quiet Thanksgiving holiday. As the
infant city had no church, ironically the largest building to hold a
community holiday service was the Criterion Saloon.

On the day of the trial, December 4, 1860, the dirt streets of Denver
City were filled with spectators. It was the biggest event the city had
ever hosted to date. As the honorable presiding judge, William M.

Slaughter, called the People's Court to order, the prosecuting attorney, James E. Dalliba, faced a formidable team of four attorneys for the defense. Dalliba's opening statement to the jury was a promise to prove that Hill's death was an act of murder. Hiram P. Bennett, one of the defense attorneys, countered by stating the act of his client, Harrison, was self defense. After a day of conflicting testimony from eye witnesses, some who saw Hill draw a gun, and some who didn't, the prosecution rested. The defense attorneys took two days presenting their case and witnesses, including Sheriff Wynkoop, and Doctor Bell. Finally Charley Harrison took the stand in his own defense. He retraced the night's events for the jury, remaining calm and forthright in his testimony, and never wavering under cross-examination by the prosecutor.

After fourteen hours of deliberation, the jury being deadlocked on a verdict, ten to two for acquittal, Judge Slaughter dismissed the jury. Prosecutor Dalliba, in a statement to the press, said in part, "In view of the difficulties...encountered in procuring a new trial, together with the publicity already given in the newspapers, I prefer to abandon the case." Thus, the case was dropped and Harrison was freed of all charges.

Outrage at the dismissal came from a not so surprising source by this time, William N. Byers. His editorial in the *Rocky Mountain News* screamed for justice in "the cold blooded act of murder." Harrison replied to Byers in a letter to the editor, and was somewhat vindicated by yet another editorial.[12]

In April 1861, the Civil War broke out. During that summer in Denver City, tensions ran high between the loyalists on both sides. Military personnel were called out to patrol the streets. In the middle of this tension was Charley Harrison, who actively held meetings for the Confederate cause at his saloon. On a hot August evening, a confrontation between the soldiers and Charley Harrison and his employees at the Criterion, resulted in a full-blown fight. Gunfire wrecked the saloon and people on both sides were injured.

Harrison, along with several others, was arrested for an act of rebellion. A hearing before Commissioner William Larimer resulted in bond for Harrison, but a trial was set. A two-week trial ended with the jury finding Harrison guilty of a lesser charge of obstructing military officers. Yet Judge Hall was not finished with Charley Harrison. In his statement to the defendant upon sentencing, he said:

> *Charles Harrison, it is the decision of this court that you shall pay to the Territory of Colorado a fine of five thousand dollars. Further, it is decreed that you shall have two days, within which time you must conclude all your affairs in this territory, after which you shall depart from Colorado for the rest of your natural life. If you are found within these borders after sundown of September nineteenth, the military is authorized to arrest and imprison you and hold you for summary sentencing.*

The next day, Harrison paid his fine, sold the Criterion Saloon and settled the remainder of his affairs. The following morning, September 19, he left Denver City on a stage headed east.

The dapper gambler who rode into the frontier town of Denver City in 1859 knew his hand was called. He folded. Yet in the end, Charley Harrison etched his mark in Denver's history.

The Fugitive
Runnin' On Empty

The summer of 1860 was a bloody one in early Denver history, despite the good intentions of the People's Court. On July 12, less than a week following the shooting death of Charles Stark at the Criterion Saloon, James Gordon, who had been present at that shooting, committed murder, fled the territory, and caused a controversial manhunt that is still debated by historians. Jerome Smiley, in his excellent *History of Denver*, described the episode: "The next act in the fearful drama, after Harrison killed Stark, was one of the most thrilling, throughout its long stages, that is found in the early annals of Denver."[13]

A young man, recently graduated with a degree in civil engineering, Gordon came from a well-established ranching family in Iowa. Unfortunately the youth still had wild oats to sow. In a local bar, an inebriated Gordon became involved in a barroom brawl which resulted in Gordon stabbing a man. Whether or not the incident played a role in their decision, the Gordon family relocated to the Rocky Mountain region.

On the family ranch a few miles north of Denver City, James Gordon worked hard for a time. That is, until he discovered the saloons and gambling establishments in town. Gordon did well enough at gambling that he gained a favorable reputation for a time. He even had a stake in the Cibola Hall for a short while.

As the summer grew hotter, Gordon's taste for women and whiskey did as well. On the night of July 18, a Wednesday, an inebriated Gordon, firearm in hand, sauntered recklessly through the town, carousing in the saloons and causing mayhem among bystanders. Eventually, and with no one hurt thus far, Gordon made his way to Ada LaMont's house of ill repute. Unfortunately for everyone in the house, Gordon wasn't in the mood for a paying visit. In an attempt to force himself on one of the working girls, who resisted, he pulled his gun and threatened everyone in the room. The house bouncer, a man by the name of Frank O'Neil, approached Gordon in an attempt to calm the situation. Gordon, who would have none of it, pulled the trigger and put a bullet into O'Neil, who fell to the floor. For good measure, Gordon shot him again before leaving the premises.

The following morning, a somber and somewhat sober Gordon made a personal apology to O'Neil, who was recovering from the two bullet wounds. Gordon even offered to pay all the medical expenses for his recovery. His somber mood didn't last long.

The very next day, Gordon hooked up with drinking pals, John Rooker, recently acquitted of the murder of Jack O'Neill, and a gambler by the name of Fitzpatrick. The trio went on a two-day drunken binge throughout the town's saloons, pulling obnoxious pranks, shooting out bar lights and mirrors, all the while backslapping each other in congratulations. At one point, after leaving the Elephant Corral, the trio headed over to Blake Street, with pistols in hand. No one stood in their way. Suddenly, Gordon encountered a miner in the street with his dog. In a cursing rant, Gordon shot the dog, not once but twice. Laughing all the way to the Louisiana Saloon, the trio ordered a round of drinks. Evidently displeased with the bartender's performance, Gordon grabbed a liquor bottle and threw it at the back of the bar. Pandemonium broke out in the packed saloon as patrons immediately headed for the door.

One of those who didn't make it out the door was John Gantz. Gordon stopped Gantz and offered to buy the man a drink. When Gantz muttered his "No thanks," Gordon flung him to the floor. Gantz got up, tried for the door again and Gordon grabbed him again. Throwing him down again, Gordon jumped on top of him and pointed his revolver in his face. Witnesses described what happened next in a scene that is hard to imagine.

Gordon pulled the trigger, but the gun didn't fire. Gantz, a German immigrant, pleaded for his life in his broken English. Gordon again pulled the trigger, again the gun did not fire. Frustrated or furious in his drunken state, we will never know. What we do know is Gordon fired the gun three more times. The fifth time proved to be the magic bullet, for it shot straight into the brain of John Gantz, killing him instantly. Gordon must have thought of this as another prank, for he left the saloon in fits of laughter. Incredibly, as he made his way to yet another saloon, no one stopped him.

The next day, Charley Harrison heard of the killing and went looking for Gordon. Speaking with witnesses who claimed Gordon was too drunk to mount a horse, Harrison deduced he was still in town. Sure enough and a step ahead of the law, Harrison found a very hungover Gordon in the alley behind the Cibola Hall. Aware of boiling tension over the horrendous murder of an innocent man, Harrison actually provided a horse for Gordon to get out of town.

Meanwhile, the citizens had formed a posse and set out on horseback to find the murderer. Eventually he was spotted near Fort Lupton where a member of the posse managed to shoot Gordon's horse. However, Gordon got away, and with nightfall the posse returned to town. The following morning, citizens were called to a meeting held at the corner of Blake and G streets.[14] A new posse was formed headed by A. J. Snider and Sheriff H. H. C. "Ki" Harrison, (no relation to Charley Harrison.) This posse was instructed to bring Gordon to the city, dead or alive. The new posse was formed in large part because the citizens felt the first posse may have been a ruse to allow Gordon to escape. This second posse followed a dead or wrong trail, and again returned to Denver City. The controversy continued.

Word soon reached Denver City that Gordon had been spotted at Bent's Fort on the Santa Fe Trail, and was headed for the Kansas prairies. Finally the city officials appointed William H. Middaugh as sheriff and directed him to leave immediately for Leavenworth, Kansas, where he would receive the proper authority and credentials under territorial law to pursue Gordon outside of the Rocky Mountain region of the territory.[15] Middaugh managed to receive an appointment as a deputy United States Marshal. Working closely with local law enforcement, Middaugh, acting on a credible tip that Gordon was heading for the Missouri River by train, received a warrant for Gordon's arrest and headed east to Coffey County, Kansas Territory, along with Leavenworth Deputy Abel Armstrong. The two managed to intercept Gordon at the small town of Ottumwa, Kansas. The news of Gordon's capture reached the citizens of Denver via the *Rocky Mountain News* in its August 28, 1860 issue, which read in part:

> *Gordon appeared to be overwhelmed with astonishment when he found himself overtaken and captured, and is said to have given himself up to complete despair. We sincerely hope that our citizens will take active steps to have Gordon's trial conducted in a manner strictly in accordance with the principles of law and justice. The trial ought to take place here, and if such a course can possibly be adopted, it will meet the approval we believe of our citizens.*

Editor Byers was obviously writing to appeal to the government powers of the Kansas Territory, for the manhunt and capture of James Gordon was about to take on a new level of controversy.

When Middaugh returned to Leavenworth with his prisoner, he was assured by the officials that Gordon would be transported to Denver City for trial. As it turned out, the governor of Kansas, for whatever reason, did not recognize Middaugh's authority as a U.S. marshal, or the warrant he was issued by the Kansas officials. Therefore, the U.S. Court ruled that Gordon be released from custody on a writ of habeas corpus. Editor Byers' as well as the citizens of Denver City's worst fears were realized.

When the German population of Leavenworth learned of Gordon's release, they immediately formed a mob and managed to apprehend Gordon. With the noose already around Gordon's neck, it was William Middaugh and the Leavenworth deputies who secured his release. The stunning account reached Denver by dispatch from the *Daily Leavenworth Times*, dated September 18, 1860:

At about three o'clock yesterday afternoon, the court, after having heard an elaborate argument, gave an able opinion, upon the question of jurisdiction, and discharged Gordon. The prisoner was now free to go where he pleased, but dare not leave the Courtroom for fear of the angry crowd without. It was now apparent that an attempt would be made to lynch him. Mayor McDowell was prepared with a large posse to preserve the peace. Accordingly, under the charge of the mayor, he (Gordon) was moved to the county jail. When he entered the hall a scene of the wildest excitement commenced. The seething, tossing crowd surged to and fro, pressing against the officers and striving to get at the prisoner, it was a commotion such as only a mad crowd of human beings can get up. Down into the street they went, the crowd yelling 'hang him, hang him!' Finally by the dint of great firmness, the Mayor landed him safely in jail. The crowd increased around the jail and became more and more furious. Men armed with muskets and revolvers and knives gathered thick and fast, and as the shades of night came on, large bonfires were built up all around the jail. During all this time, Mayor McDowell made several speeches, urging obedience to the law and requesting the people to return home in quiet. It was finally agreed between the Mayor and the ringleader of the riot that Gordon should be delivered over to Sheriff Middaugh, and that all further disorder and riotous proceedings should cease on that being done. Gordon was brought out of the jail and turned over to Sheriff Middaugh. Now commenced a scene that begs description. The crowd rushed upon Gordon crying like demons. They forced him down into the narrow and rocky glen north of the jail. But the brave officers stood by the prisoner and sometimes almost overborne they still recovered and pressed forward, holding their prisoner safe in their charge. Several times the crowd had a halter around his neck, but each time an officer cut the rope. Then followed a tumult and strife between the officers and rioters that was desperate to the last degree. The contest, for half an hour, was fierce and terrific. The din, howl and confusion was now worse than pandemonium, the prisoner begging to be hung, killed or anything to take him out of such agony. By this time, every stitch of clothing was torn off of him, and he had nothing on his body but his clanking chains. After a desperate struggle, the prisoner again safely landed from the fury of the mob. Gordon is very badly bruised, cut and lacerated. To Mayor McDowell we cannot award too much praise for his firmness, intrepidity and cool judgment during all of this lamentable affair. There are many rumors of a number of persons being badly injured. We learn of two Germans, one of whom badly wounded by a stab in the side, and the other by being pushed off a high bank on the river. Sheriff Middaugh is badly hurt. We have not learned the extent of his wounds, but from what we are informed, suppose him to be seriously injured.

The *Rocky Mountain News* responded in the September 24, 1860 issue, with this headline:

Violent Mob! Intense Excitement!
Attempts to Hang Gordon!

> *By the arrival of the C.O.C. and P.P. coach at 11 o'clock last night, we are placed in possession of the Leavenworth Times of the 18th, by the hands of Dr. Arnold who was present during the trial, and the subsequent mob violence. Dr. A. assisted in dressing the wounds of Sheriff Middaugh, and saw him in the following morning, when he was doing well and would be able to return here in a few days. We have the full proceedings of the trial now before us. The evidence was conclusive, and Gordon was liberated for want of jurisdiction - a nice point which the Kansas officials could not see (?) when Gordon was arrested to be brought back here.*

Meanwhile, a detachment of U.S. military troops took a badly bruised Gordon, who had begged for his life, to the military hospital at Leavenworth. Incredibly, the authorities in Kansas still refused to return Gordon to Denver City. Sheriff Middaugh returned to Denver to secure affidavits, warrants, witness testimonies, and other evidence pertinent to the murder of John Gantz at the hands of James Gordon.

When Editor Byers learned of the new developments first hand from Middaugh, as well as from subsequent news dispatches from

Leavenworth, he fired a scathing editorial in the September 25, 1860 issue of the *Rocky Mountain News*:

Mob Law

*The (*Daily Leavenworth*) Times cannot more deprecate such action than we do, but does it consider fairly and impartially the case? In the first place, the Times never condemned the retention of Gordon in that city, when he should have been sent immediately here. If public opinion, and the Press of Eastern Kansas tacitly permits officers, under the cloak of "jurisdiction," to wrest forcibly, prisoners from officers having them properly in their charge, to hold them for a time, and then turn them loose upon the world, she must not complain if she sometimes reaps some of the evil consequences of popular outbreaks, And pray from what judicial tribunal was authority wrenched? Did not the U.S. District Court turn the murderer at large in your midst, and do you prize such accessions to your population? If so, we earnestly hope he will remain a denizen of Leavenworth. There is no excuse for Leavenworth taking up the cause of people seven hundred miles away. The Times closes with the following: 'They will not ask us, and we cannot go into lawless measures to redress their grievances.' No, we do not ask Leavenworth to depart from the 'even tenor of her way,' to assist us in the punishment of our criminals, but we do ask that when those criminals, of ours have been pursued hundreds of miles, arrested and started back, that citizens and officers of Leavenworth allow them to be returned to us and not interpose their bogus authority to take them from our officers, detain them and then turn them loose upon the world.*

Whether the newspaper wars made a difference in the eventual return of the prisoner to Denver City, or the unpopular decision by Kansas authorities to release him in the first place, will never be known. However, Middaugh's diligent work did produce enough added evidence that eventually secured the prisoner into his custody. Yet controversy continued throughout the lawman's journey with his outlaw prisoner back to Denver City.

Middaugh escorted Gordon, shackled in chains and with three guards, out of Leavenworth. At a train connection in Kinnekuk,

31

Kansas, Middaugh was strangely denied passage and forced to lay over. The following morning, Kansas authorities arrived and produced a warrant charging Gordon with horse theft, and again took charge of the prisoner. By that very afternoon, the charges were not substantiated and the Kansas authorities once again were forced to return Gordon to Middaugh's charge.

By this time, the funds to Middaugh, provided by volunteers in Denver City, were limited. Middaugh, with no additional guards, managed to return Gordon by coach, to the city. When he finally returned with his captive, he had traveled over three thousand miles in pursuit of the murderer over a long two month period.

It was two o'clock in the morning of September 28, 1860, when a weary Sheriff Middaugh arrived with a bruised and beat up James Gordon back to the city where the crime occurred. By noon, charge of the prisoner, hand-cuffed and chained at his feet, had been handed off to John H. Kehler and his deputies at the new hastily constructed jail.[16] A motion by the People's Court set the trial for James Gordon at two o'clock that very afternoon. While the wheels of justice were slow and strange in Leavenworth, they were swift in frontier Denver City.

Promptly at two o'clock that afternoon a crowd of nearly six hundred citizens assembled at a grove of cottonwood trees near Blake Street. Dr. McDowell was chosen as presiding judge and the sheriff selected twenty-four men from the crowd from which the judge would then choose twelve to serve as jurors. Next, the attorneys for the defense were selected.

The defense dream team of the day included future Colorado territorial governor, H. C. Hunt, attorney and later a member of the Territorial Court system; John H. Sherman, who would later become a territorial judge; W. P. "Park" Mclure, a prominent city leader with a fine future ahead; Seymour W. Waggoner, who had served as the judge on previous trials; and the future mayor of Denver City, John C. Moore.

Selection of the prosecuting attorney, representing the citizens as well as the deceased John Gantz, commenced. The well regarded attorney, who would later become a state delegate to the U.S. Congress, Hiram P. Bennett, was nominated but declined. The seasoned attorney knew instinctively the deck was stacked. Not only was there a strong five man defense team, the judge, and not the attorneys, would select the jury. Controversy now took on a new twist.

Even the crowd sensed that the People's Court was going above and beyond their duty to secure a fair trial. As the crowd of citizens began to voice their objections, smarter council prevailed on the People's Court. Attorney, and future Colorado territorial governor Alexander C. Hunt, replaced Dr. McDowell as presiding judge. With this change and the assurance of a fair jury selection, Bennett agreed to prosecute the case. As the crowd cheered in agreement, Judge Hunt, citing the need for time for both sides to collect evidence, adjourned the trial until the following morning.

The *Rocky Mountain News* reported the events of the day, in that day's issue, ending with:

> *The meeting then dispersed. There was the best of order and perfect quiet and apparently a cool determination to vindicate the rights of the people. When the trial resumes, let the people select their jury, men who are honest, upright and trustworthy; let them see that no unfair means are resorted to, by forestalling time, or in any other manner.*

The trial began in earnest the following morning, a Saturday, at 9 o'clock. Several hundred people were in the crowd that day, in a grove of trees below Wazee Street, between F and G streets.[17] A fair and impartial jury was selected and agreed upon by both opposing sides. Opening statements were made, and witnesses were called by the prosecution. Headed by lead attorney, W. P. "Park" McClure, and H. C. Hunt, the defense team presented a strong case for the benefit of their client. However, the testimony of the eleven witnesses called by the prosecution described in great detail the events of that night that led to the death of John Gantz at the hand of the accused. Perhaps the most explosive testimony came from Godfrey Kuster, who testified to seeing Gordon jump atop Gantz and pull the trigger of his gun five times, the final attempt producing the bullet in the head of the deceased. Kuster further testified to witnessing Gordon leaving the saloon, and on the street, Gordon yelled, "I killed a damned Dutchman, and don't care a damn, but would like to kill more." Kuster also testified that when Gordon saw him on the street, he ran toward him, but Kuster was able to get away.[18] This revelation sent a chill through the spectators and all but sealed Gordon's fate.

The defense began its case at 8 o'clock that evening. Their first witness was Robert Gordon, father of the accused. He testified in part that his son came to the ranch claiming that "some one said I killed a man last night." He needed a horse and his father gave him one. He further stated that his son was good man, but had changed after he fell from a horse. The judge continued the trial for the following day.

That night, a lynch mob formed outside of the place where Gordon was being held. Amazingly, and to the credit of the fine citizens of the city, they formed their own group and stopped the lynch mob from any violence.

By this time, the James A. Gordon murder trial was on the front pages of many newspapers across the country, covering the murder to the escape of the murderer and chase to Kansas. Now, on Sunday morning, September 30, 1860, final witness testimony, closing arguments and the jury verdict were about to be completed.

High winds that day forced the court proceedings indoors. The trial resumed at Dunn's Block on Front Street. The closing arguments for the prosecution were delivered to the jurors in an able discussion of the law, and debunked the defense's presumption of insanity due to drunkenness by reiterating the previous eyewitness testimony and ending with a jury instruction regarding malice aforethought.

The defense council began by stating the prosecution had failed to prove the their client was the actual killer! The council further stated that the testimony of John Kuster was that of a "bully witness."

Incredibly, defense attorney, John C. Moore, then made a plea to the jury, contradictory to his fellow council, that the act resulting in death, "may" have been involuntary and brought on by mental alienation, and drunkenness.

James Gordon then rose before the jury and made a long statement. He did not speak about the murder, but recounted his "departure" from the city and his subsequent arrest by Sheriff Middaugh. He said that he did not care whether he lived or died, and blamed his actions on "bad liquor." He thanked Middaugh for saving his life in Leavenworth, as well as his parents for their support.

The judge then instructed the jury as to the law regarding murder and malice. The jury quickly returned with a verdict, which was announced with great fanfare for the citizens. To hear the verdict, a large crowd had gathered in front of the Tremont House in Auraria. There, on the balcony of the establishment, Judge Hunt announced the verdict: Guilty. Nearly unanimous in agreement, the crowd cheered.

The judge pronounced the sentence as death by hanging. A motion was made and accepted that the condemned party be given time to settle his personal affairs. Judge Hunt set the date for the hanging for Saturday, October 6, 1860, between the hours of three and six o'clock p.m. The condemned prisoner hung his head in silence, and then was remanded to the custody of the marshal for proper guarding until his date with death.

During the ensuing days leading up to the execution, a petition was circulated around the city by Thomas Warren to save Gordon's life. The petition gained few signatures, but did raise a ruckus in the city. R. E. Whitsitt, a prominent citizen, openly refused to sign the petition and Warren challenged him to a duel. Cooler heads eventually prevailed and the duel was called off. On the night before the execution, the Reverend Dr. Rankin attempted to calm the city by asking the people to abide by the verdict of the People's Court, that it had been held openly and fairly.

A scaffold was built near the bank of Cherry Creek, just south of E Street.[19] It was almost the same place where Denver City's first hanging occurred in June of that year. On the afternoon of October 6, James A. Gordon was escorted under heavy guard to the gallows on the banks of Cherry Creek. Walking with him up the steps was the Reverend Rankin. Gordon knelt in prayer as the Reverend cited the twenty-third Psalm. As a last request, Gordon asked that Sheriff Middaugh serve as executioner, stating: "I would much rather a decent man drop the trap."

And so, Middaugh fastened the noose around Gordon's neck. His last words were "Oh, God, have mercy." Middaugh opened the trap door and Gordon's body dropped. As the body swung slowly, the crowd stood in silence. James A. Gordon was dead. He was twenty-three years old.

This retribution for murder sent a strong message to would-be criminals in Denver City. With the People's Court, the citizens resolved that there would be law and order. Not quite a year later, in February of 1861, the Territory of Colorado was created by an act of Congress, under President James Buchanan. Just as the war between the states broke out in the East, President Abraham Lincoln appointed William Gilpin as the first territorial governor. Under Gilpin's leadership, the first territorial legislature included among the many laws and provisions the adoption of a formal death-penalty law, by hanging.

* * *

The People's Court would have much more work to do. Moses Young was convicted by the court of the murder of William West in March 1860. Following the conviction, Young was walked to West's home, under heavy guard, and hanged from a tree in front of the West home.

The People vs. Gredler was another form of swift justice by the People's Court. Marcus Gredler and Jacob Roeder were prospectors on their way to the South Park diggings in 1860. They stopped near Bear Creek, west of the city on June 12, 1860. Some sort of dispute or fight occurred, ending with Gredler removing Roeder's head from his torso with a swift swing of an ax over the sleeping victim. Gredler was apprehended and brought to Denver where he was tried by the People's Court in the Apollo Hall on June 14, 1860. He was found guilty of murder and hanged the next day.

The last trial conducted by the People's Court resulting in an execution occurred on December 7, 1860. A hay purchase near Fort Lupton turned to murder when Patrick Waters shot Thomas Freeman. Waters then hid the body in the brush and fled to Nebraska. He was eventually captured by W. T. Shortridge and escorted to Denver where he stood trial. The trial took place at the Criterion Hall. Waters was found guilty of murder. Patrick Waters was hanged on December 21, 1860.

The People's Court was abolished when Colorado officially became a territory of the United States on February 26, 1861. Civil and criminal laws were adopted by Governor William Gilpin and the Territorial Congress. Sheriffs were appointed to each of the seventeen counties. Of the many sheriffs, Sheriff Samuel Howe of Denver would prove to be a formidable foe against crime and murder.

Assassination
Soldier Blue

Captain Silas Soule had volunteered his services to his country during the Civil War. He was admired and well liked by most of his fellow soldiers. But not everyone held Soule in esteemed regard. On the night of April 25, 1865, just weeks after the end of the Civil War, the assassination of President Abraham Lincoln, and just weeks after his wedding, Silas Soule was gunned down on the streets of Denver by an assassin's bullet.

By all accounts, and there are several, ranging from his own letters to family diaries, Si Soule, as his friends called him, was known for his sense of humor, quick wit, and fierce loyalty to family, friends and country. He came from a strong New England family with historical roots.

The Soule family descended from George Soule, a passenger on the *Mayflower*, the ship that carried the first settlers to New England. Amasa Soule was a strong abolitionist who, in 1855, moved his wife, Sophia, and four children, including his sixteen-year-old son, Silas, to a newly purchased farm at Coal Creek, very near Lawrence, Kansas. The move was for the sole purpose of aiding in the establishment of entering Kansas as a free state to the Union.

At Lawrence, Amasa Soule became a leading activist, helping to establish the first Underground Railroad station in the area, for the escape of slaves. Young Silas was beside his father in these activities and within a year, he became one of the original "Jayhawkers," an anti-slavery group who actively worked against the pro-slavery forces. These conflicts would become known in history as the "Bleeding Kansas" years leading up to the Civil War.

Silas Soule gained notoriety with his leading role in the 1859 rescue of a Lawrence physician, and ardent abolitionist, John Doy. Dr. Doy, traveling on a road near Lawrence, stopped to help a group of escaped slaves. A group of pro-slavery forces from Missouri, crossing into Kansas, happened upon the incident and apprehended Dr. Doy. He was found guilty of harboring slaves and given a term of five years in prison. Soule and a group of Jayhawkers broke him out of jail and took him by boat across the Missouri River to safety back in Kansas. Soule and his group gained notoriety in the region and were soon dubbed "The Jayhawker Ten." Because of this, Soule was asked to assist in a plan to rescue the well-known abolitionist, John Brown, from a jail at Harper's Ferry, Virginia. However, the rescue attempt never occurred as Brown refused to be rescued.[20]

Soule spent some time in Philadelphia, Pennsylvania, before returning to Kansas. He had several meetings with Eastern abolitionists, including the increasingly popular poet, Walt Whitman. The two became friends.

When Soule arrived back in Lawrence in the spring of that year, he found that most of his friends and even his brother William had left for the Rocky Mountain region and the new gold rush. Determined to join his friends on a new adventure, Soule left for the mountain region west of Denver City with a group of several heading west under the slogan of "Pikes Peak or Bust."

Prospecting near today's towns of Empire, Evergreen, Idaho Springs, and Grant, Soule helped establish Geneva Gulch, and Central City, where he settled for a time. Evidently tired of prospecting, or down on his luck, he wrote to a friend on July 21, 1861. The letter included the observation: "...getting Damn sick of this God forsaken place." [15] The future for Silas Soule was about to change, and the decision he would make would not only lead to historic controversy debated to this day, but would also end with his assassination.

The Colorado Territory had been created and granted by the U.S. Congress on August 1, 1861. William Gilpin, selected by President Abraham Lincoln, became the territorial governor. One of Gilpin's first acts was to organize the First Regiment of Colorado Volunteers. The purpose was to aid in the war effort, as well as protect Colorado citizens against increased crime from roaming bandits and marauding Indians.

The summer had been a hot one with rumors swirling of a Confederate attack. Posters were hung at street corners with offers to buy percussion caps and ammunition for use against the Confederate

"CAMP—WELD" C.T.

Camp Weld was established west of Denver to protect citizens from roaming bands of Indians.

Denver Public Library, Western History Department

forces. At the same time hostile Indian tribes were capitalizing on the chaotic situation, intensifying their aggression against white settlement.

Governor Gilpin had sent several requests to Secretary of War Simon Cameron, detailing the situation and asking for help from Washington. Cameron, overwhelmed with the raging war in the East, was unable to grant Gilpin's requests. Although he had no official authority from the War Department, Gilpin went forth with his plan.

One of the largest recruiting centers in the territory was at Central City. Captain Samuel Tappan, with his persuasive persona effected the enlistment of over one hundred men in a twenty-four hour period. One of those men, Silas Soule, not only chose to enlist with the First Colorado Volunteers, he actually fully supported the effort by recruiting fellow miners to the cause. For his efforts, he was awarded a commission as first lieutenant of Company K, under the command of Colonel John P. Slough.[21]

Another man eager to enlist with the First Colorado Volunteers was the former sheriff of Denver, Edward Wynkoop. Enlisting on July 31, 1861, he received a commission as second lieutenant. He would later say in a letter to his son Frank, "I went into the service to help my country in her time of trouble, not to play soldier."[22] Those words would play out not only in his military future, but for Silas Soule, as well.

The citizens of Colorado Territory rallied around the First Colorado Volunteers. On August 10, 1861, several women of the mining town of Eureka, near Central City, hosted a benefit for the recruits. Captain Samuel Tappan led a parade march of his troops down the dirt street. Also in attendance were Silas Soule and Edward Wynkoop. After speeches by Tappan and Wynkoop, the women presented bibles to the troops. On this day, Soule and Wynkoop formed a bond that would last through the events to come and change both of their lives forever.

Soule's duties during his first year of service were primarily in recruiting. He traveled often between Central City and the newly-constructed Camp Weld, on the southwest outskirts of Denver. By the end of that summer, John P. Slough had been promoted to colonel, commanding the First Regiment of Colorado Volunteers. Samuel Tappan had been promoted to lieutenant colonel and requested Wynkoop be given a promotion to captain of A Company.[23] Soule now reported directly to Captain Wynkoop. For the remainder of 1861 Lieutenant Soule worked at garrison duty at Camp Weld, still under construction.

Meanwhile, John Milton Chivington, a Methodist preacher from Ohio who arrived in Denver the previous year, had been asked by Governor Gilpin to serve as regimental chaplain. However, the large, overbearing, gun-toting man of the cloth wanted a fighting commission. Gilpin agreed to the request, granting him the rank of colonel.

In February 1862, rumors of Confederates invading the Rocky Mountain region for the gold were swirling. The Army of the Confederacy had plans to invade the area in an effort to drive out the Union forces. Confederate Brigadier General Henry H. Sibley, with little knowledge of the military ability in the region, boldly moved forward with his plans. His troops, over a thousand, were known as Sibley's Brigade.

The First Regiment of Colorado Volunteers drilled daily. The order finally came to march south and the untested military unit proved its strength and worth to the country. In one march, the men traveled ninety-two miles in thirty-six hours. They reached Fort Union, over four hundred miles from Denver, in thirteen days.

In the encounter against Sibley's Brigade, dubbed as the "Gettysburg of the West," they defeated the Confederate forces at Glorieta Pass in New Mexico Territory over a two day battle. Colonel Chivington led a bold circular maneuver taking his men, including Silas Soule, to the rear of Sibley's line. With his supply lines destroyed, Sibley's men were forced to retreat. Chivington and his men returned to Denver as heroes.

Surprisingly, Silas Soule also became the talk of the local media: "He [Soule] handled himself well in battle." His sense of humor and keen wit made him popular with all who came in contact with him, and his natural ease with the media made him a darling among the reporters. Ovando J. Hollister later reported: "Robbins, Soule and Hardin were here, every one of them as cool and collected as if on parade."[24]

Soule described his fighting experience at Glorieta Pass in triumphant prose to his friend Walt Whitman:

As soon as we heard of the battle we made a forced march to the rescue. We marched a Reg [sic] of some 350 miles in 14 days. We marched 120 miles in three days and 80 miles in 24 hours. I think we made the biggest march on record. We understood that Sibley was making an attact [sic] on Fort Union. The word came to us about sundown after the men had marched 40 miles and had not had their supper and they threw their hats in the air and swore they would march 40 miles farther before they slept and they did. They started off singing the Star spangled banner, [sic] Red white and blue and yankee doodle [sic] so you can imagine what kind of material this Reg is composed of.[25]

So great was Chivington's popularity that by May 1862, both Colonel Slough and Colonel Tappan had tendered their resignations to Brigadier General Edward R. S. Canby, setting up a perfect promotion for Chivington which eventually would make him commander of the entire military district. It was also at this time that the First Regiment of Colorado Volunteers officially became the First Colorado Cavalry.[26]

Under Chivington's command, several officers received field promotions, including Silas Soule and Edward Wynkoop. Canby promoted Wynkoop to major of the regiment, who in turn promoted Soule to captain of Company D.

Continuing his service with the First Colorado Cavalry, Soule served under Wynkoop throughout 1863 at Camp Weld. In January 1864 he was largely in the field with his troops fighting Indians, quelling skirmishes, and generally doing his duty to protect the citizens, from forts such as Garland in Colorado, and Fillmore in New Mexico.

Perhaps the most ardent supporter of the First Colorado Cavalry, William Newton Byers, editor of the *Rocky Mountain News,* never missed an opportunity to report of their accomplishments. A humorous report involving Silas Soule appeared in the August 6, 1864 issue of the paper:

Soule is reported to have had a most successful skirmish lately with a corps of mosquitoes on the Arkansas, making them hunt their holes and mortally maiming more than one of 'em. Still later advice states that three dead bodies were picked up on the field next morning but whether they met their untimely end by alighting on the Captains very auburn hair and getting scorched or by listening to his sweet Irish brogue and getting charmed, deponent knoweth not!

Captain Soule served as acting assistant adjutant general for the First Colorado Cavalry in July 1864, and accompanied Major Wynkoop, with his new assignment as commander of Fort Lyon, along the Arkansas River, in May 1864.[26] At the fort, both men learned that a band of peaceful Southern Cheyenne, under Chief Black Kettle were camped near the fort. In an effort to clarify his duty, Wynkoop wrote to Chivington: "I would like to receive from headquarters full and thorough instructions in regard to the course I shall adopt in reference to the Indians."[27] Chivington replied with commands to reinforce the military detachment, to be ready for an enemy advance from the Confederates. This was a ruse on the part of Chivington. The winds of war were blowing ever stronger.

Denver Public Library, Western History Dept.
Captain Silas Soule refused to fire on the Cheyenne camped at Sand Creek. Following his testimony against his commander, Colonel Chivington, Soule was assassinated on the streets of Denver.

In early September, Captain Soule accompanied Major Wynkoop into the Kansas Territory to meet with Chief Black Kettle, a meeting that Wynkoop believed would lead to peace for all parties. At the end of the meeting, Black Kettle agreed to return four white children held hostage by the Cheyenne Dog Soldiers.

Captain Soule accompanied his commanding officer, Major Wynkoop, to the peace council held at Camp Weld on September [28], 1864. Wynkoop had informed Chivington of his meeting with Black Kettle and the surrender of four prisoners in exchange for peace. Wynkoop had personally brought in Chiefs Black Kettle and White Antelope, among the many members of both Indian tribes. Rows of army wagons brought the Indians as well as four captives into the city on that fateful morning.

Also forced to attend this meeting was Governor Evans who held a cold reception. Black Kettle spoke of his desire for peace. Chivington informed the chiefs that peace negotiations were to be made "when you lay down your arms...for the time for treaties has passed."[28] Chivington then instructed the Indians to return with Wynkoop and Soule to Fort Lyon.

The influential press, led by Byers and his *Rocky Mountain News*, called for the "immediate extinction of the Indians."

> *The most revolting, shocking cases of assassination, arson, murder and manslaughter that have crimsoned the pages of time have been done by the Indians, in former days and recently-nevertheless we are opposed to anything which looks like a treaty of peace with the Indians...The season is near at hand when they can be chastised and it should be done with no gentle hand...*[29]

With a stroke of predictive journalism, editor William Byers clearly stated the views of many citizens of the Colorado Territory. Territorial politics reached an explosive level by August 1864. The powers at large, primarily in Denver, lobbied Washington for a second time for admission to the Union. The stakes were high and the obstacles were numerous, particularly regarding the Indians. Foremost on the minds of political hopefuls, particularly Governor John Evans and Colonel John M. Chivington, were the recent Indian uprisings. Now, with the support of the influential newspaper editor, the course was clear: eradicate the "Indian problem."

In the crisp autumn of 1864, roving bands of young Cheyenne and Arapaho warriors had raided eastern Colorado and western Kansas, causing alarm among the white settlers. When the Nathan Hungate family were found murdered just south of Denver, their scalped and horribly mutilated bodies were brought to Denver and displayed before the public. Mass hysteria gripped the town.[30]

Governor John Evans found himself in a political pressure cooker. The safety of the citizens as well as secured land prospects that would lead to eventual statehood were at risk. To this end, he clearly needed a military victory against the Indians, for the Colorado citizens, as well as his own political future. Governor Evans called for an additional military militia to end the Indian problem. He wired an urgent plea to Secretary of War Stanton: "Extensive Indian murders, the Indian war begun in earnest." Washington gave Evans the authority to enlist citizens for a regiment not to exceed one hundred days. In less than a month's time, the Third Regiment of Colorado Volunteers were in force against Indian hostility, under Chivington's command.

Governor Evans then issued a general proclamation dispatched to the Indian camps by messengers, ordering all peaceful Indians to assemble at Fort Lyon. Those Indians who did not comply with the order would be killed. The order authorized the citizens of Colorado Territory to:

> *Go in pursuit of all hostile Indians on the plains...kill and destroy, as enemies of the country, wherever the Indians may be found.* [31]

Startled by this proclamation, nevertheless Wynkoop met with the acknowledged peaceful chiefs Black Kettle, White Antelope, Little Raven and Left Hand, who came into Fort Lyon in an effort for peace. Wynkoop told the chiefs to bring their people, along with the Arapaho tribes, to the fort for peace negotiations. Wynkoop then instructed the tribes to camp along Sand Creek, some forty miles from the fort.

When Evans heard of the proposed peace talks, he was enraged. Wynkoop later testified that Evans said: "...it would be supposed at Washington that he had misrepresented matters in regard to the Indian difficulties in Colorado, and he had put the government to a useless expense in raising the regiment; that they had been raised to kill Indians and they must kill Indians." [32] Thus the stage was set for what became the worst tragedy in Colorado history.

Shortly thereafter, Wynkoop was suddenly relieved of his command and replaced with the previous commander of the post, Major Scott Anthony. With this military move, Evans and Chivington proceeded with their plan.

On the morning of November 28, 1864, just two days after Wynkoop had left for his new assignment at Fort Riley, Kansas, Captain Silas Soule was on a reconnaissance mission with twenty troops of the First Colorado regiment, along the Arkansas River. Ten miles up river from Fort Lyon, Soule and his command came upon a mule team on the north bank of the river. In casual conversation, the driver delivered a stunning piece of news to Soule. He had passed Colonel Chivington and a dozen companies of soldiers further up the river. Curious, as no one at the fort had prior knowledge of such a large military force, Soule traveled further upstream. After a few miles, Soule came up to an advancing four column of cavalry soldiers, complete with artillery wagons. Chivington, in the lead, asked Soule if anyone at the fort knew he was coming. Soule replied in the negative. Soule returned to the fort, following Chivington's advance.

Denver Public Library, Western History Dept.

Colonel John M. Chivington ordered the Indian attack at Sand Creek on November 29, 1864. Chivington may have later ordered the assassination of his nemesis, Captain Silas Soule.

Once at the fort, Chivington immediately took command and sealed off the fort. No one was allowed in or out. Meeting with Major Anthony, Chivington revealed his plan of attack on the Indians. Anthony then organized his troops accordingly.

Soule later wrote a letter to Major Wynkoop:

> *"As soon as I knew of their movement I was indignant as you would have been were you here and went to Cannon's room, where a number of officers of the 1st and 3rd were congregated and told them that any man who would take a part in the murders, knowing the circumstances as we did, was a low cowardly son of a bitch. Capt. Y. J. Johnson and Lieut. Hardin went to camp and reported to Chiv, Downing and the whole outfit what I had said, and you can bet hell was to pay in camp."*[33]

Captain Silas Soule immediately went to his commanding officer,

Major Anthony, asking the major to dissuade Chivington of such an action.

I talked to Anthony about it, and he said that some of those Indians ought to be killed; that he had been only waiting for a good chance to pitch it to them. I reminded him of the pledges he had made them, and he said that Colonel Chivington had told him that those Indians in the camp should not be killed; that the object of the expedition was to go out to the Smoky Hill and follow the Indians up. Anthony told me that I would not compromise myself by going out, as I was opposed to going.[34]

Obviously this was not the case. Lieutenant Joseph A. Cramer also made a case for reconsideration to Chivington who replied in part, "...damn any man that is in sympathy with Indians." Both Cramer and Soule were put on notice to steer clear of Chivington. Their orders stood. At eight o'clock that night, nearly seven hundred troops comprised of the First Colorado Cavalry, including Soule, as well as the Colorado Third Infantry under Colonel George L. Shoup, and the additional troops from Fort Lyon, under Major Anthony, marched north from Fort Lyon to the banks of Sand Creek and into infamy.

Dawn broke cold and foggy on the barren prairie along the banks of Sand Creek on November 29, 1864. Camped in the ravine near the creek were some six hundred Indians, primarily women and children, along with chiefs Little Raven, White Antelope, Left Hand and Black Kettle.

Chivington divided his forces into a three-pronged attack of the village from the south, the east and west. Rounding out the armed troops were four twelve-pound howitzers. As the sun rose, Chivington's troops began their charge into the sleepy Indian village, a fight that would last over six hours. White Antelope, hearing the shots, left his lodge with arms extended, in the traditional sign of peace. He was shot down in a single round of fire.

Major Anthony's First Colorado Regiment were used as reinforcements along the battle lines. On a ridge a short distance from the village, Captain Silas Soule watched in horror as the slaughter of human beings went on and on. When he was ordered to lead Company D into the battle, Soule steadfastly refused. Lieutenant Joseph Cramer also refused to send in his troops.

As a military operation, the battle was a horrible bungle. Military command was lost early in the day, as soldiers were caught in their own crossfire. The surprised Indians, a few chiefs and warriors who were in camp, were ill-armed, but managed to hold their own and kept the soldiers at bay for quite some time. Meanwhile, nearly five hundred Indians were able to escape across the prairie, including Black Kettle, who carried his bullet-riddled wife to safety north toward the Smoky Hill River.

Those Indians who could not flee the bloody insanity died on the spot, primarily women and children. Eye-witness testimony estimated the number just under two hundred, while Chivington would boast six hundred "hostiles" killed. "When the sun was high in the sky," as the Indians later recounted, the battle was over. Later that afternoon, Major Anthony ordered Soule to accompany him back to Fort Lyon. Soule led the supply team back the miserable miles to the fort in silence. Chivington and his men remained at battlefield site of the slaughter. He would later return to Denver and a hero's welcome.

Back at Fort Lyon, Soule and several soldiers spoke quietly of their disdain for what had happened at Sand Creek. Colonel Tappan, who was at Fort Lyon at the time of the attack recuperating from a leg injury, heard the talk of the soldiers and began making inquiries. Meanwhile, Soule and Cramer took on a letter writing campaign to get the truth out. As more and more soldiers began to open up, it became clear the battlefield was not the only site of atrocity.

In a lengthy letter describing the horrible events of the day written to Wynkoop dated December 14, 1864, Soule said in part:

> *Jack Smith was taken prisoner, and murdered the next day in his tent by one of Denn's Co. "E". I understand the man received a horse for doing the job. They were going to murder Charlie Bent, but I run him into the Fort. They were going to kill Old Uncle John Smith, but Lt. Cannon and the boys of Ft. Lyon, interfered, and saved him. They would have murdered Old Bents family, if Col. Tappan had not taken the matter in hand. Cramer went up with twenty men, and they did not like to buck against so many of the 1*[st].[35]

Through detailed reports received by Secretary of War Stanton, an investigation by the Joint Committee on the Conduct of War began on

January 10, 1865. Ultimately there would be several investigations, however, the most comprehensive and dramatic investigation occurred in Denver. The military panel, headed by Colonel Tappan, was hotly contested by Chivington, who by this time had been mustered out of service. The first order of business was on January 14, when Tappan placed Wynkoop as commander of Fort Lyon; again.

Captain Silas Soule was the first to testify on February 11, 1865. He described in graphic detail the brutal killings of the innocent Indians camped at Sand Creek, and in damning testimony related the previous peaceful negotiations by Wynkoop and continued under Anthony, to allow the the tribes to camp at Sand Creek. With Soule's testimony, which lasted for three days and was supported by other soldiers of the First Colorado Regiment, as well as officers including Cramer and Wynkoop, the U. S. Congress opened a full investigation.

Meanwhile Captain Soule had been transferred to the Denver Provost Guard. By testifying against Chivington, which destroyed Chivington's reputation, Soule became the target of Chivington supporters, a strong group in Denver. Although aware of the threats this group posed, by all accounts Soule performed his duties as Provost Marshal without incident, and remained a favorite topic in the *Rocky Mountain News*.

> *The Regimental Band and Capt. Soule, too, were musically on it yesterday — thanks to their good taste and generosity for a glorious serenade, now mellow as St. Patricks [sic] day.*[36]

On April 1, 1865, Silas Soule and Hersa Coberly were married in a private ceremony by Reverend Kehler, the chaplain of the First Cavalry. And again, the *Rocky Mountain News* covered the event in the April 5 issue:

> *Married. In this city, at the residence of H.J. Rogers, on the 1st inst., at 8 o'clock A.M. by Rev. Mr. Kehler, Capt. Silas Soule and Miss Hersey [sic] A. Coberly.*

On Sunday evening, April 23, 1865, Silas Soule and his bride of three weeks had just returned to their home on Curtis Street, around 9:30, when shots rang out. As provost marshal, Soule left to investigate. He walked along Lawrence Street, crossed at F Street, and proceeded to Arapahoe Street, where he was confronted by a man who instantly shot him in the head. Captain Silas Soule fell to the street, dying instantly.[37] He was twenty-six years old.

Although the assassin fled the murder scene on foot, eyewitnesses stated the murderer was Private Charles W. Squiers, of the Second Colorado Cavalry, formerly under Chivington's command. Squiers had previously been accused of attempted murder, however he was released from the charges based on the recurring obstacle of proper territorial jurisdiction.

Authorities learned from tips and informants that Squiers had left for New Mexico, proudly claiming to his friends he had killed Soule.

It was widely suspected that Squiers was either an agent or an assassin paid by Chivington himself. Shortly before Soule was killed Chivington had given a speech where he offered to his supporters five hundred dollars to any person who would kill an Indian or one who sympathized with them. Flame-throwing rhetoric to be sure, however soldiers and officers of the First Colorado Regiment had previously testified to overhearing Chivington's threats against Soule and Cramer at Fort Lyon. Therefore, a posse was sent to New Mexico to track Squiers and return him to Denver.

Meanwhile, the *Rocky Mountain News* covered the horrific assassination in the April 24 issue under the headline:

The Homicide Last Night

> *Our city was thrown into a feverish excitement last evening by the assassination of Captain S. S. Soule, of the Colorado First. The sad affair took place about half past ten o'clock, and was evidently coolly and deliberately planned, and as systematically carried out. For some time past the Captain had been in charge of the provost guard of the city and neighborhood, and his duties in that capacity had, as a natural consequence, created many enemies. Threats against his life have been freely and frequently made — so we are informed — and no longer ago than yesterday he said that he was expecting to be attacked. In the evening he and his wife were visiting at the house of a friend and returned home between nine and ten o'clock. Shortly after, a number of pistol shots were fired in the upper part of the city, evidently to decoy him out, and the Captain started to ascertain the cause. Whilst passing along Lawrence*

Denver Police Museum

David J. Cook was perhaps the most successful lawman in Denver's early history.

Street, Near F, and directly in front of the residence of Dr. Cunningham, he seems to have been met by the assassin, and the indications are that both fired at the same instant, or so near together that the reports seemed simultaneous. Probably the Captain, expecting to be attacked, was in readiness, and when the other man presented his pistol, he did the same, but the intended assassin fired an instant soonest, with but too fatal effect.

The ball entered the Captain's face at the point of the right cheek bone, pressing backward and upward, and lodging in the back part of the head. He fell back dead, appearing not to have moved a muscle after falling. The other man, from the indications, was wounded in the right hand or arm; how severely is not known. His pistol was dropped at his feet and he immediately started and ran towards the military camp in the upper part of the city, leaving a distinct trail of blood where he passed along. When the shots were fired they were standing about four feet apart, face to face. Within less than a minute after the fatal shot, one of the provost guard and Mr. Ruter reached the spot. The Captain was already dead, and his murderer had disappeared. They alarmed Dr. Cunningham, and a guard was sent for.

A number of persons, soldiers and civilians, soon gathered around, and after a few minutes the body was removed to the building occupied by the officers of the Headquarters of the District. The excitement this morning, when the facts became generally known, was intense. Hundreds of citizens visited the scene of the tragedy, and it has formed the burthen of conversation throughout the city all day. Patrols were dispatched in every direction, and it is hardly possible that he will escape more than for a day or two. Probably he will be overtaken to-day. Of his identity we shall at present refrain from speaking, though there is scarce a doubt but it is clearly known. The cause is said to have grown out of an arrest made by the Captain in the discharge of his duty as Provost Marshal.

Captain Soule was highly respected by his brother officers, and beloved by the men in his company.

He was married in this city on the 1st inst., and consequently leaves a young wife to mourn this terrible and untimely fate.

It is the hope of all that his murderer and his accomplices will be speedily brought to judgment, and a punishment meted out to them such as the base crime deserves."

A few interesting points in this news article are worth mentioning. First, it was no secret that Editor Byers backed Chivington and defended his actions in the paper. The fact that Byers chose not to release the name of the suspected murderer to the public is highly suspect of proper journalism of the era. Second, it was a well-known fact that threats had been made against Soule specifically because of his testimony against Chivington. The insertion into the article that the cause of the shooting was "said to have grown out of an arrest made by the Captain in the discharge of his duty as Provost Marshal," is an inaccurate statement and must have been inserted as a distraction to the obvious assassination that it was.

As the military investigation into the Sand Creek matter, and Chivington in particular, was still ongoing in Denver, the following statement was entered into the official record:

The members of the Commissions having been requested to assist in making arrangements for the funeral of the late lamented Silas S. Soule, commission adjourned until Thursday morning April 27th, 1865 at 9 o'clock.

The funeral for Captain Silas Soule took place in Denver on Wednesday, April 26, at St. John's church. One of the largest funerals to date in the city, the church was crowded with many citizens who knew of the jovial provost marshal by his fine reputation in the city.

Also in attendance, surprisingly enough given the political dynamic, was Governor John Evans.[38]

The *Rocky Mountain News* covered the funeral in the April 27 issue in the obituary section, saying in part:

> As a military funeral, this was the finest we have ever seen in the country. The officers and soldiers and Lt. Wilson's Company, made an appearance of style and discipline most "military" indeed. A long line of carriages — almost all the public and private ones in town — were in the citizen cortege. Deceased was about 27 years of age, descended from Irish parentage. His sister and mother reside in Lawrence, Kansas. His young widowed bride - has been draped in weeds before the orange blossoms scarce had time to wither.[39]

Captain Silas Soule was buried with full military honors at Mount Prospect Cemetery, or the City Cemetery as it became commonly known. A group of generous citizens began a collection drive for a proper memorial for his grave site.[40]

There is some evidence that in early July, Wynkoop learned of Squiers' exact location in Las Vegas, New Mexico, and alerted the military forces in that region. In any case, Squiers was arrested in Las Vegas, New Mexico, where Lieutenant James Cannon traveled to bring the prisoner back to Denver to stand trial for the murder of Captain Soule.

Cannon and his prisoner arrived in Denver on July 11, where Squiers was taken in cuffs and chains to the provost jail on Larimer Street, to face a military trial for murder. The recently completed jail was, ironically, constructed during the tenure of the late provost marshal, Silas Soule.[41]

Meanwhile, Lt. Cannon took a room at the nearby Tremont House, where three days later he was found dead in his room. An incomplete autopsy ruled the death a natural cause. However, several members of the military pushed for an investigation. The *Daily News*, a small Denver paper, reported in their July 14, 1865 issue: "Mysterious Death of Lt. Cannon — Evidence before the Coroner's Inquest." Sheriff O. O. Kent served as the coroner. As mysterious as the death may have seemed, so was the subsequent coroner's inquest. No reports ever appeared in any of the newspapers. However, the *Rocky Mountain*

News did report Cannon's burial, in the City Cemetery, the very next day after the inquest was held.[42] Major Wynkoop would later write what he had always believed, that Lt. Cannon was poisoned.[43]

Squiers spent his time in the provost jail in chains as he awaited his trial. However, just days before the trial was set to begin, Squiers escaped. The *Rocky Mountain News* reported the incident in the October 10, 1865 issue:

> *It is supposed he [Squiers] was aided from the outside, as the large padlock at the back door was picked. Two men are under arrest for aiding in the escape, one of them, a blacksmith, charged with furnishing the chisels for removing the shackles from the limbs of the prisoner.*

Accounts vary as to where Squiers went; the fact is he was never seen in Denver again and thus never held accountable for the assassination of Captain Silas S. Soule.

No direct evidence was ever presented implicating Chivington in either Silas Soule's murder or Squiers' escape from the provost jail. However, following the very convenient escape, even the most ardent Chivington supporters came to believe he was behind both crimes. Perhaps Major Wynkoop said it best:

> *"...Col. Chivington never dared to place Capt. Soule in arrest but some months subsequently had him murdered at night in the streets of Denver by an assassin whom he hired for that purpose."*[44]

The Italian Mob Murders
Sunday, Bloody Sunday

In 1873, under Mayor Joseph Bates, Denver hired a town marshal and several deputies to patrol the streets. Many of this group would become members of Denver's first official police force, formed in April 1874.[45]

One of these men would go on to have a distinguished career and a place in Denver history. He was David J. Cook. Elected sheriff of Arapahoe County in 1869, he was appointed as the major general of the Colorado Militia in 1873, under the same auspice as the Denver appointments. At the same time, Cook formed the Rocky Mountain Detective Association, a group of sheriffs, police chiefs, and marshals across the western states that worked together in law enforcement. It was in this capacity that he was able to apprehend the killers of the bloodiest murder in the history of Denver's first century.

For several days in the cool autumn air of October, 1875, neighbors in the 600 block of Lawrence Street began complaining of an increasingly vile odor in the area. As the odor intensified, police officers were called to investigate. The officers were drawn to a building at 634 Lawrence Street, where thousands of flies swarmed around the windows and doors. The building seemed to be empty, so the police entered through an unlocked front door. Immediately the officers noticed the blood. It was everywhere. There were bloodstains on the floor, on the walls, and even dried pools of blood in the kitchen.

Investigation of the kitchen led to the discovery of a trap door in the floor. Opening the trap door, the most foul effluvial vapor nearly overpowered the officers. Continuing on, they descended the rickety bloodstained steps.

Dirty mattresses were heaped in a corner, obviously placed to cover something...or someone. Under the mattresses were four decomposing naked male bodies. Their throats had been slit from ear to ear. The wide gashes on each of the bodies were infested with maggots. Their bodies were riddled with deep knife wounds. Amid the clutter of the basement, which included several musical instruments, were found some of the weapons used in this quadruple murder. Among the weapons the police found were a bloody hatchet with clumps of hair secured in the dried blood, and several bloody knives.

By this time the neighborhood was filled with rumors and speculations as to what had occurred; the who and the why. The police had the same questions and began interviewing the neighbors. It was learned that several Italian immigrants had moved into the building some months previously. No one seemed to know who they were by name, yet knew that they were musicians from observations of their daily activities. Further interrogation of the neighbors revealed no one had seen them or any activity from the house since the previous Sunday.

When the news of the murders hit the streets of Denver, Giuseppe

Cuneo, Denver's Italian consul, told the *Rocky Mountain News* in an interview dated October 19, 1875, that he believed it was disgruntled laborers that had "...hacked a 'tyrant' boss' to death." The article added a bit of journalistic prose: "He reminds us of the artistic grace the Italian throws even into his crime."

As the four bodies laid unclaimed in the county morgue, eventually a local shoemaker identified the adult male only as "Uncle Joe," a customer, and also identified the shoes retrieved at the crime scene as those of "Uncle Joe's," which he had repaired. In addition, he said the other three bodies, all young males, were known to him as sons and a nephew of "Uncle Joe."

Still, the murder case was a mystery. As the coroner's jury began their investigation, David J. Cook, sheriff of Arapahoe County, began his own investigation. His due diligence and keen skills led to the identity of the deceased. Guiseppe Peccorra, along with his two sons, Guiseppe, Jr. and Giovanni, and his nephew, Luigi, were the four victims of the brutal murder.

Further investigation by Cook revealed that the deceased men had been frequent associates of Filomeno Gallotti and Michiele Ballotti, known as the leaders of a Denver Italian mob, who ran their various operations, including a "tin-shop" out of a building at the lower end of Fifteenth Street.[40] Cook talked to as many people as he could when he found this building was now vacant. The names of two other men, Leonardo Alessandri and Silvestro Campagne, were repeated in his conversations with several people.

Gallotti had seemed to disappear, but Cook did learn from inventory lists and account receipts that many items were missing. Of particular interest were tools, knives and hatchets. Cook believed he had a working theory on the murder and the murderers. Two teams were put on the case, one to learn everything they could about Gallotti and the other to track him down.

It seemed Gallotti was a victim of the very crime element he became the head of. As a young boy in Italy he was allegedly stolen by a mob gang. Growing up under such circumstances, it was only natural that he would become a gangster as well. In the years before he emigrated to America, he rose to some prominence in the mob. He was known as cold-blooded and it was a widely held belief that he had committed several murders, forcing him to leave the country.

Members of Denver's Italian mob were photographed by Denver police following their capture, led by David J. Cook.

Meanwhile, Cook learned the other three murder victims that had been identified as family members of Peccorra, were in fact, young boys Peccorra had lured into working for him. They were sent out to work the streets as musicians for money, which was given to Peccorra in exchange for their scant living conditions. Cook also learned that Peccorra may have been using this operation as a ruse, and that he may have been involved with Italian mobs as well.

On a tip or a stroke of luck, Cook learned that the vanished men might be making their way to the Mexican border. In an effort to intercept them, as well as alert officers along the border, Cook sent out a series of cablegrams to all ports of entry. At about the same time, he received information that three men matching the descriptions Cook had of the alleged murderers were seen boarding the southbound train at the Littleton depot. He immediately sent his top men, W. Frank Smith and R. Y. Force, to track them down.

After three weeks of following leads, the officers walked into an Italian bar in Trinidad, Colorado. With another stroke of good luck, Smith and Force found all three of the men they were searching for. On stage performing for the patrons of the bar were Alessandri, Balloti, and Campagne. The officers presented themselves to the musical trio and placed them under arrest. Taken to the local jail, the three men were searched. The men's undershirts were stained with blood.

Interrogated separately, the men eventually turned on each other and divulged the entire scheme that led to the murders in Denver. The next morning, the officers secured the men in chains and boarded the train for Denver.

The news had already reached Denver even before the suspected murderers arrived.

Alessandri Confesses!

This was the headline of the *Denver Daily News* of November 9, 1875. The train was expected back in Denver at five o'clock that evening. As a throng of people gathered at the depot, awaiting the arrival of the murderers, Cook took action to avoid a potential vigilante mob. Guards were placed along a passageway where the heavily guarded prisoners passed through unharmed. Undaunted, the crowd, now shouting, "Hang them!" and "Get a rope," followed the horse-drawn omnibus containing the prisoners, all the way down to Blake Street, where they were successfully taken into the jail. Cook and his men, with Winchesters in hand, held off the vigilantes.

Through further interrogation of the newest jail inmates, Cook learned of the involvement of two additional men, Leonardo Deodotta, and "Old Joe" Pinachio. It seemed these men knew of the money taken from the house during the night of the murderous event. Cook arrested Deodotta, still in Denver, and Pinachio at his home near Sloan's Lake. Cook strongly urged the men to tell all they knew. And tell they did. Cook learned that Pinachio's Sloan's Lake residence was the underground place where the money was held and controlled by Gallotti and the mob. When the attempt to rob Peccorra of the money turned to murder, the men hid the money. Cook took both men to where they said the money was hidden. After a few attempts, Deodotta located the blood money. Deodotta further stated that Gallotti would soon be in contact with him for the money.

With this evidence in hand and the confession of the two men, Cook now had a motive. He set out to bring in Gallotti. Luck seemed to be with Cook once again when an informant passed a letter to him, detailing the travel plans of Gallotti. With two of his mob members, he was headed south to Mexico. It further said that a fourth mob member had been sent back to Denver to retrieve the money. Cook put officers on watch for the returning member, while again sending his top man, W. Frank Smith, south to track down Gallotti.

Along with Smith was James Lewis, who knew Gallotti and spoke Italian. The men tracked the alleged murderer to Taos, New Mexico, where they learned a man matching Gallotti's description had been frequenting a local shop, buying a gun with a twenty dollar gold piece, as well as selling gold to the proprietor. The officers, with the cooperation of the shop owner, lured Gallotti into the shop with the pretense of a desire to buy more gold.

When Gallotti entered the store, suspecting nothing, he was greeted by the officers who placed him under arrest. The officers returned to Denver, with their prisoner in chains.

Gallotti was safely housed in the county jail and under the protection of newly-hired Denver police officers. As the news that Gallotti was in the jail, there were several attempts by lynch mobs to enter the jailhouse. Cook and his men held them off.

Cook informed Gallotti of the confessions made by Pinachio and Deodotta. Gallotti then made a full confession to Cook of the quadruple murder. Among his many statements are those that detail the murders. He said:

> *"I commenced the job at the card table, by catching 'Old Joe' by the hair and sawing my knife across his throat until he was quite dead. I helped to kill one of the boys, as the others were making a bad job of it. I then put up my knife and watched Anatta, and Ballotti cut the other two. They are as guilty as I and deserve as severe a punishment"*[46]

This confession led to even more arrests in the quadruple murder. On December 4, 1875, a grand jury was impaneled to hear testimony. John Anatta, implicated by Gallotti's confession, turned state's evidence. Indictments for murder were issued for the seven arrested men.

On February 8, 1875, the alleged murderers were arraigned and their trials were set. Gallotti appeared before the District Court on May 20, 1875, pleading guilty before the court.

The prosecuting attorneys were able show that, under Colorado

Denver Police Museum
An 1873 hanging in Denver, attended by David J. Cook.

law of 1870 the defendant could be tried for murder despite his plea of guilty, but could not receive the death penalty. Future Colorado governor and U.S. senator, Charles S. Thomas, served as Gallotti's defense attorney. Thomas was able to successfully argue that no jury could be impaneled following a defendant's guilty plea, with the death penalty as a possibility. With this successful argument, the prosecuting team reduced the possible sentence from death to life in prison.

The murder trial of Filomeno Gallotti, eventually held in the spring of 1876, ended with the jury finding Gallotti guilty of murder. He was sentenced to life in prison.

Accomplices in the murder, Ballotti and Valentine were also sentenced to life in prison under Colorado law, while Anatta, Alessandri and Campagne were each sentenced to ten years in prison. The remaining accomplices in the murders were acquitted.

In August 1876, Colorado achieved statehood. The Centennial State's first legislature adopted both the 1868 death penalty statute as well as the 1870 provision amending it.

* * *

As the city of Denver entered into the next decade, law enforcement had greatly improved. The Charter of Ordinances of the City of Denver, created in 1862, while noble in theory, placed a number of requirements on the lawmen. Forced to comply with the many city ordinances upon a frontier town full of saloons, gambling establishments, and bordellos, the job was overwhelming for a lawman who worked alone. As in any newly established town or city, there was little money to pay forcement, not to mention protection of the citizens. As with any police force, try as they may, they could not be everywhere.

Notes for Part I

1. Quote from William N. Byers' *Hand Book to the Gold Fields of Nebraska and Kansas*, D. B. Cooke of Chicago, 1859.
2. *Pikes Peak Gold Rush Guidebooks of 1859*, edited and republished in 1941 by Aurther H. Clark and Company.
3. *The Rocky Mountain News*, April 23, 1859. It should also be noted that at this same meeting a motion was passed to organize a new "State or Territory."
4. Historians have used various spellings of the surnames of both the victim and the murderer. As there are no legal records preserved, I have chosen to rely on the personal diary of William Larimer Jr., who along with his father, founded the first cemetery in the settlement. Larimer Jr.'s diary records the first burials as they occurred including the entry; "April 9,1859: Aurther Binegraff, German, murdered by Jn. Stuffle," and "John Stuffle, German, Hung after a fair trial." Both men were buried on the same day. Further, in covering the murder, the *Rocky Mountain News* in their first issue, April 23, 1859, omitted both names. In the January 9, 1878 issue of the paper, a recount of the murder includes the names spelled as "Biencroff" and "Stoefel." There is no accounting for the source of these respective spellings in the issue of the paper.
5. *Lynching in Colorado 1859-1919*, pg.17.
6. *History of Denver*, pg. 339.
7. *The '59er's Roaring Denver in the Gold Rush Days; The First Three Years*, pg. 23.
8. *The '59er's Roaring Denver in the Gold Rush Days; The First Three Years*, pg. 15.
9. Some historians spell the surname O'Neil.
10. Ferry Street is today's 11th Street.
11. F Street later became 15th Street.
12. *Rocky Mountain News* issues of December 11 and 18, 1860.
13. *History of Denver*, pg. 343.
14. G Street later became today's 16th Street.
15. Colorado did not become a territory until 1861.
16. Kehler would later serve as chaplain of the First Cavalry. John H. Kehler Collection, CHS.
17. F Street would later become 15th Street and G Street, 16th Street.

18. *The Rocky Mountain News*, October 1, 1860.
19. Today's 14th Street.
20. "An Attempted Rescue of John Brown From Charlestown, Virginia Jail," Kansas State Historical Society, Vol. VIII, pg. 213-226.
21. From the Anne Hemphill family collection.
22. First Regiment of Colorado Volunteer Records and Company Muster Roll, CHS.
23. Wynkoop Collection, Chavez History Library.
24. Company Muster Roll of July 29 through August 31, 1861. Transcripts of the Colorado Volunteers records, State of Colorado, Division of the Archives and Public Records.
25. Hollister, *Boldly They Rode*, pg. 70.
26. Letter dated March 1862, Charles E. Feinberg Whitman Collection, Library of Congress.
27. Colorado State Archives. This change occurred in November of 1862 and is an important distinction. Many authors have interchanged the two regiments in accounts of both Glorieta Pass and the Sand Creek Massacre. The change was specifically made to convert from infantry to cavalry by the War Department to be "more effective for Indian-fighting purposes," Glorieta Pass being military prior to the conversion.
28. Ironically, Chivington had replaced Major Scott Anthony with Major Edward Wynkoop, a move he would later reverse.
29. Congressional Testimony, Wynkoop, March 20, 1865.
30. Congressional Records, "The Rebellion Records," Series I, Vol. XLI.
31. *The Rocky Mountain News*, September 28, 1864.
32. The Cheyenne Indians were later found innocent of the murders.
33. United States Congress, Report on the Conduct of War, including testimony,1865.
34. ibid.
35. Roberts and Halass, *Written in Blood*, pg. 328-331.
36. Sand Creek Massacre Testimony, 1865.
37. ibid.
38. Letter held in its entirety at the Denver Public Library, Western History Department.
39. The March 18, 1865 issue of *The Rocky Mountain News*.
40. In November of 2010, the Colorado Historical Society placed a memorial plaque in honor of Captain Silas Soule on the building at the northwest corner of Fifteenth and Arapahoe streets in downtown Denver. It was at this exact location where Soule was assassinated on April 23, 1865. The plaque reads: "Silas S. Soule. At this location on April 23, 1865, assassins shot and killed First Colorado Cavalry officer Capt. Silas S. Soule. During the infamous Sand Creek Massacre of November 29, 1864, Soule had disobeyed orders by refusing to fire on Chief Black Kettle's peaceful Cheyenne and Arapaho village. Later, at army hearings, Soule testified against his commander, Col. John M. Chivington, detailing the atrocities committed by the troops at Sand Creek. His murderers were never brought to justice."
41. *Kansas State Historical Quarterly*, November, 1939 Vol. 8, No. 4.
42. Perkins, LaVonne. "Silas Soule and His Widow Heresa [sic], and the Rest of the Story." *Denver Westerners Roundup*, Vol LV, no.2, Mar-Apr, 1999.
43. Mrs. Hersa Coberly Soule was twenty years old at the untimely death of her husband.
44. A six foot tall obelisk was placed on Soule's grave on June 19, 1866. When Soule and many other bodies were removed to Riverside Cemetery beginning in 1893, the obelisk was not and, thus is lost to history. Perkins, pg. 13.
45. Wynkoop unfinished manuscript, Colorado Historical Society, Kraft, Wynkoop, pg. 151. Although Wynkoop by this time was on his way back to Fort Riley, the message could have been sent.
46. *The Rocky Mountain News*, February 9, 1865.
47. *The Rocky Mountain News*, July 15, 1865.
48. Wynkoop's unfinished manuscript, Colorado Historical Society.
49. *The Denver Police Department Pictorial Review and History, 1859-1985*.
50. ibid.
51. "Hands Up" Cook, David J. pg.7.
52. "Hands Up", Cook, pg. 26. 'Old Joe' is actually "Uncle Joe" Peccorra who was murdered that night. Whether it was a misstatement by Gallotti or misreported by Cook is not known.

Part II

1880 - 1899

A s Denver entered the next decade, the city experienced an economic boom that resonated across the state. Colorado's mining industry led to financial wealth that brought the Union Pacific and Kansas Pacific Railroad to Denver in 1870. As Denver became the railroad hub for the state's commerce and business, the city grew in size and population. From the northern edge of the city, where the Omaha and Grant Smelter operated, to the south, along the South Platte River, factories, warehouses, and the bustling railroad yards contributed to the growth of the city.

With such an economic boom, employment opportunities abounded. As the labor market soon tightened, racial tension became an increasing issue in Denver.

* * *

The Chinese Riots
Race Riot & Murder

Racial tensions in the city, and across the state for that matter, had been brewing for quite some time. With the strong economy many immigrants came for employment opportunities, competing for jobs that common American laborers were also seeking. Added to this tension were the labor organizers who also wanted to capitalize on the state's growing economy. Very early on both the Chinese and the Italian immigrants were targeted by labor leaders in the city.

Joseph Buchanan, a Denver labor leader, was particularly against the Chinese encroachment into the city, saying that, while he believed in the "Brotherhood of Man," regarding the Chinese people he believed in "Brotherhood of Limited."[1] Denver's Italian vice consul, Giuseppe Cuneo, denounced the Chinese as "a class of creatures my people are

63

Denver Public Library, Western History Department
Denver's Larimer Street scene, circa 1880.

sold to every day — a curse to their own people, a disgrace to their country and a stain upon any country that gives them hospitality."[2]

This sort of attitude soon gained favor throughout the city and even in the realm of politics by 1880. It stemmed from Territorial Governor Edward M. McCook's speech to the territorial legislature of January 31, 1870, which convened in Central City. In this speech, he said that Colorado needed the Chinese labor and should welcome them. He said in part, "They are exceedingly muscular: and if we can first avail ourselves of their muscle, we can attend to their morals afterwards." Many Colorado businessmen, particularly railroad and mine owners, agreed with the governor.

In 1880, there were just under one thousand Chinese immigrants living within Denver's city limits. The majority of these immigrants lived in lower downtown, primarily on upper Holladay Street, (the heart of the red light district) north to Twentieth Street. While legitimate businesses did exist, such as laundry services, Chinese markets, and restaurants, there were also several opium dens in the area. The largest concentration of the opium dens were found in the alleys of the 2000 block between Holladay and Blake streets, an area known as Hop Alley.

Forbes Parkhill, a young reporter for the *Denver Post*, who would go on to write books and articles on early Denver history, later wrote of his experiences in Hop Alley:

> *On either side of a dim, narrow corridor the visitor found tiny, windowless, board-partitioned cubicles, barely large enough for a cot and a taboret containing the opium-smoking layout. As a police reporter, I once took part in a raid on these firetrap opium joints. The raiders were empowered to make arrests only when they discovered a smoker in the act of 'hitting the pipe.' The patrolmen would boost me up to look over the transoms. If I found an addict actually smoking, he was arrested. The raid netted a number of white men, a few Negroes, two Chinese, and no women. The only woman addict I ever knew of was 22-year-old Eva Latour, one of Mattie's [Silks] girls, who killed herself with opium. Once smelled, the sweet odor of opium smoke is never forgotten. Sometimes this not-unpleasant odor seemed to fill Market [Holladay] Street.*[3]

The *Rocky Mountain News* wrote of the horrible living conditions of the area in the July 15, 1880, issue:

> *Outhouses, crowded together near the sleeping and eating compartments, their contents overflowing into the yards, filled with piles of ashes, decayed vegetables, chicken feathers and other refuse...a combination of smells the most horrible.*

Thus, racial tensions were fanned throughout the city. The year 1880 was also a local and presidential election year. Chinese immigration became an important political issue for both parties. Republican presidential candidate James Garfield favored Chinese immigration. In opposition, Denis Kearney, an Irish immigrant and founder of the Workingman's Party, led a campaign to ban Chinese immigration. Fearful that cheap Chinese labor would threaten the white working class, Winfield Hancock, the Democratic presidential candidate, supported the ban on Chinese immigration.

In Colorado, and Denver in particular, in an effort to take political control away from the Republicans, who favored the Chinese labor, the Colorado Democrats ran a campaign against Chinese labor. The *Rocky Mountain News* followed suit with several editorials attacking

Denver Public Library, Western History Department
One of the many opium dens in Denver's Hop Alley.

the opium dens. In particular, the October 23, 1880, issue referred to the Chinese population in Denver as the "Pest of the Pacific." The paper ran a small article in the October 28, 1880, issue reporting "on good authority" that there was open talk in the city of running the Chinese out.

Then, on Saturday night, October 30, 1880, several members of the Democratic Party organized a march through the streets of Denver. Many carried anti-Chinese banners. Little did they know these actions would ignite a firestorm of anti-Chinese sentiment among Denver's working class. It would take less than twenty-four hours.

On an otherwise peaceful Sunday afternoon, October 31, 1880, Denver's racial history took a tragic turn. Newspaper accounts differ as to how the riot began on that afternoon. Historians differ on who started the horrifying event. What is known is that it began in John Asmussen's saloon, located in the 1600 block of Wazee Street. An argument broke out between two Chinese immigrants shooting pool and a few intoxicated white customers. One of the men reportedly confronted the two Chinese men playing pool, hitting one of them with a cue stick, and was promptly shot at by the other pool player. While the pool player missed his shot, the white customers immediately exited the saloon and quickly spread the story that a Chinaman had killed a white man.

"Within a matter of minutes," according to *Denver Post* police reporter, Forbes Parkhill, a mob descended in Denver's Hop Alley area of lower downtown. They broke into the businesses, destroyed everything they could and even beat the owners. As the rage continued, many of the Chinese proprietors slipped out their back doors, only to be caught and severely beaten.

Denver's police force quickly rushed to the scene, but were unable to control the rioting masses. By two o'clock that afternoon, the mob had increased to over three thousand strong. Mayor Richard Sopris ordered all Denver bars to close in an effort to subdue the crowd. He also called in reinforcements from the fire department to help control the growing crowd. Fire Chief William Roberts was made an acting deputy sheriff.

When the mayor addressed the crowd asking them to disperse, he was promptly shouted down. Mayor Sopris then ordered the fire department to turn their water hoses on the unruly mob. This only enraged the crowd, but they did disperse, right back to the businesses in Hop Alley.

As afternoon turned to evening the rioting intensified. More businesses were ransacked and more innocent victims were attacked. By nightfall, the angry crowd began torching everything they could. Chinatown was soon on fire. Then the lynching began.

One such victim that lived to tell the tale was Sing Hey. He had fled the carnage, finding safety in an outhouse. When he chose to escape the stench-filled hideout, he was immediately discovered by the crazed mob. The *Rocky Mountain News* covered the story in a small article in the November 1, 1880, issue:

> *A rope was put around his neck and he was dragged about the ground.*

Fortunately for Sing Hey, cooler heads prevailed and Hey was eventually released.

However, the eight policemen on duty that fateful night were unable to gain control, despite the additional help from the fire department. The Denver Police Department had been without leadership since the suspension of Chief Hickey. With the city clearly in crisis, Mayor

Sopris appointed General David J. Cook, former city marshal and currently the head of the Rocky Mountain Detective Association, as acting police chief. General Cook immediately assembled two militia units, the Governor's Guard and the Chaffee Light Artillery, with a volunteer recruitment totaling nearly five hundred men.

The militia units fanned out in an effort to gain control of the situation. Cook and one group arrested several men attempting to torch a building. As the arrests were underway, a mob of rioters tried to rush the militia. General Cook instructed his men to fire their weapons into the ground, then point the smoking muzzles of their guns toward the mob. The presumed threat worked well as the mob quickly dispersed.

While the militia units were able to quell the violence in some areas and rescue innocent victims, they were not able to immediately stop the riot raging in the city.

Of the many Chinese laundry businesses set on fire that night was one owned by Sing Lee, located at Nineteenth and Lawrence streets. The mob broke the door and windows by wielding axes and hatchets, throwing bricks and rocks. Once inside, they found one of Lee's employees, Look Young, hiding under a bench.[4] Men grabbed the helpless laundryman and dragged him outside of the business, as they set a torch to it.

With the building going up in flames, the men beat Young unmercifully. Then they placed a rope around his neck and dragged him, all the while beating him with a large oak branch, to the corner of Nineteenth and Arapahoe streets. Attempting to hang him from a light pole proved more difficult than they thought, so they proceeded to drag him down Arapahoe Street, looking for a better opportunity. Along the way, a few brave men stopped the brutal act, including Doctor Cotton C. Bradbury.

Look Young was placed in a wagon and taken to Dr. Bradbury's office.[5] Young was beaten so severely that there was was very little the doctor could do but to make him as comfortable as possible. A reporter for the *Rocky Mountain News* was in the room as Young died. He filed his report which ran in the November 1, 1880, edition of the paper:

> *Blood was issuing freely from his mouth and nose. An examination showed a face and neck much swollen, the signs of a rope being visible on the latter. The teeth had been knocked*

Denver's Chinese riots as depicted in the *Rocky Mountain News*.

or kicked out. There was a deep wound on the top of the head that had apparently penetrated the skull. There were bruises all over the body, from hand to foot.

Finally in the early morning hours of November 1, 1880, General Cook received additional help in the form of a five-hundred-man volunteer posse. The men, all registered Republicans, obviously wanted to help end the riotous situation. They may also have seized upon a bit of a political opportunity of their own, as the election was just days away. In any case, with the help of these possemen, as well as Cook's own militia units, several arrests were made, including those suspected of beating Look Young to death. During the roundup of instigators, several of the Chinese were also taken to the Arapahoe County jail for their own protection.

When the streets of lower downtown were finally restored to some sort of safety, the *Rocky Mountain News,* which had helped fan the racial hatred with their inflammatory editorials, covered the story in the November 1, 1880, issue. However, its previous editorial position had evidently not changed, as the following report appeared:

> *Chinatown no Longer Exists*
> *Washee, washee is all cleaned out in Denver*

Nowhere in the paper's coverage of the previous night's horror was there a story of the beating death of Look Young.

There were many acts of bravery during the anti-Chinese riot of October 31, 1880. Several citizens hid the Chinese in their homes, including Denver's mayor, Richard Sopris.

A local gambler with a shady reputation, Jim Moon, leveled his revolvers at a group of rioters who were about to assault a Chinese laundryman. Moon told the angry men, "This Chinaman is an unoffensive man, and you shant touch him, not a one of you."[6] Moon then took more than a dozen Chinese to the Arcade gambling hall for safe refuge.

Lizzie Preston, the owner and madam of a brothel at Seventeenth and Holladay streets, along with nearly a dozen of her "girls," boldly confronted the rioters. Armed with shotguns, fireplace pokers, champagne bottles, and even shoes, the brave women defied the angry mob and sheltered some thirty-four innocent Chinese. Historian Roy T. Wortman described the scene:

Liz Preston, a madam of a local brothel, was protecting four cowering Chinese with a shotgun.[7]

The mob finally dispersed when William Roberts, acting deputy sheriff, arrived on the scene with a group of his men. According to Roberts,

> *The four Chinese were secured for protection in the side parlor of Miss Preston's brothel. By the end of the riot the madam had sheltered thirty-four Chinese.*
>
> *That day the pariahs, the outcasts of society, the denizens of Holladay Street, the center of the red light district, put themselves in the hall of fame. And perhaps the recording angel gave them one white mark.*

The aftermath of the anti-Chinese riot had far-reaching political ramifications. Three days later, on election day, the Republicans were overwhelmingly voted into office, largely due to the Democratic party's ill-conceived campaign against Chinese labor.

The local newspapers waged a war among themselves regarding the riot and the subsequent fall-out. The *Denver Republican* editorialized that the Democrats, backed by the *Rocky Mountain News,* were the cause of the racial riots. The *Rocky Mountain News* countered in editorials that it was the fault of Mayor Sopris, who, in their opinion, did not take charge of the situation early on.

On November 4, the day after the election, the Chinese immigrants, who had been held for their safety, were released, only to find their businesses and homes destroyed. The estimated damage in Hop Alley was over $53,000. The Chinese consul requested reparation payments from the city of Denver, as well as the federal government. However, U. S. Secretary of State James Blaine denied the request, and the city of Denver promptly followed the government's lead.

Most of the suspects arrested for their alleged involvement with the beating of Look Young were eventually released, due to a "lack of evidence." Those bound over for trial were later acquitted in February 1881.

Denver's first recorded racial riot was one of the hundreds of anti-Chinese riots that swept across American cities during the 1870s and 1880s. The three largest and most violent incidents occurred in Los Angeles, California in 1871, Calgary in 1892, and Denver in 1880.

David J. Cook and his deputies. This photo, courtesy of the Denver
Police Museum, has never before been published.

As Denver city officials scrambled to recover from the dark day
of shame, the U. S. Congress passed legislation to create the Chinese
Exclusion Act of 1882, which essentially restricted additional Chinese
immigration.

Yet in Denver, no local or federal law would deter those bent on
racial prejudice and the crimes and even murder that would continue.

* * *

During the decade of the 1880s, Denver became the fastest-
growing city in the nation. Within that decade, Denver's city limits
had stretched south of 6th Avenue. By 1880 Denver's southern edge

was Alameda Avenue. With that increase in growth was an increase in crime, and yes, murder.

The city police force had grown as well, and improved exponentially over the years. For the most part, law enforcement worked well in containing crime in the city. However, in 1886 a senseless murder led to a hanging affair, and the last legal hanging in the state, at least for a time. It also led to another round of debates surrounding the death penalty.

A Hanging Affair
"Crime Doesn't Pay"

On the night of May 19, 1886, an attempted robbery on a Denver street car went horribly wrong. Joseph C. Whitnah, employed as a driver for the Denver City Railway Company, was robbed by two men. During the confrontation, a gun was pulled. In the next instant, Whitnah was dead.

An eyewitness, Frank O. Peterson, was detained by police for questioning, originally suspected of being involved in the crime. He was later released.

That very morning two men, Richard Conley and Richard Morgan, had escaped from the Arapahoe County Jail. Chief Austin W. Hogle sent men to search and guard all avenues in and out of the city.

As the Denver police force searched for clues to the identity of the killers, Leonard DeLue, an associate with David J. Cook's Rocky Mountain Detective Association, received a tip from a patron in a local saloon. He stated that he had overheard a conversation between two men concerning the recent street car murder. DeLue reported the information to Cook, who in turn forwarded the information to the Denver police department. Together, DeLue, Cook and Chief Hogle worked the case.

The *Rocky Mountain News* reported on the investigation in the issue of May 21, 1886:

> *Rewards amounting to $1,000 have been offered by the Governor and street car company, and it is hoped that the assassin will be brought to justice.*

According to the tipster and witnesses who corroborated the events, the detectives learned that on May 20, the day following the murder, two young men having a conversation in the G.A.R. Saloon, located at 561 Larimer Street, discussed the murder of the previous evening in great detail. The information the detectives learned from those who overheard the conversation led to the arrest of the alleged accomplice in the murder. The media learned of the conversation, and rushed to print the story regardless of the on-going murder investigation. The alleged conversation reported in the press is as follows:

"I had to kill - (him)"
"What do you mean?"
"The street car driver. I mean."
"What in time did you want to kill him for?"
"I told him to throw up his hands and he reached for his hip pocket, when I shot. Then I began to holler, and I jumped closer to him, held the gun lower and down, and shot again."
"What did you do that for?"
"I wanted that money box. I heard a man running, and thought it was an officer. I was afraid to get into the boot, for fear the man who was running would see me, and see I was a colored man. Than I ran after Withers, hollering after him, and threatening to shoot him, unless he kept his mouth shut."[8]

On Monday, May 24, the detectives arrested John "Kansas" Withers. Under interrogation at the Arapahoe County Jail, Police Chief Hogle pressed Withers for details of the night in question. Eventually Withers confessed to the crime. He said in part:

"I met Green on the corner of Nineteenth and Larimer. He asked me where I was going and I told him I was going home. He told me to come on and go with him. I asked him where he was going and he said he was going to get some money owing to him. I asked him where it was and he said Broadway. He didn't say anything about robbing anyone and never mentioned a street car until we got way out there and I said to him you go and get your money and let's go back to town. It was before we got to the turntable when I said this. The street car was coming, I walked on ahead of Andy and he walked to the street car. I must have been 100 feet ahead of him. I heard a shot and

This trolley at Broadway in downtown Denver, is representative of the one Andrew Green attempted to rob, which ended in murder.

someone holler then. I heard another shot and another holler. I suspected of what had been done, so I broke and run as fast as I could."

With this information, the police had a solid lead on who committed the murder of Joseph C. Whitnah. Chief Hogle recalled seeing an "Andrew Green" on the previous day's police report dated Sunday, May 23, 1886. Green was already in custody, serving time for vagrancy, drunkenness, and carrying a concealed weapon. Hogle sent a patrol detail to the site where the prisoners were working to pay off their various fines. Green was taken back to the county jail for a new set of questions.

While Green was undergoing further interrogation, again the media rushed an unsubstantiated story to print:

Murderer Caught

It appears that a negro named Andrew Green, on Wednesday last, met another negro named John Withers and asked (him) to go out with him. Withers had no idea what was the other man's object, but accompanied him as requested. The pair went out on Broadway and took a stand near the turntable. The next car which came up was Whitnah's, and Green approached it, went to the driver and demanded the money box. The request was denied, and Green then fired at and killed Whitnah.[9]

The *Rocky Mountain News*, not about to be left out of the fierce competition of media coverage surrounding this murder story, ran an editorial calling for the closing of the G.A.R. Saloon, stating in part that the establishment in question was: "a dive and den of vice and crime, said to be a resort for the very worst cutthroats, thieves, burglars, gamblers, prostitutes, and vagrants, white and colored." The editorial went on to say that, while Green and Withers patronized the G.A.R., "The honest, hard-working colored men of the city, who have families growing up...are very earnestly demanding that this hellish plague-spot of iniquity shall be wiped out." Evidently the editorial carried some weight, for the city Board of Aldermen revoked the G.A.R.'s liquor license. Denver city supervisor, Thomas Nicholl eventually closed down the stained establishment, most likely due to public sentiment.[10]

When the news of Green's arrest hit the streets of Denver, a mob of over three hundred masked men marched over the Colfax Avenue bridge to the Arapahoe County jail demanding Green be turned over to them.

It was 1:30 a.m. on the morning of May 27, 1886, when Sheriff Frederick Cramer, gun in hand, confronted the mob, with a simple demand: "Hold Up!" Cramer then had the following advice for the crowd: *"The first man who breaks in the door is a dead man, I'll kill him. Don't come a step nearer, you fellows, or we'll shoot."*[11]

Suddenly, someone did shoot, and then others in the crowd began shooting. Three shots were fired through a window of the jail and Jailer Hopkins returned fire into the crowd of masked men. At about that time, a police wagon arrived full of reinforcements for Cramer and his deputies. Sheriff Cramer again addressed the angry mob: *"Boys, you had better go home. I know how you feel and don't blame you for it. The man will be hung legally and that is all there is of it."*[12]

The group soon scattered.

The following day, in an interview with Denver's undersheriff,

Andrew Green was caught and convicted of murder. He was hanged in Denver.

John M. Chivington responded to a question regarding the lynch mob of the previous evening. Stating that he did not see a reason for a lynching as he believed the man would be found guilty and thus, the death penalty would apply, he further commented that should that not be the case: *"I am not sure that I would not be willing to help put the rope around the fellow's neck myself and help lynch him."*[13]

This statement was indicative of the atmosphere in the city surrounding this murder case. Tensions were obviously high. Sheriff Cramer of Arapahoe County hired more guards to protect both the accused and the jail.

Meanwhile, twenty-six-year-old Andrew Green was still being interrogated by the police department, with no additional charges filed when the newspapers printed their stories to the contrary.

At first, Green told the authorities he was nowhere near the crime scene on the night in question. "How could I be, I've been in jail for the last six months...[f]or the larceny of a stove from Lewis & Scott. Justice Jeffries sentenced me for 200 days, and I only completed my sentence about two weeks ago."[14]

Because the murder had occurred just five days previous, the detectives sensed deception and pressed on with their questioning. Detective Martin Watrous informed Green of the statement Withers had made, implicating Green as the killer, as well as the witnesses at the saloon, who overheard Green's own account of the murder. Green then recounted the events of the night to the officer. Curiously, when Green was asked why he was currently in jail, he responded:

"I was arrested Sunday night. I had heard everybody talking

about the murder and had read the paper regularly. I thought Peterson's being arrested would squash the whole thing. If I had thought there was any danger I would have skipped. I thought Peterson would be discharged and that would end the whole matter."

Green ended his statement by saying: *I "am awful sorry I killed him. I didn't intend to kill him. I wanted to scare him and get the money."*[15]

With this information in hand, and the two confessions by Green, the Denver District Attorney's office filed a charge of murder against Andrew Green. Perhaps due to the social outcry for justice, the trial date was quickly set.

Both Andrew Green and John Withers were arraigned on six separate felony charges. Green was also charged with first degree murder, which allowed for the death penalty, despite a plea of "guilty" or a confession.

This change in the law was amended in 1883, following what the public deemed as injustice in the murder trials of the Italian mob murders in 1875, some of whom pleaded guilty to avoid the death penalty. The 1883 amended law also, for the first time, created "degrees" of murder. Conviction of first degree murder allowed for the death penalty, while second degree murder meant life in prison or less, depending on a jury's verdict.

Thus, Andrew Green was charged with murder in the first degree. The indictment read before the court on the opening day of the trial stated that Green did "feloniously, willfully, deliberately, with premeditation, and of malice aforethought kill and murder Joseph C. Whitnah."

The trial began on June 22, 1886. With Judge Victor A. Elliot presiding, LeDru R. Rhodes led the prosecution team, while thirty-two year old Edgar Caypless led the defense team, including George W. Miller, who also represented Withers in a separate trial.

The prosecution was able to introduce Green's background, revealing that at the age of twelve, Green had shot his father, who later recovered. A few years later the young man served time in prison in both Colorado and Missouri for larceny. Larry L. Fouts recalled for the jurors his conversation with Green at the G. A. R. Saloon and

Denver's new Arapahoe County Jail shortly after construction in 1891. It was later the site of a racial riot that ended in a lynching.

Green's admission to killing Whitnah. James Price, a co-worker with Withers, testified that both Withers and Green had told him about the murder. Next to take the stand for the prosecution were the police and detectives who cracked the case including David J. Cook, and Chief Austin W. Hogle and Detective Martin Watrous of the Denver police.

Of particular note was Watrous' testimony regarding the confession of Green as well as his interrogation of Green regarding the murder weapon. Watrous explained for the jury how he and his colleagues had put together the case with eyewitness testimony and he told Green that Withers had confessed to his involvement in the crime that ended in murder. On cross-examination of the witness, defense attorney Caypless was unable to get Watrous to admit to any sort of coercion or undue influence regarding the confession.

Next, the issue of the murder weapon was raised by Rhodes and the prosecution team. Watrous explained he showed the gun to Green during questioning and Green denied knowing anything of the gun. Watrous further stated that Green later wished to change his statement regarding the gun. When Rhodes asked the witness to state for the jury the changed statement, the defense attorneys objected.

Robert Smith testified that the gun in question belonged to him. He said that approximately ten days before the murder, Green asked to borrow the gun. Smith also said that when he lent the gun to Green, it was fully loaded. When the gun was returned to Robert Johnson, Smith's roommate, two shells had been fired. Johnson was called to the stand, repeating the same episode and stated that he had replaced the spent shells with new ones.[16]

The prosecution then submitted Green's written confession into evidence. Immediately the defense team objected. Lead defense attorney Caypless claimed he had not seen it! Caypless argued that Green could not have made the statement voluntarily, but was coerced to do so. This set up a fire-storm in the courtroom. Finally, Judge Elliot asked Cook, Hogle and Watrous a series of questions regarding the manner in which the confession was obtained. All testified that Green's written confession was not forced. In the end, Judge Elliot ruled the confession was admissible into the court record. The confession included Green's words: *"I didn't mean to kill the car driver, I merely wanted to hold him up."*

Detective David J. Cook was again called to the stand. He testified that Green recounted during the interrogations that Green had "turned the gun toward the driver's head and it went off accidentally. He fired the second shot to prevent being identified." This is corroborated by Fout's description of the saloon conversation when Green said: "I told him to throw up his hands and he reached for his hip pocket, when I shot. Then I began to holler, and I jumped closer to him, held the gun lower and down, and shot again."

With this testimony, the prosecution rested.

After a series of motions and clarifications by the court, in another amazing moment by the defense team, Caypless called his one and only witness. Charles M. Thompson, a reporter for the *Rocky Mountain News*, took the stand. Thompson was present when Green gave his confession. He testified for the defense that while Green did fire a second shot into Whitnah, it was Thompson's impression that he did so because he "was afraid."[17] Final arguments began the following morning, June 25, 1886.

Judge Elliot instructed the jurors on the law regarding the difference between first and second degree murder, as well as the issues of law pertaining to an act of murder while committing a crime, and reasonable doubt. Final arguments by both sides were presented before the jury who then retired to reach a verdict.

A reporter for the *Tribune-Republican* managed to ask Green a few questions. His reply was printed in the next issue of the paper:

"Oh, I feel first-rate. I give that jury about fifteen minutes to return a verdict against me in the first degree, but if any of the crowd expect me to faint or raise any racket when I receive it, I'll fool 'em, I will. I'm too game for that. A man has to die sometime, anyhow."

The jury took just over an hour to reach a verdict. Green was found guilty of first degree murder. Defense attorney Caypless immediately filed a motion for a new trial.

Meanwhile, John Withers, Green's accomplice in the crime-turned-murder, pleaded guilty to second degree murder, and was sentenced to life imprisonment at the Colorado State Penitentiary.

On July 2, 1886, the defense attorney argued before the court several motions for overturning the guilty verdict and, therefore, a new trial. The judge denied all motions and then rendered his sentence of the convicted murderer. Andrew Green rose from his seat as the judge sentenced him to death by hanging.

The execution date was immediately set by the judge for July 27, 1886. With a little over three weeks to file their appeals, the defense team had a tough job. Newspapers across the state covered the high profile murder case and its aftermath. With the final appeal rejected by the Colorado Supreme Court, the news media now focused on a renewed debate of the death penalty.

As the execution date neared, the focus in the media became that of the moral decency of a public hanging. The debate would continue on well after the execution, eventually leading to legislation signed in 1889 that relegated all future executions in the state to the premises of the state penitentiary at Canon City.

Weighing in on the public argument was Sheriff Frederick Cramer. Quoted in the July 10, 1886 issue of the *Daily Denver Times*, he said:

In view of the great excitement and interest which has been created in this case, and the cold-blooded way in which the murder was committed, I am inclined to think the public demands a public execution, and, at present, think I shall so order it.

Denver Public Library, Western History Department
An early execution by hanging in Denver.

As the date of July 27, 1886 neared, Sheriff Cramer released through the media the site of the execution of Andrew Green. The location would be along the west side of Cherry Creek, where a open space of land was ideal for the expected crowd.[18]

In the early morning hours of that fateful day in Denver history, a city work detail, headed by John Yates, assembled the gallows at the site. The gallows used the latest technology, whereby weights, gauged to be greater than the weight of the criminal, were attached to a rope. When the rope would be cut, the weights would fall, thus causing an instant break in the neck of the criminal.

As the construction continued, several vendors lined up with popcorn, candy, and hot dogs to sell at what would arguably be the most attended event of the summer in Denver. By noon, in the heat of a day simmering on several levels, the crowds of spectators quickly gathered, some 15,000 in total, including many families with young children. Several in the crowd, clamoring to obtain the best view, led one attendee to observe: *"Socially and morally this place is an enigma to a stranger."*[19]

Meanwhile, Green received his last meal shortly after 6 a.m. The meal, consisting of steak and eggs, fruit and coffee, was delivered by Undersherrif Chivington. Green spent the rest of the morning with

82

various visitors to the jail including the Reverend Dr. I. W. Triplett of Shorter African Methodist Episcopal (A.M.E.) Church, and several members of the press.

Shortly after 1 p.m. several sheriff deputies escorted a neatly attired Andrew Green from his jail for the last time. Dressed in a black suit and tie purchased by Sheriff Cramer, Green walked slowly, his ankles being bound by chains. From the jail, Chief Hogle and a few officers took the prisoner to the execution site alongside Cherry Creek. Green uttered nary a word as the officers escorted the condemned man to the gallows.

The crowd, nearly wilted in the summer heat, suddenly came to life with the glimpse of Green at the gallows. Famed Denver detective Sam Howe, who was in the crowd that day, later reminisced for a reporter at the *Rocky Mountain News* in an interview published in the October 18, 1904 issue of the paper: "in those days a hanging was a big event."

A hush filtered through the crowd as Sheriff Cramer brought a solemn Green to the scaffold and read the death warrant issued by the Arapahoe County District Court for all to hear:

> *The said Andrew Green shall be remanded to the place from whence he came, the common jail of Arapahoe County, there to be confined until the twenty-seventh day of July A.D. 1886, between the hours of 9 o'clock in the forenoon and the setting of the sun on the same day, by the Sheriff of Arapahoe County, taken from the place of confinement to some convenient place of execution and there be hanged by the neck until he shall be dead.*[20]

Sheriff Cramer concluded by saying:

> *I hereby certify that I have duly executed the within warrant at 2 o'clock and 20 minutes P.M. on this 27th day of July A.D. 1886, by hanging the within named Andrew Green by the neck until death did ensue as I am herein commanded. This done at the City of Denver in the County of Arapahoe and the State of Colorado.*

An assembled choir then sang a song, and Green seemed to enjoy singing along. Reverend Gray read a few bible verses and then announced that Green wanted to make a few remarks before the crowd. The crowd surged forward in an effort to hear every word.

With his hands still cuffed, but no chains on his ankles, Green stepped forward on the platform and began reading a few remarks he had prepared. He began by saying:

> *I am here now to pay the penalty of the crime I committed on the 19th of May, 1886. Of course there is no use for me to say I am not guilty, as I am. As proved by the laws of Colorado, I am guilty, but of what? Of murder in the first degree? No; but of murder in the second degree. My life has been sworn away here on earth, but it cannot be sworn away in Heaven.*

For the next fifteen minutes Green went on to recount his misdeeds and what led him to this point, blaming the law, his friends (Price and Withers) and Judge Elliot. He finished by thanking his attorney, Caypless, and even Sheriff Cramer and Undersheriff Chivington for their kindness. It wasn't clear if Green was finished when shouts from the crowd erupted: *"Put the rope on him."*

Sensing a disgruntled crowd, the sheriff motioned to the Reverend Triplett who led the assembled group in prayer.

Sheriff Cramer removed the cuffs from Green's hands and tied his hands behind his back. Deputy Sheriff Hollingsworth secured his legs and gave him a final drink of water. Then Cramer placed the rope over Green's head and around his neck, placing the knot just below the left ear to ensure a clean break of the neck. Hollingsworth placed the traditional black hood over Green's head.

The crowd had become quiet and subdued during the solemn actions of the officers. It was as if the group of onlookers were startled out of a trance when a loud thump from the gallows was heard all across that field along Cherry Creek.

In an instant, Green's body was jerked into the air. The body fell a few feet and dangled. Ghastly contortions of the hanging body led the crowd to gasp in horror. The body didn't fall further, but hung in the air. Green's legs rose up, and his shoulders shook as the rest of his body twisted. It was clear to all that neither the rope nor the weights worked to break Green's neck. He was strangling to death.

For nearly fifteen minutes, the crowd watched Green slowly die by strangulation. Doctor McLaughlin finally asked that the body be lowered to determine death. Upon examination, he suggested the body be left hanging a bit longer.

The method of hanging Andrew Green was known as the "twitch-up" method. A weight greater than that of the condemned man's body was attached to the rope, strung through a series of pulleys on a horizontal beam. The theoretical method was that as the weight fell, the man's body lifted, taking with it the slack in the rope around his neck, thus causing death by hanging. However, in Green's case, the executioner attached a three hundred pound weight to the rope, nearly twice of what Green weighed. Thus, when the weight fell, Green shot up nearly four feet into the air. However, the method failed to break Green's neck, as was the intent, hence the slow strangulation.[21]

Green's body was cut down and loaded into the black wagon belonging to the mortuary firm of Tidball and Farmer. The funeral took place the following day. The leaders of the Zion Baptist Church, Denver's prominent African American church, chose not to hold the service at their church, as Green was a convicted murderer. Thus the informal service was held at the local city skating rink. Burial followed unceremoniously at Riverside Cemetery.

Following the hanging of Andrew Green, the subject of public executions became a topic in the media, and with the citizens of Denver. The *Denver Tribune* of July 28, 1886, the day after the hanging, editorialized: "[We] predict that there will never be another public legal execution in Colorado. The next legislature will be asked to pass a law to provide for the private execution of criminals." The editorial concluded with, "It would be well to have a suitable place provided within the walls of the State Penitentiary."

The editorial proved to be prophetic, for on January 11, 1887, six months after the hanging of Andrew Green, Governor Benjamin H. Eaton, himself a former prison commissioner, declared in a speech before the Colorado General Assembly at the state capital, that:

The public execution of criminals sentenced to death should be expressly prohibited by law. It is not the intention of the law to make the agonizing atonement of the condemned furnish forth an entertainment for the depraved. The execution should take place in seclusion, attended only by the executioner and a regularly impanelled jury.[22]

Nearly three years after the public hanging of Andrew Green, in January 1889, Colorado lawmakers passed legislation remanding all executions to be carried out under the jurisdiction of the warden at the Colorado State Penitentiary. On April 19, 1889, Governor Job A. Cooper signed the bill moving all executions to within the walls of the state penitentiary in Canon City.

Thus, the execution of Andrew Green was the last public hanging in Denver.

Murder at the Palace Theatre
"Emotional Insanity"

Denver's red light district was the site of many crimes, including murder, as the city entered the booming 1880s. A decade earlier, the business of prostitution had been moved from the downtown financial district, to Holladay Street. It was a long street, running north to approximately the 2200 block. Lined on both sides of the street were several houses of ill-repute. At the northern end, where the cribs were located, Denver's criminal underworld lurked to take advantage of the seamy side of the city. Murder was a regular occurrence, often overlooked by the press, primarily due to the nature of the business in the district. Life on the "row" and particularly the dangerous crib area is best described by one who lived it:

> At the bottom of the underworld, can be found the lowest type of poverty stricken humanity; it is composed of all shades, grades and colors huddled together. These places of existence are called cribs, dives, dens, holes and nests. These hellholes catch all kinds of girls on the drift, who do not realize their fate, of that they are with the scum of the earth, until too late. It would not be possible to escape even had they a desire to do so.[23]

While Holladay Street was Denver's "official" red light district, there were plenty of "leg art" show places on Denver's Blake Street. By 1876, more than sixty saloons enjoyed brisk business in Denver. Nearly all of these establishments offered variety shows, in the form

Denver Public Library, Western History Department
The Palace Theatre was the scene of murder.

of burlesque and minstrel performances, where female entertainers danced and showed a lot of "leg."

Denver's gambling boss, "Big Ed" Chase, owned three of the most notable and notorious establishments: the Arcadia Hall, the Cricket Hall, and the Palace Theatre. While all three businesses had their fair share of underworld crime, including gambling and back room city politics, the Palace Theatre was known all across the Western frontier.

Located on the west side of Blake Street (1443-1459) between Fourteenth and Fifteenth streets, the Palace Theatre was famous for its wide variety of entertainment — from elegant buffets and fine wine, to gambling and racy female stage performances. It soon became a favorite hangout for locals, including city journalist, Eugene Field. Due to the excellent central location in Denver, the miners who came to to the city, as well as the those who just arrived from the train station, often made the Palace their first stop in town.

However, the Palace Theatre was also the scene of several murders, including three in one year. One newspaper, the *Georgetown Courier*, editorialized in part: "From the amount of blood that has been spilled in that den, its floors must be of a gorgeous, gory red color." With the connections Chase had with the city politicos, be it on a professional level or through the many payoffs he made to the corrupt law enforcement officers, the Palace Theatre continued its shady operations.[24]

One of the young showgirls employed at the Palace was pretty seventeen-year-old Effie Moore. One evening, while mingling with customers, Moore met a good-looking, charming, and wealthy gambler. His name was Charles E. Henry, who was only nineteen years old. A whirlwind courtship ensued and the two planned marriage. Rumors abounded at the Palace, as is typical in such atmospheres, and soon young Charlie was half-crazed with jealousy as well as alcohol. He confronted Effie with one of the rumors that she was already married, which she quickly denied.

On the night of November 13, 1887, according to police records, a drunken Charles Henry entered a private upper level box at the Palace Theatre. During the variety performance on stage, four gunshots resounded from the box. Below, Effie Moore lay dead in a pool of blood. Charles E. Henry was immediately arrested with a .32 caliber revolver still in his possession.

As the funeral arrangements were being made, Henry, as well as Palace owner, Ed Chase, offered to pay all expenses. The newspapers reported more than 4,000 mourners attended the services.

During police interrogations, Henry said he had no memory of shooting Effie Moore. Nevertheless, he was charged with murder.

The trial of Charles Henry began in February 1888. The defendant pleaded not guilty by reason of "emotional insanity." During the trial the defense attorney introduced evidence, supported by doctors, that his client suffered from "transitory frenzy," a form of temporary insanity. Further testimony revealed that Effie Moore was a married woman when she agreed to marry Henry. The jury returned a verdict of not guilty based on the initial plea of "emotional insanity."[25]

This paticular insanity plea proved to be one of the first successful in American jurisprudence.

The *Denver Republican* dated February 26, 1888, condemned the Palace Theatre as:

...[a] human slaughterhouse, the scene of four murders during the past 13 months...a thoroughly tough, hard place, frequented by a class of desperate, depraved men and women. The employes [sic] are, almost without exception, of the worst possible character.

The *Rocky Mountain News* reported in the issue dated July 19, 1888, that Henry had been found unconscious in his hotel room at the Brunswick Hotel. The paper said Henry had ingested great amounts of alcohol and laudanum in an attempt to commit suicide. However, Henry recovered and by 1892 he was living in Dallas, Texas. There, he murdered another showgirl with whom he had become "madly infatuated." The *Denver Republican* of April 22, 1892, reported that the girl, Irene Russell, had been shot through the heart. The outcome of this second act of emotional insanity is unknown.

Prostitute Murderers
Girls Gone Wild

Blanche Morgan (alias Pearl Smith) was one of many who lived and worked in the northern section of the tenderloin district. Although located near the crib area, her bordello was a bit nicer than the typical one-room cribs. Morgan ran her two-room crib at 2235 of Holladay Street. She actually employed a few girls, including one Ardell Smith, who along with Morgan, ran another business of sorts that included drugging customers and even murder.

The criminal element of Holladay Street caused high anxiety in 1884. The customers of the crib area seemed to be disappearing in frightening numbers. Detectives eventually began a surveillance of the area after receiving tips from the underworld. The modus operandi of the girls was to mix morphine into the customers' drinks and then rob them. In the spring of 1891, Blanche and Ardell went too far and were eventually arrested for murder.

William Joos made the mistake of entering 2235 Holladay Street on the afternoon of May 27, 1891. Joos, a single man in his early thirties, had traveled to Denver for some relaxation and fun, from his home in Golden, where he was employed at the brewery. After negotiating for a thirty minute "visit" with Ardell Smith, Joos and Ardell entered a back room to complete their business. While the two were engaged, Blanche Morgan obtained a bucket of beer from a nearby bar. From fellow madam, Mollie White, Blanche obtained a packet of morphine, which she mixed into the beer. Following the rollicking time with Ms. Smith, Mr. Joos eagerly accepted the offer of the bucket of beer. When

89

Joos subsequently lost consciousness, the girls relieved his pockets of several gold pieces and deposited his limp body in the alley behind their establishment.

Police detective Sam Howe discovered Joos' body that evening. The *Denver Republican* ran this headline in the May 28, 1891 issue:

Murder By Morphine.

Detective John L. Leyden, along with Howe, arrested Morgan, Smith, White and another prostitute by the name of Mattie Fisher for murder. When the case finally went to trial, nearly six months later, Smith, Fisher and White were convicted of involuntary manslaughter, spending only one year in the county jail.[26]

Blanche Morgan was released and served no time for her part in the death of Joos. However, less than two weeks later, she was arrested for robbery.[27] She had evidently enticed a passerby into her establishment, whereupon she and a few cohorts robbed the man of all his money, and then kicked him out the door. For this act, Blanche Morgan did receive jail time. Shortly after completing her jail sentence, she left Denver for good.

* * *

Another denizen duo of Holladay Street, Bell Warden and Mattie Lemmon, also committed their share of violence and murder. The two had a small bordello in the 2200 block. Their crime spree would earn them a long term in the state penitentiary. The final act, ending in murder, occurred on March 20, 1884.

According to police reports, John Fitzgerald, a Leadville businessman, either met Mattie Lemmon at the bordello or in lower downtown. Friends, co-workers and family members never heard from Fitzgerald again.

On May 18, 1884, Fitzgerald's badly decomposed body was discovered carelessly buried along the sand banks of Cherry Creek, near the Colfax Avenue bridge. The coroner's report revealed that the victim's throat had been slashed. After good detective work by Denver police, particularly Sam Howe, Warden and Lemmon were arrested for murder, as were accomplices Anthony Delph, also known as Charles Smith, and Barry Gates, the denizens' lovers.

The *Rocky Mountain News* of November 12, 1884, in an exclusive

Denver Public Library, Western History Dept.
Mattie Lemmon was convicted murder in a prostitution ring and sent to the Colorado State Penitentiary.

interview with Charles Smith, printed his confession to the murder. He said that it was Gates who slit the "black barber's throat." He also admitted to relieving Smith's dead body of over one hundred dollars in gold and a fine gold watch. Smith said he then took the body to an empty house near Cherry Creek for hiding before the two buried it at the bank of the creek.

During the murder trial, which began on December 26, 1884, all four defendants pleaded innocent. Smith, who took the witness stand in his own defense, denied any involvement in the murder. All four defendants were found guilty of murder and sentenced to ten years each at the state penitentiary.

Mattie Lemmon, age thirty-two, and Bell Warden, age twenty-five, entered the prison system on December 28, 1884. Their previous occupation on the prison log sheets is listed as "hairdresser." After serving three years in prison, Mattie Lemmon died in 1887. Bell Warden served six years and was paroled on April 18, 1891.[28]

* * *

During Denver's formidable years, Holladay Street was first named McGaa Street, for William McGaa, a Denver pioneer. It was later named Holladay Street in honor of Ben Holladay, a pioneer in travel and stagecoach operations. However, by the 1870s, upper Holladay Street had gained a reputation as "...one of the Wickedest streets in the West."[29] Thus in 1888, the Holladay family asked the city council to rename the street. They did; to Market Street, so named, according to the council, for the meat markets located on the lower end of the street. For a sense of logistics of the area today, Twentieth and Markets streets are within a stones throw from the pride of the Colorado Rockies, Coors Field.

* * *

Ida Mae Jones operated a small bordello at 1040 Market Street. Known as "Black Ide," for her viciousness, she was one of the worst on the "row," and most people feared her very presence. Ms. Jones had a wide reputation of drinking and violence, and it was common knowledge along Market Street that her drunkenness often ended in ball bat swinging episodes against her particular adversary of the moment.

On August 1, 1890 Ms. Jones followed Stephen Zimmer, a stonemason from Nebraska, down Market Street, confronting him at the corner of Twentieth and Market streets. There she stabbed him to death.[30] The Denver police were immediately called to the scene and gave chase. Meanwhile, Zimmer bled to death on the streets of Denver. Jones was quickly apprehended and charged with murder.

The *Rocky Mountain News* reported the sordid details of the murder that very day. In the August 1, 1890 issue of the paper, it was reported that Zimmer, despite the "spree that had cost him his life," was a family man, and his death left behind a wife and six children in Nebraska. In his coat pocket was a letter written in German, intended to be sent to his wife.

Ida Mae Jones pleaded not guilty to the murder charge and claimed self-defense. During the murder trial, Jones' attorney argued that Zimmerman's death was caused by the delay in proper medical attention. Following closing arguments, the judge, in keeping with the self-defense claim of the accused, instructed the jury to decide "if the blow was struck for revenge, or in passion, or for self-protection." In fairness and according to the law, he further instructed the jury, "not to allow the fact that the prisoner has been in the habit of practicing fornification, to weigh against her and that the unchaste and the chaste in criminal matters have equal rights and are entitled to equal protection of the law."[31]

Following a short and swift deliberation, the jury returned a verdict, finding twenty-five-year-old Ida Mae Jones guilty of second degree murder. She was sentenced on October 31, 1890, to fifteen years in the state penitentiary at Canon City.

Jones entered the penitentiary on November 23, 1890 and became inmate #2388. Prison life did not seem to tame her nasty disposition. She was reprimanded on numerous occasions for insubordination, fighting with inmates, and destruction of prison property. Incredibly, she managed to earn an early release. Serving nearly nine of her fifteen year sentence, Jones was released on August 13, 1899.

Black Ide not only returned to Denver and Market Street, but to her old ways as well.

One incident occurred in 1901 when she took a ball bat to Jennie Thompson, striking her several times. An unidentified newspaper clipping in the personal files of Denver detective Sam Howe reported that Ms. Jones leveled the bat: "with all the strength which has made her reputation...as one of the most dangerous in the city."[32] In August 1901, she was arrested for beating one Jessie Smith nearly to death. The *Denver Republican* reported in the August 30 edition of the paper:

The negro population of Market street from Nineteenth to Twenty-first streets is terrorized by Ida Jones.

How this did not violate her prison parole is unclear. In any case, a few weeks later, she was arrested again for menacing, having pulled a gun on one of her customers, a miner by the name of Charles Peterson. He had accused her of stealing over two hundred dollars from his money pouch. The money was never recovered. Another customer, Henry Fitschen, reported to the police the theft of more than one hundred dollars during a visit to Black Ide's establishment.

In 1902, Black Ide was charged and convicted of larceny and returned to the state penitentiary in March of that year, for a second term, this time serving ten years. Ida Mae Jones was the first female inmate at the Colorado State Penitentiary at Canon City to be pregnant. Prison records report the birth of her child, but nothing further. Ida Mae Jones, aka "Black Ide," was released from prison in 1905, and disappeared from history.

A Moral Dilemma
What's A Woman To Do?

On the morning of July 24, 1891, sixteen-year-old Gertie Harris nearly died from an operation that went horribly wrong. Racked by convulsions and rapidly losing blood, it took two doctors to save her life. One of the doctors, Doctor Holmes, alerted the authorities. His professional medical opinion indicated that Miss Harris' condition was the result of an abortion.

As Miss Harris recovered and slowly gained her strength, the Denver police were allowed to question her. After explaining her sad circumstances and the events leading up to that hot day in July, Harris reluctantly gave the investigators the name of the person she had sought out to help remedy her situation.

Georgiana South, who also went by the name of Madame Astle, ran a sordid business out of her home at 1759 Stout Street. Newspaper advertisements listed her occupation as "chiropodist," treating ingrown toenails and other ailments of the feet. However, word on the street was that she also performed abortions for a fifty dollar fee. Miss Harris confirmed this fact with the Denver police. The police arrested South and charged her with attempted manslaughter. The Denver district attorney later dropped that charge and substituted a charge of "using an instrument with intent to procure abortion." It was an obscure law seldom used under even more obscure law.

At the time, Colorado statutes relating to abortion were fairly clear in two key aspects. The law specifically stipulated that a person convicted of "attempting to procure the miscarriage of any woman then being with child," was eligible under the law to be sentenced to prison for "a term not exceeding three years." Should such an attempt result in the death of the mother, the act was then deemed manslaughter "unless it is apparent that such miscarriage was procured or attempted by or under the advice of a physician or surgeon, with intent to save the life of such a woman, or to prevent serious and permanent bodily injury to her."[33]

The law, controversial to be sure, was seldom enforced with the exception of the few incidents that specifically met the provisions outlined in the statutes.

Perhaps the best known criminal case to fall under this state statute was that of Doctor Mary Solander, who was convicted of manslaughter in an illegal abortion procedure which had resulted in the death of the mother.[33] While Solander was a popular figure and often advertised her medical services in the local newspapers, during her trials (it would take two) she was never able to produce evidence of any professional medical training.[34]

The circumstances leading up to the tragic death were recounted by the prosecution in detail and fortified with the testimony of the county coroner. His detailed report recounted the sworn statement made by Solander that "she had administered four powders to the patient." The coroner further testified that the cause of death was that of "uterine hemorrhage caused by a procured abortion." Perhaps a harbinger of the future social debate, the trial ended with a hung jury.

In the second trial the prosecution presented the same witnesses with one additional witness. The testimony of Clement Knaus, who had brought the victim to Solander for her services, was quite damaging to the defense. He testified that as Fredericka Baunn withered in agony three days after Solander administered the powders, he went back to Solander for help. On the return trip to Baunn's home, Knaus recounted for the jury the conversation between he and Solander:

> On the road she asked me if a child came from Baunn. I told her yes. She said that if the woman should die, that the medicine would be the cause. She told me to put the child where no one would find it. Baunn was dead when we got there. Mrs. S. went right back to find a lawyer.[35]

After three hours of deliberation, the jury returned a verdict of guilty of manslaughter. Judge E. T. Wells sentenced Solander to three years at the state penitentiary in Canon City.

However, local sentiment sided with Solander. After a series of letters and signed petitions, Territorial Governor Elbert pardoned Solander after five months of incarceration.

Solander's conviction was a watershed event for the current state statute, as it provided precedence for future cases. As such, the outcome of the case of Georgiana South was nearly a forgone conclusion.

Within a month of her arrest, the trial began in a downtown Denver courtroom. The prosecution team presented witnesses who stated that South often used instruments during her "delicate" procedures. While the defense objected and later offered their own witnesses who testified to the contrary, it was the testimony of the victim and her attending physician that sealed the fate of Georgiana South.

Sixteen-year-old Gertie Harris testified before the jury that

Georgiana South did indeed use a medical instrument on that tragic day in July. Her testimony was backed up by that of Doctor Holmes who saved Gertie's life.[36]

The jury returned a guilty verdict. Georgiana South, inmate #2819, was processed into the state penitentiary where she spent the next three years of her life.

As the moral debate surrounding abortion continued into the next century, the first concerted effort to overturn state laws prohibiting abortion began in 1957, with an organized group of attorneys and judges. Through the efforts of the American Law Institute, the "model penal code" called for abortion to be legal in cases where there was "substantial risk that continuance of the pregnancy would gravely impair the physical or mental health of the woman, or that the child resulting from pregnancy would be born with grave physical or mental defect, or in cases of pregnancy resulting from rape or incest."

Colorado Governor John A. Love was the first governor in the nation to approve the new abortion law, effectively amending the Colorado law on abortion that had been on the books for over one hundred years.

Upon signing the legislation into law, Governor Love's remarks to the press reflect the sentiment of many Coloradans to this day. "The action of the Legislature in passing a bill which seeks to amend Colorado law in regard to the legal termination of certain pregnancies has presented to me one of the more important and difficult decisions of my experience in office."

Murder and A Barroom Brawl
Diamonds in the Rough

The underworld criminal element in Denver's history, while colorful with the names of Jefferson Randolph "Soapy" Smith, Edward "Big Ed" Chase and Lou Blonger, was also an ugly history. Not only were these men involved with swindling the public, there was corruption, crime, back-stabbing and murder.

Gambling halls, saloons and variety theaters such as Chase's Arcadia Hall, the Cricket Hall and the Palace Theatre, were notorious as dangerous places. There were other establishments with similar reputations, such as the Missouri Club, the Bucket of Blood, Smith's Tivoli Club and Johnny Murphy's Exchange.

With so many establishments competing for business it was only a matter of time before there would be a violent encounter. It happened on October 11, 1892.

Early into that fateful evening, Tom Cady entered the Missouri Club for a game of poker. Cady, a well-known associate in "Soapy" Smith's bunko operations, also had a reputation for his nasty disposition. Evidently his disposition was particularly nasty this evening, as it wasn't long before an argument broke out. Words were exchanged involving poker chips, between Cady and the owner of the establishment, Jeff Argyle, as well as a gambler by the name of James B. (Jim) Jordan. Cady struck Jordan in the face with his cane. Argyle pulled his pistol. Aiming at Cady, as Argyle pulled the trigger, a patron grabbed Argyle's arm. Thus, the bullet lodged into Cady's chair. Both Cady, the instigator, and Argyle were arrested for assault, and taken to jail.

Having enough excitement for one night, or so he thought, Jordan went over to Murphy's Exchange, also known as the "Slaughterhouse," at 1617 Larimer Street.[36] The Exchange was busy that night and as bartender Mark Watrous could hardly keep up with the drinking demands. The owner of the establishment, Johnny Murphy, was behind the bar lending a hand.

Jordan found old friends and joined them for a drink at their table. Among the group were local gamblers William (Bill) Crooks, Cortez (Cort) Thomson and Clifton (Cliff) Sparks. Thomson, who spent a good deal of time at the Exchange, was nevertheless best known in the crowd as the paramour of Denver's foremost madam of the red light district, Mattie Silks. Sparks had a bit of notoriety among the crowd as well. A recent arrival from St. Louis, Missouri, the dapper gambler never went anywhere without wearing his prized possession, a diamond-studded stickpin said to be worth over two thousand dollars.

Meanwhile, "Soapy" Smith, having learned of Cady's arrest, bailed his friend out of jail. The two men then proceeded to Murphy's Exchange for a drink. Shortly thereafter, Jordan joined Smith and Cady. During their conversation, Jordan apologized to Cady for the previous ruckus at the Missouri Club. Cady's nasty disposition

Denver Public Library, Western History Dept.
Jefferson Randolph "Soapy' Smith was indicted for murder but the charges were later dropped.

evidently had not improved, for he made a snide remark and again swung his cane in Jordan's direction.

In a split instant, guns were drawn all around. Bullets blazed and in the aftermath, as the smoke cleared, Cliff Sparks lay mortally wounded on the barroom floor. Crooks rushed forward and knelt in grief beside his dying friend. Grabbing Sparks close to his chest, Crooks, while in a sobbing display, bit off the prized diamond stickpin from the man he claimed to be a friend.

Cort Thomson, as an eye witness to the events, was said to be impressed by the slick maneuver. Whether or not he shared this new-found technique with Mattie Silks is not known, however it did find its way to the bordellos and cribs along Market Street. Not long after the murder, customers of the red light district businesses complained of having jewelry such as stickpins, scarf pins, and expensive buttons stolen from their clothing. Forbes Parkhill recounts in his book, *The Wildest of the West*, that a local dentist increased his profit margin by making steel "biters," clamped to the back of the patient's front teeth. It was all the rage for a time. Apparently it ended in 1894, when a soiled dove by the name of Minnie Darley was arrested for stealing a gold scarf pin by biting it off of the clothing of her customer, Frank Le Fevre.

Many of the eye witnesses were interrogated by the police that night, including Murphy, the owner, and Watrous, the bartender of the Exchange. Subsequently, Tom Cady, Jim Jordan, Johnny Murphy and Cort Thomson were all arrested, pending possible charges of "accessory to murder." Jordan's gun was taken as evidence. Smith, who managed to slip out the back door undetected, turned himself in, along with his gun (containing six fresh rounds of ammunition) to the authorities the following day. Mattie Silks put up the bail to get Cort Thomson out of jail on the same day. Murphy and Cady remained in custody until some time later that day. The *Rocky Mountain News* of October 12, 1892, reported the murder:

> *Cliff Sparks, a gambler, was killed in Murphy's Exchange at 11:50 last night. He was shot through the body by either Jim Jordan, another gambler, or by Jeff Smith, known more familiarly as 'Soapy.' Sparks had been a gambler in Colorado and Denver for fourteen years. He was forty years of age and unmarried. He was dressed finely and wore good jewelry. His father is a physician in St. Joseph.*

As the Denver Police Department worked to identify the killer, the city officials, for undetermined reasons, ordered the closing of Smith's Tivoli Club and McEvoy and Dale's gambling hall, located on the second floor of the same building housing Murphy's Exchange, yet let the Exchange (the scene of the murder) continue to operate.

A coroner's inquest was convened the day following the shooting. For six hours, the panel heard from several witnesses. Conflicting testimony abounded. Much of the testimony would later be parsed out in selective form in the local newspapers.

Bartender Watrous testified that both Jordan and Smith drew their pistols. Watrous then pushed Jordan away from the fray, toward the front of the saloon. Jordan broke away and managed to fire off a shot. He also stated that he saw Smith pull a gun. He heard a shot ring out and saw Sparks fall to the floor.

John W. Murphy, proprietor of Murphy's Exchange, testified for an extended period of time and gave several details, some of which were contradictory to the other witnesses' testimony. He said that following the altercation when Cady yielded his cane to Murphy at Jordan's direction, he shoved Cady away at the same instant Watrous pushed Jordan. He said as he pushed Cady, he shouted to Sparks for help. At the same instant, he heard shots ring out. Stunned, he let go of Cady who ran toward Sparks and leveled a blow to his head. He said he heard Smith shout to Cady, "Tom let's get out of this." As they hurried toward the rear of the saloon, Murphy said he followed them. He said he knocked Cady down and turned toward Smith. Cady then picked up the cane Murphy had dropped and hit Murphy in the face. He concluded by saying that he thought Cady fired the shot that killed Sparks.

Cort Thomson testified that he saw Sparks facing both Cady and Smith when he was shot, that he saw Smith pull his gun, yet could not say who fired the fatal bullet.

The *Rocky Mountain News* published yet another version of events as learned, the reporter noted, "from a well known witness." While the witness is not named in the article, the piece reads in part:

> *Jordan drew his revolver to avenge an old fancied wrong. He drew to kill either Smith or Cady. He cared but little which. He was nervous and saw his enemies, each with a weapon. Before he could raise to gain aim, his finger pressed the trigger and the ball flew in a wrong course. The weapon fired at him was used in equal haste. Neither party desired to take any chance, and their bullets went wild. A witness well known and whose word cannot be doubted stated that Jordan's revolver belched forth its leaden ball when he was holding it on level with his wrist. The same witness is quite sure of the course of this death messenger. Jordan's bullet, he says, killed Sparks.* [37]

Through all the testimony, conflicting as it was, the coroner's jury released their verdict late that night.

> *The deceased came to his death in Murphy's exchange, (sic) 1617 Larimer street, Denver, Arapahoe County, Colorado, about 11:50 p.m. October 11, 1892, by a gunshot wound caused by a pistol ball fired from a revolver in the hands of James Jordan. We further find that said shooting was felonious, and that Thomas Keady or Cady was accessory to the same.*

Jordan, Cady, and surprisingly enough, Smith, were all held on charges of murder and accessory to murder, respectively. With the news of the arrests, the *Rocky Mountain News* of October 13, 1892, published the following report:

> *Groups of well-known gamblers yesterday discussed the shooting in all the downtown saloons and the general impression prevails that the scene enacted in Murphy's exchange [sic] on Tuesday night will prove but a prelude to a bitter warfare*

between a well known gang of men who live by their wits and dollars gained by fleecing. The ill-feeling has been smoldering of late and needed but slight provocation to fan it into a blaze of crime.

The murder trials of the three accused finally reached court a year later. Nearly all of the witnesses who testified before the coroner's jury again testified in all three of the trials. The testimony was the same; no one could agree on an accurate account of the shooting resulting in the death of Cliff Sparks.

Thomas Cady was the first to go on trial for the murder of Sparks. On October 28, 1893, he was found not guilty of murder. Jefferson Randolph "Soapy" Smith pled not guilty. His attorney, James Belford, evidently had some influence with the presiding judge, for within two months, the murder charge against Smith was dropped. Likewise, James Jordan's attorney was able to get his client acquitted for lack of evidence.

Who murdered Cliff Sparks? A question that remains unanswered in the annals of Denver's homicide history.

The County Jail Mob Lynching
Racial Tensions Run High

Despite law and order which eventually came with statehood in 1876, Colorado's capital city of Denver suffered setbacks when a few citizens took the law into their own hands. Such was the case on an extremely warm July evening in 1893, when an Italian immigrant, Daniel Arata, was taken from the county jail, viciously attacked by an angry mob, stabbed, then lynched not once, but twice, on the streets of Denver.

Daniel Arata, a hard-working man with a tough guy attitude, quickly rose from menial jobs to become the manager of the Hotel D'Italia, a popular drinking establishment among the Italian immigrant population. The saloon and adjacent boarding house, located in lower Denver at 1545 Wewatta Street, was in a rough, rundown area next to the railroad tracks.

The Hotel D'Italia was a tough hangout. Fights were nearly a nightly occurrence. Arata was often the instigator of such barroom brawls. On the evening of July 25, 1893, Arata started yet another brawl, this time ending in murder.

Arata had been drinking throughout the slow business day and for whatever reason, took an interest in a saloon patron who entered the establishment at approximately 6 p.m.

Benjamin C. Lightfoot, a sixty-year old veteran of the Civil War, stopped in the saloon for a beer on his way home from his job as a contracted plaster worker. After hoisting a cold one at the bar, Lightfoot headed for the door when he was confronted by Arata. Witnesses said a friendly conversation transpired between the two and Arata "suggested" that Lightfoot should stick around and have another beer. Considering this an invitation from Arata, Lightfoot agreed.

As he finished the beer and again headed for the door, Arata stopped him for the second time. This time in a most unpleasant tone, Arata demanded Lightfoot pay for the beer. An argument ensued whereby Lightfoot said he took the invitation to stay and have another beer as a complimentary one. Arata became visibly agitated as he nearly bellowed he did not give away beverages for free. Lightfoot further explained he did not have the money to pay for the second beer.

The argument escalated to the point where Arata threw a punch which landed on the side of Lightfoot's head, knocking him to the floor. Arata didn't stop there; he began kicking Lightfoot unmercifully. He didn't stop until blood was running from Lightfoot's body. What happened next is truly astonishing, even in the annals of Colorado's most gruesome murders.

Arata calmly walked away from Lightfoot's limp body, returned to the bar, washed off what blood he could and poured himself a drink. After a few moments, he retrieved his pistol and slowly walked back to Lightfoot who still lay unconscious on the floor. (There is no record or testimony as to whether anyone in the bar attempted to help the injured man.) Arata raised his pistol and fired a bullet into the chest of the nearly lifeless Civil War veteran. He then dragged the dead body behind the building in an attempt to hide it.

A few hours later, on an anonymous tip, the police arrived at the Hotel D'Italia. Finding the saloon in disarray and evidence of blood everywhere, questions were asked of Arata who replied in a drunken state that he had cut himself. Further investigation by the officers led

Daniel Arata was arrested on charges of murder. A mob stormed the Arapahoe County Jail and hanged Arata from a nearby tree.

to the body of Lightfoot hastily placed behind the building.

Arata was arrested on suspicion of murder. A visibly inebriated Daniel Arata had to be physically hoisted into the police wagon. He was taken to the Arapahoe County Jail at 1448 Kalamath Street.

The year 1893 was the beginning of an economic depression in the state. The repeal of the Sherman Silver Purchase Act caused a near overnight collapse of Colorado's number one industry: mining. Thousands of miners were out of work and the ripple effect was felt throughout Colorado's businesses. Businesses failed and entrepreneurs lost millions.

A natural unrest among the citizenry ensued and simmered in deep unplaced resentment during that hot summer.

Word quickly spread throughout the following day of the murder of a Civil War veteran in lower downtown. That very evening a meeting had been scheduled in the vicinity of Eighteenth and Market streets, regarding high unemployment in the city. As the citizens gathered for the meeting on July 26, 1893, the main topic of conversation was the murder of Benjamin C. Lightfoot. The conversation soon turned to outrage at the murder of an innocent bystander, not to mention a Civil War veteran. Further outrage seethed within the group when it was learned Lightfoot was murdered by an Italian immigrant, a group many believed were stealing the few available jobs.

The anger sparked an all-out group march to the county jail. As the incensed group of citizens made the mile-long march to the jail, their group swelled as more citizens joined. When the crowd arrived at the county jail, at approximately 9 p.m., the number had swelled to 10,000 according to the *Denver Times* report of July 27, 1893. According to that same *Denver Times* article, the group shouted out, "Death to the Dago," and, "We're going to lynch the Dago."

Police Chief Aaron Kellogg, along with Sheriff William K. Burchinell and a group of officers, met the angry crowd on the steps of the jail entrance. Seeking a calm atmosphere the chief suggested the crowd break up and go home, as they surely were not going to get into the jail.

The assembled group would have none of the chief's words and soon began an assault on the jail. In an effort to stop the group the guards turned water hoses on them and turned off the lights inside the jail. When this didn't stop the group, a few of the officers fired their guns, wounding two in the crowd. Now, the situation was out of control.

The infuriated group of men took on a mob-like mentality. Someone obtained an iron rail from the nearby streetcar line. Using this they were able to bust down one of the doors to the jail. They eventually found Daniel Arata. Removing the hinges from the cell door, members of the mob hauled Arata out of the cell. One of the men stuck a knife into his abdomen and then hauled the bleeding man out of the jail.

The mob then followed the men carrying the bleeding Arata to a nearby cottonwood tree where he was immediately hanged. A few members in the group, evidently not satisfied, fired four bullets into Arata's limp body. One of the shots broke the rope and Arata's body fell with a thud to the ground. The *Denver Republican* account of the lynching, in the July 28, 1893 issue, included the following: *The crowd laughed and cheered and yelled, 'Burn him, burn him.'*

The mob then dragged Arata's dead body through the streets of Denver to approximately Seventeenth and Curtis streets. There, they tied Arata by rope, to the top of a telegraph pole and left the hanging body. It was nearly 3 o'clock in the morning before police arrived on the scene and cut the body down from the pole.

Arata's corpse arrived at the Arapahoe County morgue where the coroner, John M. Chivington, previously commander of the First Colorado Cavalry who led the attack at Sand Creek on November 29, 1864, examined the body. Chivington's determination was that Daniel Arata died of strangulation. He was buried unceremoniously at Riverside Cemetery.[38]

As the local papers reported the mob lynching, the national

media soon picked up on the event. A Denver county commissioner was quoted in the *Denver Times* of July 28, 1893, as saying that the lynching "was a mighty cheap job for the county." Evidently the racial tensions of the economic times were good copy nationwide. The event was dubbed nationally as the "Dago Death Affair."

Boy Murderer
Anton Woode

Anton Woode was only twelve years old when he entered the Colorado State Penitentiary at Canon City on August 8, 1893. Convicted of first degree murder, At that time, Woode was the youngest person in the United States to be convicted of murder and sent to prison.

Anton Woode was the son of German Russian immigrants, Thomas and Michelin (Maggie) Woode, who arrived in America in 1873. First working in New Jersey, the couple, along with six-month-old Anton, migrated West for better opportunities in 1882. They settled near Brighton, Colorado, where Thomas found work in the sugar beet fields twenty miles north of Denver.

Young Anton enjoyed roaming the countryside surrounding his family farm and hunting small game. He was a good shot, nearly always bringing home food for his mother's table. His weapon was an old black powder musket, nearly as tall as he was.

On the morning of November 2, 1892, ten-year-old Anton left the farmhouse with his trusty musket for a day of hunting. Meanwhile, three hunting buddies from Denver, Alexander Baker, Joseph Smith and Harry Wyman, had arrived in nearly the same area for a few days of duck hunting. It was near noon when the hunting trio from Denver decided to split up and cover more ground. Wyman went off alone as Baker and Smith tended to their horses.[39] Woode approached the men as they were tethering the horses. After a short conversation, Woode told the two men he would lead them to an area where there were plenty of rabbits. In no time at all both Baker and Smith had shot a rabbit. At that point Baker elected to go after ducks and set out to find Wyman. By mid-afternoon, Baker and Wyman had reconnected, with Smith and Woode not far behind them.

The following events were recounted in the murder trial of eleven-year-old Anton Woode. Baker and Wyman both heard a shot behind them. The men turned to see that Smith had shot another rabbit. Within a few moments another shot was fired behind Baker and Wyman, but neither of the men could see Smith or Woode from their vantage point.

Toward dusk, Baker and Wyman returned to the agreed point where the three would camp for the night. When Smith had not returned, his fellow hunters set out to search for him. After a three hour search, the evening plunged into complete darkness. Baker and Wyman agreed to resume the search in the morning.

Shortly after daylight, the two set out again in search of their friend. On a small hill in the low-lying prairie, they soon found the dead body of their hunting partner. He was lying on his back, his eyes open and his arms outstretched. Realizing their friend was dead, Baker searched for clues as to what happened. They noticed Smith's shotgun was gone. Careful as he was to not disturb a potential crime scene, Baker searched the deceased man's pockets. When he could not recover Smith's cherished gold watch and chain, the two friends knew a murder had been committed. The men immediately returned to Denver to report the crime.

Arapahoe County deputy sheriffs Albert Hollaway and T. J. Thompson, along with Arapahoe County coroner, John M. Chivington, left Denver with Alexander Baker for the scene of the crime. Locating Smith's body, the deputies noted footsteps in the snow. A single bullet had hit Smith near the right shoulder blade. The blood saturating the ground beneath Smith's body indicated he had bled to death.

Baker and Wyman recounted the events of the previous day which suggested Woode was a suspect. Following the footsteps in the snow, the sheriffs were led almost to the very front steps of the Woode farm house, less than a mile away.

Mrs. Woode eventually let the men enter the house, but explained Anton was not at home. It wasn't long, however, when one of the deputies found the young boy hiding under his bed. After a few calm, yet direct, questions Woode produced the gold watch and chain that belonged to the dead man, Smith. When asked about Smith's shotgun, Woode said his father took it from him. Soon the deputy found it between the mattresses of Woode's bed.[40] Then the boy confessed to the lawmen that he had indeed shot Smith. The sheriffs arrested

Woode and transported him to the Arapahoe County jail in Denver.

The Denver newspapers splashed the story of the "Boy Murderer" on their front pages. The public was shocked by the news and more stories ran leading up to the trial. It became the most sensational murder trial of the century in the state of Colorado, and received national coverage as well.

Never one to stay out of the national spotlight, the coroner of Arapahoe County, John M. Chivington, gave an interview to the *Colorado Sun* newspaper. Stating his opinion of Woode, he said:

Denver Public Library, Western History Dept.

Anton Woode was ten years old when he murdered a hunter for his shotgun. Woode was the youngest person ever to be convicted of murder and sentenced to life imprisonment at the Colorado State Penitentiary.

There is something in the surroundings of this youth, Woode, that tended to make him as he is. He was born out there amid the rough, bleak hills. The boy has simply partaken of the surroundings. He is physically sapped and morally barren. He never had anything nice himself; he saw the poor murdered lad with a beautiful gold watch; he coveted it, and the price seemed cheap to him. It was only a lad who stood in the way of his possession of what every boy most wants, a watch and a gun.

Nationally, the *Evening News* of Lincoln, Nebraska, covered the Denver story, running this headline in their issue of April 24, 1893: *A Murderer at Eleven.*

The trial began in a Denver court room on Monday, February 27, 1893. The courtroom was filled to capacity as the curious watched as the young blond boy defendant entered, led by an Arapahoe County sheriff. He was dressed neatly, even sporting a tie. As he took his seat next to his attorneys, his feet barely touched the floor.

The prosecuting attorney, Booth Malone, chose not to seek the death penalty. He began opening arguments for the government's case, "The People vs. Anton Woode", before Judge David V. Burns. Woode was represented by attorneys John A. Converse, John A. Deweese, and Henry S. Johnston.

Testimony for the prosecution began with Smith's hunting companions Baker and Wyman. Both recounted the meeting with Woode, the separation from Smith, the gunshot, and the finding of Smith's body the following day. Arapahoe County Coroner John M. Chivington testified to his participation in the investigation and identified Woode's musket that fired the fatal shot, as well as Smith's stolen shotgun. Arapahoe County sheriff deputies Albert Hollaway and T. J. Thompson, testified to their encounter with Woode, the discovery of the missing watch and chain in his possession, and the subsequent confession. Holloway further testified that he obtained a second confession from Woode during a visit at the jail, this one in the presence of Assistant District Attorney H. G. Benson. Finally, Doctor J. T. Eskridge, who conducted several interviews with Woode, testified as to the intelligence and understanding of Woode. In a direct question with regard to the legal understanding of what Woode faced, the doctor answered, "I concluded that he (Woode) knew the difference between good and evil."

"The boy was remorseful," Eskridge said. "He cried and said he was very sorry."[41]

The defense team called several witnesses to the stand including Woode's parents. However, their key to the defense of Woode, in direct opposition to the prosecution's witness, was Doctor Eugene Grissom, who testified that it was his opinion that Woode could not be "perfectly sound," and further stated that it was his opinion that Woode "was emotionally insane."

Once again the Denver newspapers sensationalized the trial. An example is an article in the *Denver Republican* of March 1, 1893, which stated in part that Woode was "a freak of nature, in intellect and soul, though not in body."

In his closing argument, defense attorney Deweese stated to the jury, "In the instructions of the court, you see that you are forbidden to find a verdict of guilty in either the first or second degrees of murder unless the people have proven beyond any reasonable doubt that the act was committed with malice and premeditation," and he finished with the words, "You will readily see that this has not been done." After three days of testimony the jury began their deliberations.

The following evening, March 2, 1893, shortly before six o'clock, the jurors indicated to Judge Burns that they were unable to reach a verdict. Whether the final words from the defense attorney had the weight intended will never be known. Or could it have been a case where the jury were simply reluctant to convict a child of murder? In any event, the judge certainly was not happy. Addressing the jury members, he said, "Gentlemen, it is a matter of regret that you are unable to agree. There is no probability that in any future trial of this case, the evidence will be any stronger." His anger showed in his final words to the jury, "A later jury which will consider this case will have no lighter task than has fallen to you. You are discharged."

The following day, the *Rocky Mountain News,* in their coverage of the trial and failure to reach a verdict, opined that it was a "sickening sentimentality," that led to the trial outcome.

The district attorney's office set the retrial date of Anton Woode for March 20, just two weeks after the first trial. Meanwhile, Woode remained in the county jail where he had recently observed his eleventh birthday.

Woode's second trial began much as the first trial had. Defense attorneys were again Deweese and Johnston. The prosecution team was again headed by Malone. Both sides delivered their opening arguments, however the defense team introduced a new theory as to the actions of the then ten-year-old Woode on that fateful fall day four months previous.

The defense of young Anton Woode now seemed to be a physiological disorder due to syphilis contracted by Anton's father and passed onto his mother and thus inherited by Anton. The theory was supported by the defense's expert witness, Doctor F. G. Yocum, who testified that would effect his mental stability. On cross-examination, the prosecution attorney, Malone, reminded the doctor of a previous conversation where the doctor had concluded that Woode was indeed able to know right from wrong. He was also able to get the doctor to admit, under oath, that he had not actually examined Woode's parents and therefore, did not actually know for a fact the definitive evidence of syphilis.

Confident in discrediting the defense witness, the prosecution bolstered their case by recalling their previous expert witnesses on the subject of Woode's mental state. Again, Doctor J. T. Eskridge testified that during his numerous examinations of Woode, he concluded that Woode knew the difference between good and evil. Further pressed by the attorney, Eskridge stated that in his opinion after his many examinations of Woode, there was no evidence of a syphilis inheritance.

The trial continued fairly rapidly throughout the day, ending with closing arguments late in the night. At 9:45 p.m., that very night, the case was given to the jury.

In an amazing twelve-hour turn around, the members of the jury filed into the court room at 9:45 a.m. the following morning with a verdict. The clerk of the court read the verdict: *"In the case of the 'People vs. Anton Woode.' we, the jury, find the defendant guilty of murder in the second degree."*

On April 5, 1893, Judge Burns heard final appeals from the defense council, before passing sentence on the convicted murderer. The judge ruled that because the verdict was guilty of murder in the second degree, the defendant was not eligible for the death penalty. Thus Judge Burns, under Colorado law, sentenced Woode to twenty-five years at the state penitentiary in Canon City.

On April 8, 1893, eleven-year-old Anton Woode experienced his first train ride; to the iron gates of the state prison. Despite his young age, Woode was processed into the prison as all inmates were. He was patted down, fingerprinted, and interviewed for vital information records. He was then given a shower, his head was shaved, and he was sprayed for bugs. Finally his official prison "mug" shot was taken. The photo would be that of any innocent twelve-year-old boy were it not for the inmate tag, #3199, pinned to his striped shirt.

Life in prison was routine and somewhat mundane for Woode. He was placed in a six-by-eight foot jail cell which for a time he occupied by himself.[42] Woode had little contact with his fellow inmates, as he preferred and the warden agreed. In this self-imposed solitary confinement, Woode turned to books and began to educate himself. However, he was expected to work at the prison, as all inmates were.

Due to his age and obvious lack of skills, Woode worked various jobs in the prison office, the library, and the kitchen. As he grew older, Woode was required to work a more intensive labor schedule.

He had worked the night shift in the boiler room for some time when he became a part of one of the most notorious prison breakouts in the history of the Colorado State Penitentiary. It happened just a week after his eighteenth birthday, significant in the repercussions that would follow.

On the night of January 22, 1900, Woode, along with inmates Thomas Reynolds, Charles E. Wagoner, and Frank "Kid" Wallace, were finishing their dinner break when Reynolds gave a signal to Wagoner and Wallace, killed the prison supervisor, and the three inmates coaxed Woode into joining their plan of escape.[43]

By all accounts, including later prison interrogation reports of Wallace and Woode as well as the written report of Warden Clarence P. Hoyt, Woode was in the wrong place at the wrong time; a victim of the circumstances. Nevertheless, Woode escaped with three other inmates.

The *Canon City Record* broke the news the next day and fear gripped the town. The headline in the *Denver Post* issue of January 23, 1900, "The Boy without a Conscience," declared what many thought of Anton Woode: "The lad was practically devoid of conscience and moral instinct." The article concluded with these words:

A perfect type of the born criminal or criminal degenerate is Anton Woode. There is no doubt about that.

After three days of searching, on January 25, Woode and Wallace were surrounded by law enforcement officials near the stage road between Canon City and Cripple Creek, otherwise known as the Shelf Road.[44] Cold, wet and hungry, the inmates readily surrendered. With tensions high, the authorities returned the prisoners hidden in a horse-drawn wagon filled with hay.

For his part in the murder and prison escape, Anton Woode, now an adult, was charged as an accessory to murder. Once again, John Deweese defended Woode in the trial, which took place in January 1901. Woode was acquitted due to a lack of evidence. However, because of Woode's voluntary escape and eluding the authorities, he lost all the benefits of time already served. According to state law,

Woode had little hope of ever being granted an early parole from prison.

During the next few years Woode studied several languages, excelled in math, learned to play the violin, and enjoyed art classes. He stayed to himself as much as possible, perhaps learning a valuable lesson from his past deeds, that and from maturity. In the early summer of 1903, that maturity as well as quick thinking would lead to a fundamental change in the future of Anton Woode.

On the morning of June 22, 1903, an explosion at one of the prison gates along the south wall signaled the beginning of one of the most spectacular breakouts in the history of the penitentiary.

Shortly before the explosion, Woode, who was working alone in the deputy warden's office, observed a scuffle in the yard involving three men and a woman. Woode immediately rang the prison bell alarm system. As the prison officials were thus alerted, so too were three inmates facilitating their planned escape. One of those inmates, Kirch Kuykendall, exploded into the office and threatened Woode with a knife. Woode managed to exit from the office unscathed and alerted the prison guards that an escape was underway.

Unknown to Woode and the prison guards, earlier in the morning six inmates had reported to the Cell House Three prison guard, Clarence Cleghorn, that they were ill. The prison doctor, along with a staff member of the prison hospital, arrived before the roll call of the morning to examine the ill men. Suddenly, three of the inmates wielded homemade knives and demanded the guard and the two medical men to disrobe. Three of the inmates then traded their prison uniforms for the ordinary clothes of the three men while the other three left to perpetuate the explosion.

As the escapees headed toward the main gate, they encountered a woman. This was the confrontation Woode witnessed from the office window. Unknown to Woode at the time, the woman was Mrs. Annie Cleghorn, the wife of the prison warden, John Cleghorn, and the aunt of the prison guard, Clarence Cleghorn. The inmates took Mrs. Cleghorn as hostage in their escape. With a knife at Mrs. Cleghorn's throat, the inmates made their way to the gate. With a rag presoaked with nitroglycerin, Kuykendal shoved it into the gate lock and lit a match. The gate exploded.

Shots were fired and Mrs. Cleghorn collapsed to the ground.

Leaving their hostage, the inmates rushed through the gate. Within an hour all six were either apprehended or dead.

Because of the effort Woode displayed in alerting the prison officials to the escape, Warden Cleghorn, along with the members of the prison board, lobbied the governor for a pardon of Anton Woode. A letter dated June 22, 1903, and signed by Louis King, President, H. L. White, Secretary, Thomas M. Bowen, and Warden John Cleghorn, asked for the governor's consideration:

> *Whereas, We consider that great assistance was rendered this institution by the prompt and fearless action of Thomas Helster, #4839, and Anton Woode, #3199, in the attempt to escape made this morning by the six desperate criminals confined herein; and, Whereas, We further consider had it not been for their efforts and prompt action great injury or death might have resulted to Mrs. Cleghorn and others connected with the institution. Therefore be it Resolved, By the board of penitentiary commissioners now in session, that we most respectfully recommend His Excellency, James H. Peabody, governor of Colorado, to extend executive clemency to said Helster and Woode, as a reward for their services and meritorious conduct.*

On October 13, 1905, Governor James Peabody granted Anton Woode a full pardon. The boy murderer had served twelve years, four months, and twenty-eight days behind bars for his crime.

After literally growing up in prison, life on the outside was not what Woode expected. Through charitable benefactors such as the Cleghorns, Woode was allowed to leave the state and learn a suitable craft at the Roycroft Colony in New York. The generosity of his benefactors was evidently lost to the now twenty-three year old Anton Woode. He wrote a letter to Warden Cleghorn just six days after his arrival, saying; "I am entirely dissatisfied with my location." Receiving no response, he wrote to Governor Peabody, again with no response. However, word of the pleading letters reached the media and his letters were printed. Public sentiment turned against Woode once again.

Woode remained in New York, eventually found work as an

artist, married and lived a quiet life until his death in Minneapolis, Minnesota, on March 8, 1950.

Strangler's Row
High Anxiety

The fall of 1894 brought on a bloody and chilling episode in Denver's early history. Within three months, three working women in the tenderloin district had been strangled, each one in their own place of "business." Fear gripped the city, while the soiled doves of Market Street lived in terror.

The Denver newspapers only added to that citywide fear when they dubbed Market Street, "Strangler's Row." Suddenly the headlines of the Denver newspapers screamed with sensationalism; "Jack The Ripper," the papers wrote, now stalked the streets of Denver.

There were reasons to be concerned; all victims to date had been murdered on "The Row," and all had been strangled, and all had been found with a towel in their mouths. Moreover, with no sign of forced entry, a stranger in the form of a customer now became the invisible suspect.

With the constant media focus, and no leads or suspects, the pressure was intense at the Denver Police Department. The detectives were looking at anyone and everyone, while private detectives were actively working to collect the one thousand dollar reward for the capture of the killer or killers, as reported in the *Denver Evening Post*.[45]

On September 3, 1894, Lena Trapper, of German descent, was found choked to death in her one-room crib at 1911 Market Street. Her lifeless body was on the bed with a piece of her skirt shoved down her throat. There was no forced entry, nothing was taken or disturbed in the residence, and no sign of a struggle.

The police detectives felt they had enough evidence against Richard Demady to charge him with the murder of Ms. Trapper, who had been in a long-term affair with Demady. The charges were later dropped.

The next month, another murder by strangulation was discovered.

In the wee morning hours of October 28, a Denver policeman, Tony Saunders, ran from his home in the 1900 block of Market Street, frantically blowing a whistle. Three officers near the location heard the whistle as a signal for help and rushed to the scene. Pushing through the sizable crowd which had formed, the officers gained access to the private residence at 1925 Market Street.

In the bedroom just off the parlor was the body of prostitute Marie Contassot. The twenty-three-year-old, had been choked to death, leaving her face grossly discolored and swollen, and her eyes bulging from their sockets. Her neck was badly bruised. A large piece of rope was found near the body. There were no signs of forced entry.The murder was nearly the same as the Trapper murder.

Investigators learned Marie and her sister, Eugenie, were brought to America from their native France, by one Charles Chaloup, who was also French. Chaloup, as it turned out, was also a Denver-based pimp with a less than good reputation. Marie and Eugenie served the Market Street clientele under Chaloup's ruling iron fist. He would soon fall under suspicion of murder by the Denver police.

However, another person of interest quickly became the number one suspect during the murder investigation. He was Tony Saunders, the Denver police detective who had first alerted police to the crime scene. Saunders also went by an alias, Antonio Santopietro, previously unknown to his fellow police officers.

It seems Antonio Santopietro was well known on Market Street as a pimp, but not as a cop. He had been involved in a personal relationship with the late Ms. Contassot for quite some time. Obviously, this led to many raised eyebrows in the police department. However, according to police reports, while under interrogation, he professed his love for Marie, and swore (in broken English and Italian) he had nothing to do with her murder. He further stated they had been lovers for over seven months and that she had just moved in with him less than a week earlier.[45] Eventually, he was released due to lack of evidence.

The police continued their investigation, now refocusing on the Market Street pimp, Chaloup. It had been revealed that Chaloup and Marie's sister, Eugenie, had just recently returned from a trip to Paris, where Chaloup had purchased real estate. The sisters were about to inherit a fortune from an ailing relative in Paris. Neighbors and friends of Marie Contassot, interviewed by police and newspapers, claimed

Denver Public Library, Western History Department
Denver's Market Street was the scene of several grisly murders.

Eugenie and Chaloup planned to get the entire fortune, leaving Marie with nothing. While Eugenie told the police she had planned another trip to Paris, she would not confirm or deny the family fortune. Meanwhile, Chaloup denied any knowledge. Chaloup, no longer under suspicion, seems to have faded from the list of suspects, while sister Eugenie, interestingly enough, never was a suspect.

As the fear mounted in the city, Market Street madams took matters into their own hands to protect themselves and their working girls. Denver's most famous madam, Mattie Silks, who owned a fancy parlor house just down the way from the latest murder, led the way in protecting the tenderloin district. To protect her girls, Mattie had iron bars installed on all the windows. Other madams followed suit, even placing locks on doors and windows.

Just two weeks after the Contassot murder, on November 13, nineteen-year-old Kiku Oyama, was found dead by her boyfriend, Imi Oyama. In similar fashion as the Trapper and Contassot strangulations, Oyama had been strangled, a towel shoved in her mouth, and left for dead on her bed at 1957 Market Street. Ms. Oyama had only arrived in the United States a year earlier. Denver had very few Japanese prostitutes and the murder of one so beautiful and so young set the women of Market Street into further terror.

1880 - 1899

Another legendary madam, Laura Evans, was so shaken by the strangulations by "Jack the Ripper" that she eventually left Denver for good. In an interview, she stated:

"The reason I left Denver when I did was because Jack the Ripper was cutting the wombs out of some of the girls."

For a time, most of the finer parlor houses along the row shut down or limited their business hours. Only the one-room establishments, or cribs, remained open, and even these women were terrified. The killer, or "Jack the Ripper," as the press called him, was never found. The police department eventually closed the case on the strangulations on Market Street.

But was it really over?

Notes for Part II

1 Buchanan, *The Story of a Labor Agitator.*
2 *The Denver Times*, February 18, 1879.
3 Holladay Street, named for pioneer Ben Holladay, was changed to Market Street, at the request of the Holladay family, in 1888.
4 Parkhill, "Scarlet Sister Mattie," *Denver Westerners Brand Book*, 1948.
5 Various written accounts have confused the murdered victim, Look Young, with the proprietor of the laundry, Sing Lee. The correct account is documented in the U.S. State Department, Foreign Relations, 1881.
6 U.S. State Department, Foreign Relations, 1881.
7 Wortman, *Denver's Anti-Chinese Riot,* 1880.
8 ibid.
9 *The Denver Tribune-Republican,* May 25, 1886.
10 *The Daily Denver Times,* May 24, 1886.
11 *The Rocky Mountain News,* June 21, 1886.
12 ibid, and Secrest, *Hell's Belles,* pg. 149.
13 King, *Going to Meet A Man.*
14 ibid.
15 *The Rocky Mountain News,* May 28, 1886.
16 King, *Going to Meet A Man,* pg. 39.
17 ibid.
18 See Part I.
19 King, *Going To Meet A Man,* pg. 75.
20 ibid pg. 83.
21 The area is the vicinity of today's West 10th Avenue and Elati Street.
22 Colorado used this method until 1933, when lethal gas became the method of legal execution.
23 Briggs, L. Vernon, in a self-published account printed in 1932.
24 Colorado State Archives.
25 Radelet, University of Colorado.
27 Colorado State Archives, Messages of the Governors.
28 Josie Washburn worked in such a place at age nineteen, in 1871. See T*he Underworld Sewer: A Prostitute Reflects on Life in the Trade,* 1871-1909.
29 Noel, *The City and the Saloon,* pg. 90.
30 *The Denver Republican*, February 26, 1888.
31 Secrest, *Hell's Belles,* pg. 137.
32 According to police reports, and Howe's personal records, Ardell Smith had a rap sheet dating to at least 1889.
33 *The Denver Republican*, October 15, 1891.
34 Colorado State Penitentiary Records. It is interesting to note that while some historians have

spelled Warden's first name as Belle, all prison records spell the name as Bell.

34 Parkhill, *The Wildest of the West.*

35 Sam Howe Scrapbooks, CHS.

36 Arapahoe County District Court Records, Case # 6054.

37 ibid.

38 General Laws of the State of Colorado, Section 42, Offenses against the person of individuals.

39 Solander was convicted in 1873 and entered the prison system as inmate #60.

40 McGinn, *Female Felons*, pg. 4.

41 Colorado State Archives, and the *Boulder County News*, Januray 10, 1873.

42 *The Denver Times*, August 26, 1891.

43 Parkhill, *Wildest of the West*, pg. 92.

44 *The Rocky Mountain News*, October 13, 1892.

45 See Part I.

46 To this day, there is no headstone at the grave site of Daniel Arata. Riverside Cemetery records.

47 Kreck, *Anton Woode; Boy Murderer*, pg. 2.

48 ibid.

49 ibid.

50 Colorado State Prison Archives Correction Records list Woode as American, his occupation as Farmer, and his height at 4'7".

51 The murder of William C. Rooney is detailed in Part III.

52 *The Canon City Times.*

53 ibid, pg. 275.

54 Wommack, *Our Ladies of the Tenderloin*, pg. 116.

1880 - 1899

Part III

1900 -1919

With the dawn of a new century, social reform was sweeping the nation and had a firm grip on Denver as well as most of Colorado. It was a time of labor reform, including child labor laws, and the beginnings of the women's movement.

In this era of reform the always controversial issue of the death penalty became a key issue for the state legislators. Reformists called for the abolishment of the death penalty, believing it was an inhumane practice. Governor Alva Adams stated in his 1887 inaugural address the need to end the practice of execution and supported the efforts of the reformists. Further evidence of his support of the movement was the signing of a bill prohibiting child labor under the age of fourteen. However, the issue surrounding the morality of the death penalty simmered. Over the next decade, efforts to abolish the death penalty in Colorado continued, leading to passage by the Colorado State Senate on March 15, 1893, by a nineteen to thirteen vote. But the death penalty ban was defeated by a House vote of thirty to nineteen.[1]

On February 28, 1895, a bill abolishing the death penalty passed without debate in the state senate, but again died in the House of Representatives. Ultimately, it was Governor Alva Adams, elected for a second term in 1897, who signed the legislation abolishing the death penalty for all murder cases, reducing the penalty to life imprisonment at hard labor for defendants convicted of first degree murder.[2] Governor Adams, in his annual address to the legislature, referred to the repeal of the death penalty as "The most forward step in criminal legislation that has yet been taken in Colorado."[3]

However, a significant number of Colorado citizens took exception to the new law. Due to a belief in the concept of capital punishment, vigilante justice reemerged.

In 1900 the debate over the death penalty began anew. Over a

Denver Public Library, Western History Department
The Colorado State Capitol, circa 1900, was the scene of fierce debates regarding the death penalty. In 1900 the death penalty was abolished only to be restored a year later.

century later it is still debated. Following a sensational and very public lynching occurring in 1900, public outcry both for and against the reinstatement of the death penalty was back on the table for Colorado politicians. Newspaper editorials from Boulder to Denver and Canon City cried out for restoring the death penalty. Curiously enough, both leading papers in Denver, usually at odds, called for restoring the death penalty, such as this headline on the front page of May 4, 1900 issue of the *Denver Post*:

Capital Punishment Must Be Restored

Only to be followed by the headline in the May 24, 1900 issue of the *Rocky Mountain News*:

Restore Capital Punishment

Governor Charles S. Thomas remained opposed to the reinstatement of the death penalty. Shortly after the lynching, Colorado's Secretary of State Charles Stonaker said, "Lynching is a horrible thing. But this affair has been horrible from the start. If lynching was ever justifiable, it was in this case, but I cannot put myself in the position of endorsing [sic] it. Capital punishment will never be restored. The people have outgrown it. It was useless. It was not a deterrent of crime. It is merely an end of the criminal." [4]

The following incident of a public lynching, which Governor Thomas referred to, while not occurring in Denver, remains in the annuals of Colorado history as a reflection of the subsequent actions of the Colorado government, the seat being the capital city of Denver. The 1900 incident rocked the state and fueled the debate of capital punishment once again.

* * *

Prison Break
A Tug of War

Thomas Reynolds was thirty-four years old when he was arrested for the burglary of a store in Mesa County in 1895. It wasn't his first run-in with the law, but this time his actions earned him seven years of hard labor at the Colorado State Penitentiary. He seems to have been somewhat of a hard case, as his prisoner description, dated on entry to the prison October 16, 1895, lists several scars on both arms and hands, as well as a thick scar on the left side of his neck and a scar under his left eye. According to the physical description, Reynolds also sported several "India ink" tattoos.[5]

It seems Reynolds also possessed some leadership qualities, yet may have lacked good judgment. In January 1900, with less than two years of his sentence remaining, he began a bold plan to break out of the state penitentiary. He recruited fellow inmates Charles Wagoner and Frank "Kid" Wallace into his plan.

The three worked the night shift in the boiler room of the prison, along with eighteen-year-old Anton Woode, the youngest prisoner ever to be sent to prison in the state's history.[6]

On the night of January 22, 1900, following their 10 p.m. dinner break in the "the guard's kitchen" under the supervision of William C. Rooney, Reynolds, as ring leader, signaled to his cohorts. As Rooney started to escort the prisoners back to the boiler room, Reynolds and Wagoner grabbed Rooney from behind. One of the men (it was never proven who, and each blamed the other) produced a handmade knife and plunged it into the heart of Rooney. The twenty-eight-year-old Rooney bled to death.

While Reynolds, Wagoner and Wallace left the kitchen area calling out for Zel Humphrey, the engineer of the boiler room, Woode stayed behind, "scared to death," as Wallace would later relate. Wallace said that he threatened Woode if he didn't go along with the plan.

Meanwhile, when Humphrey appeared, along with night captain C. F. Malone, the two were immediately grabbed and tied up. The four inmates then proceeded to release the hot water from the one hundred boilers, and further disabled the boilers by pouring buckets of soapy water on the boiler belts, which effectively shut down the power generator, thus plunging the prison into darkness.

The inmates then made their escape using a makeshift rope ladder, over the northeast wall of the prison, seemingly undetected. Once over the wall, the group split up. Reynolds and Wagoner took off in a southeast direction from the prison, while Wallace and Woode went north, following the Four Mile Creek.

As word reached the citizens of Canon City, fear gripped the townsfolk. The news filtering throughout the town, scant as it was, caused a high alert of citizen awareness. A social dance to be held that night at Shaeffer Hall was disrupted by the news of the prison breakout. The local hardware stores opened their doors at the late hour, selling guns, ammunition and various items for the citizens to arm themselves.

Murder At The Penitentiary: The Night Captain Killed and Four Prisoners Make Their Escape

This was the headline in the *Canon City Times* issue of January 25, 1900. The warden of the prison, Clarence P. Hoyt, issued wanted posters with the four inmates' mug shots, which were sent to law enforcement all over the state. Both Governor Thomas and Warden Hoyt offered rewards for the return of the four escaped prisoners; "dead or alive." Hoyt offered $125 for each prisoner and the governor put up an additional offer of $500. Prison officials, as well as local and state law enforcement, set up a statewide manhunt for the escaped convicts.

Meanwhile, two days after the murderous escape, the body of young William C. Rooney was escorted to his final resting place in the cemetery at Golden, Colorado. He left behind his young bride of six months. His autopsy report revealed seven stab wounds, twice in the heart, three times to the kidneys, one to the shoulder and one to his side. The viciousness of the act only enraged the citizens and law enforcement.

Three days later, on January 25, on a tip from a local landowner along Four Mile Creek, law enforcement were immediately sent to the area. Landowner Charles Canterbury had told them his young sons had spotted two strange men stealing turnips from the turnip fields on their land. Canterbury, along with William Higgins, tracked the two strangers northwest of the area. The two men found the thieves near the stage road between Canon City and Cripple Creek, commonly known as the Shelf Road.[7] Cold, wet and hungry, the two men immediately surrendered. The men were indeed, as Canterbury suspected, two of the escaped convicts; Frank "Kid" Wallace and Anton Woode. The surrender took place close to the scene of Wallace's original crime of robbing the Florence & Cripple Creek Railroad train, which earned him the prison term in the first place.

Just before sunrise the following day, the escaped convicts were returned undetected by the public, back to the state penitentiary. Under interrogation, a very nervous Anton Woode said he was forced into the escape by Wallace, and that he would be killed if he didn't "go along." He further stated that it was Wallace who had repeatedly stabbed Rooney to death. Meanwhile, Wallace during his interrogation insisted that it was Reynolds who had killed Rooney.

Whatever the truth was, word of the opposing blame game got out to the public. With Wallace once again behind bars, Reynolds became the focal point of the public's anger.

The day following the capture of Wallace and Woode, Reynolds and Wagoner were spotted near the town of Florence, some ten miles southeast of Canon City. The pair had approached a local farmhouse asking for food. Suspicious, the lady of the house alerted the local sheriff. Later that day, the sheriff and a couple of deputies spotted the inmates, near the depot station.

When confronted by law enforcement, the two inmates fled in opposite directions. As the lawmen split up in pursuit, Reynolds was quickly captured while Wagoner managed to elude the officers. The officers took Reynolds to the city jail in Florence where he awaited the arrival of prison officials to escort him back to Canon City.

Word soon got out of Reynold's capture and an angry mob of

Florence citizens surrounded the jail. Cooler heads prevailed and the following day the prison officials, including the deputy warden, arrived to take charge of their prisoner.

Fearing a mob scene back in Canon City, the prison officials chose an alternate route in transporting their escaped convict. Entering the city from the First Street bridge, their hope was to avoid any crowds closer to the prison gates.

It was not to be. An eyewitness, W. B. Felton, who was near the prison gates at 10 p.m. the night of January 25, recounted the following events:

Just as we're all about to return home, one of the men gathers us together and says Reynolds has been captured near Florence and is being returned to the prison by three officers in a two-seated rig pulled by a bay and a gray. Hurried plans are made and soon a sizable crowd has gathered along Main Street from Fourth Street to the penitentiary gate. Several of our group have stationed themselves on the bridges and some are waiting at the pen entrance. None of us carries a visible weapon, but several in the group are toting small packages wrapped in coarse wrapping paper. Suddenly at 11 p.m. two shots ring out. The men at the prison gate overpower the guards as they try to enter the prison and take control of Reynolds, leading him quickly to the corner of Main and First Streets, where the new electric light pole stands and where the rest of us were standing. Reynolds appears to be drawn and haggard, but will not speak when given the chance. He is requesting a cigarette which he is given and coolly smokes. Then the noose is placed around his neck and the rope is thrown over the top of the pole. He is hoisted about 10 feet into the air and then he is let down and given another chance to talk and he still remains mute. He has now been hoisted high above the street where he is left to dangle in the night air and it is a solemn group of men that slowly leave the street scene and return to their homes. The hanging took place across the street from the southeastern corner of the prison which gave a clear view to most of the cellhouse windows. It is now January 26th and I understand that the prison inmates who witnessed Reynold's hanging have not expressed any sympathy for their fellow prisoner and many

A trolley on Denver's Larimer Street.

are saying he got his just desserts. Reynold's body hung until about 7 a.m. this morning, January 26 and was then cut down by Warden C.P. Hoyt.[8]

Governor Charles Thomas visited the prison shortly after the lynching of Reynolds to see if he could gain additional information. While he did not find any new information as the warden's investigation was still ongoing, he did issue a public statement regarding the lynching:

> *Violence is never justifiable. The law should have been allowed to take its course. The effect upon the inmates of the penitentiary will be only temporary. When the opportunity comes to escape it will be forgotten. It will not influence the legislature in favor of capital punishment. That is a thing of the past. It will not lessen crime. If the people think the lynching of Reynolds will have a lasting affect on them they have overlooked a part of their prison history. It is not in the nature of things that it should have.*

And so the tug of war between the two opposing sides of the capital punishment issue began anew.

Meanwhile, the manhunt for the remaining escaped convict, Charles Wagoner, was ongoing. Newspapers all across the state covered the search. The February 1, 1900, issue of the *Canon City Record* stressed that a reward of $250 for the convict was still in effect. Despite the efforts of local law enforcement and prison officials, Wagoner was never recaptured.

Anton Woode was acquitted. However, because Woode did escape and willingly eluded the authorities, he lost all the benefits of time already served.

As for Frank "Kid" Wallace, who was charged with the murder of William C. Rooney, his murder trial, held at the same district court in Buena Vista, ended with a conviction of murder. Judge M. S. Bailey sentenced Wallace to an additional twenty-five to forty-five year term in the state penitentiary on top of his original sentence.[9] On the date of the murder and subsequent escape, Wallace had just four months left to serve of his original prison term.

In his 1900 Biennial Report for the State Penitentiary of Colorado, delivered to Governor Thomas in early 1901, Warden Hoyt's report included the internal prison review of the murder of Rooney and the subsequent escape of the four inmates. The report revealed a shocking series of misconduct and dereliction of duty among several prison officials. The report read in part:

> *The four convicts had been taken from their cells, contrary to explicit orders, to make urgent repairs on the boilers. The lamentable murder of William C. Rooney, night captain, was the result of disobedience of orders by the chief engineer. At this time, officers on guard towers Nos. 2 and 3 were proven flagrantly remiss in their duties in permitting the prisoners to scale the walls near their towers without making any attempt to (stop) their escape.*[10]

The report further stated that when Wallace and Woode were captured and returned to the prison, they were given "the most severe punishment, the two were punished by the dungeon treatment for the period of 96 days."[11]

The entire incident of January 22, 1900 which culminated in murder and lynching, caused the state legislatures to once again debate the issue of capital punishment.

On February 8, 1901, the state House of Representatives voted by a forty-one to twenty-four margin, to reinstate capital punishment in the state of Colorado. The bill also passed in the state Senate on March 29, 1901. The new governor, James B. Orman, would not sign the reinstated bill, yet he also did not veto it. Thus, on July 31, 1901, capital punishment once again became effective in Colorado. It was a political calculation of the time and reflection of the citizens' will, as well as a debate that would resurface in the future.

A Poisoning Affair
Bottle of Wine - Fruit of the Vine

The holidays at the end of 1901 were a perfect time for the Gabrin family to gather at Herman Gabrin's house for feasting, camaraderie — and perhaps murder.

Herman's son, Albert, had been elected to the Colorado House of Representatives in 1900. Born in Germany in 1864, Albert had immigrated to America with his parents when he was three years old; his formal schooling ended at age twelve. He had begun working on Larimer Street and next peddled goods to farmers before he gravitated to Stars shoe store, a big business in Denver. At Stars, he was promoted to salesman. At the time of the 1900 election, he sold for the May Shoe & Clothing Company. Albert's union ties brought him many influential friends — he was a prominent member of the Retail Clerks Protective Association. He also belonged to the Knights of Pythias Lodge #41 and Woodmen of the World Lodge #1. His promise to concentrate on mining concerns in Cripple Creek was well received and the bachelor was swept into office.

Albert married the widowed Nellie Hensley, three years his senior, on June 27, 1901 and she brought two children to the marriage, Dottie and Jed. Swift Hensley, an older son of Nellie and her first husband, had died in 1900, just five days after his twenty-first birthday.

Herman Gabrin hosted the newlyweds and two of his daughters, Rosy and Agnes, at his home at 4451 Highland Avenue on December

29, 1901. New daughter-in-law Nellie brewed a festive punch for the occasion.

Albert, who had previously appeared healthy and vigorous at age thirty-five, died three days after the party, on January 2, 1902. Dr. Horan, the coroner, ruled "acute gastritis induced by fermented wine used in making a mixed drink."

The *Denver Times* revealed the punch recipe as simply a hot claret punch consisting only of claret wine, allspice and lemons. Normally Albert did not drink, smoke or chew, but to please his father he joined in the toast, drinking a small glassful and remarking it tasted very sour and bitter. The rest of the family drank two or three glasses each and Nellie later said that she thought that saved them, because they quickly became ill and vomited "very vigorously" while Albert did not vomit. Herman actually went into convulsions.

Surviving Albert, in addition to Nellie and his two stepchildren, were Herman and three sisters, one listed as Mrs. Frank Oppenheimer.[12]

Perhaps because of the premature death of Nellie's older son, Swift, who died at the tender age of twenty-one, Dr. Moses Kleiner harbored suspicions. Although the coroner had detected nothing amiss, the unusual step of removing the stomach and a portion of the internal organs of Albert was ordered. The organs were given to a Dr. Hillkowitz, along with samples of the wine punch, for chemical analysis. Hillkowitz took his time examining the organs and wine, but when he finally issued a report in mid-April, he found "there was arsenic in the stomach and three and a half grains to the tumblerful in the wine." His conclusion was "arsenical poisoning."[13]

When Nellie Garrin was questioned after Hillkowitz' findings, she reported her sister-in-law Agnes and father-in-law Herman both drank the wine and were still ill. She theorized the arsenic had previously been stored in the wine jug and the jug wasn't washed out thoroughly, attempting to divert suspicion to Thies Liquor, but the liquor store insisted they always used new jugs.

More damning evidence connected Nellie to her husband's death. A Woodmen of the World life insurance policy for three thousand dollars was changed from benefiting Mr. Gabrin's sisters to his wife only eight days before his death. Nellie claimed she knew nothing of that change, but the company flatly stated she certainly did know

After 1901, all legal executions were performed at the Colorado State Penitentiary.

because she signed as the beneficiary at the time. Nellie couldn't recall that at all.

Her poor memory extended to her son's insurance also. Coincidentally, a three thousand dollar life insurance policy had also been issued by Woodmen of the World on Swift Hensley. Nellie denied she had renewed Swift's insurance policy prior to his death, claiming "some friend took it down" and had the young man's insurance reinstated on the very afternoon of the day he died.

The official cause of Swift's death: "arsenical poisoning." Nellie countered with the fact she had seven physicians attending her son and they "suspected nothing." She added that "her first husband left her well off and Mr. Gabrin was liberal with her and she didn't need additional funds."[14]

The public was skeptical of her claims of innocence. Denver authorities convened a grand jury to look into Albert Gabrin's death, but its findings were not what they anticipated. In perhaps the shortest grand jury deliberations on record, the jury began meeting at 2 p.m. and rendered their verdict at 4:30 p.m. the same day. They complimented the police chief and the district attorney's office, but found time to censure everyone else connected to the case: Coroner Horan for using a fluid containing arsenic to embalm the body; Denver druggists for not keeping a record of the purchase of poisons; Dr. Hillkowitz for his delay in making the chemical analysis; Dr. Moses Kleiner, Albert's attending physician, for not removing his patient from the home after he suspected arsenic poisoning; Policeman Malone, the law officer investigating the incident, who actually lived in the Gabrin home. Malone became a policeman through the influence of Albert and the grand jury plainly stated that he should have suspected something. A decision to pursue an indictment would have required nine votes. The jury's decision? "The jury desires to say that while the fringe of suspicion points strongly to a certain person as being the guilty party in this case, still the evidence before us at this time does not warrant the returning of a true bill."[15]

In the end, Woodmen of the World paid Nellie the $3,000 life insurance. She responded that she intended to sue the men on the grand jury for their insinuations.

Albert Gabrin was buried in Riverside Cemetery along with Nellie's first husband, also a Woodmen of the World member.

Murder on the Row
Little Girl Lost

The red light districts attracted all types of people, and the criminal element was a constant threat. The soiled dove was aware of the clientele and took measures, as best she could. All too often she was simply overpowered.

Mabel Brown had just celebrated her twentieth birthday the day before she was brutally murdered in her crib at 1931 Market Street in Denver. A week earlier a similar murder occurred, but received little press coverage. Antoine Kenhan, a street peddler, had been found strangled to death just a few doors from the Brown crime scene.

However, with the murder of Brown, the Denver papers sensationalized the tragedy by running two page layouts of crime scene photos, drawings and even an artist's rendition of the victim tied to the bed. And again, panic gripped Market Street. The front page of the *Denver Times* dated July 6, 1903 read:

> *Horrible Deed of a Strangler: Mabel Brown Bound and Choked to Death in a Market Street Resort. This morning at*

an early hour the dead body of Mabel Brown...was found in
a bedroom in her house, 1931 Market Street. She had been
strangled to death.

Young Mabel was raised in North Denver by her father, William, following her mother's death. "Big Swede" Brown, as her father was called, was a well-known, but unsavory, saloon keeper from Chicago, who operated his saloon in lower downtown Denver. Mabel attended school in North Denver and Sunday school at Highland Park Presbyterian Church, and later found domestic work.

As "Big Swede's" shady dealings caused increased consternation, the Denver police eventually ordered him to leave town. Within a short period of time, Miss Brown found work in a crib on Market Street, where she fell in with a surly wine dealer by the name of Samuel Holzweig, operating in the red light district, as well as Harry Challis, a hot-headed local bartender. It seems a love triangle of sorts emerged, as Brown, who had been in a long-term love affair with Holzweig, broke off the relationship when she took up with Challis. The two men had a confrontation resulting in a barroom brawl. Holzweig left town after that, only to return shortly before Mabel's murder.

On the night of July 5, 1903, Challis had left his place of work during a break to inform Mabel he would be working late and to meet him at a later time, as they met every night. Unable to arouse her by a knock at the door, he opened the door, which to his surprise was unlocked. Inside, as he later told the police detectives, he found Mabel lying on the bed, dead with a cloth in her mouth.

Police reports, described in detail in all the newspapers, stated the crime scene was undisturbed. On the bed near Mabel's hand were two dollar coins, the bedclothes were ruffled, as if to suggest a struggle by Mabel. No furnishings were disturbed and nothing seemed to be missing. The police felt this was not a robbery gone bad. The *Denver Republican* dated July 6, 1903, expressed the fear and concern many in the city felt that the strangulation murders of nine years ago were happening again:

A shudder of horror swept through the ranks of the scarlet
women of the half-world when they learned of the mysterious
crime. Market Street is superstitious. There is a belief that one
such murder is bound to be followed by two others in rapid

succession. Every woman in the quarter believes this as firmly as she believes death is inevitable. Convinced of this fact, the half-world is in a state of excitement bordering on panic that nothing will assuage. A hush fell upon Market Street. Women awakened from their sleep by the first alarm dressed partially and hastened in silence to the scene of the crime. In the dim light from the street lamps they stood about in groups before the door of the house of death and talked in whispers of the tragedy.

Because Challis delayed in calling the police, he became a prime suspect, along with Holzweig, who the detectives learned, had threatened Ms. Brown's life when she left him. Holzweig had a solid alibi, as witnesses placed him at a Market Street bar at the time of the murder. Challis was cleared primarily due to lack of evidence.

Meanwhile, the autopsy revealed water in the lungs, whether to revive her, or to ensure death, will never be known. Whoever committed the murder of Mabel Brown was deliberate in their act. She had been strangled, her hands tied to the bed.

As with the Strangler Murders of nine years previous, Mabel Brown's murder went unsolved.

The Murder of the Priest
Secrets & Lies

Father Felice Mariano Lepore was not only a strong community leader, he was also an acclaimed inventor. Father Lepore also had a secret: he was a married man.

The great Italian migration to America soon followed the Irish migration. Both groups were lured as far west as Colorado by the demand for labor with the railroads, in the mines and mills, and the rich agricultural lands just east of the mountains. These emigrants were happy to have left the economic unrest and depression of their respective homelands.

Originally, the Italians settled in the South Platte River bottoms. Here, they could find cheap rent, and plenty of rich soil and water to grow vegetables. With hard work, many of these Italian families were able to afford better accommodations in North Denver. However, many already residing in the area, including the Irish, harbored prejudiced attitudes toward these swarthy immigrants who spoke a strange language.

Initially, these Italian families worshiped at St. Patrick's Catholic Church at the corner of West 33rd Avenue and Pecos Street, as this was the only Catholic parish in North Denver at the time. However, the newcomers were not welcomed by the Irish communicants. The Italian parishioners advocated for their own parish. The Irish priest of St. Patrick's, Father Joseph Carrigan, also saw the need for a priest for the growing Italian colony of Catholics in North Denver and urged Bishop Nicholas C. Matz to request such a priest.

In response, Father Felice Lepore, originally from the southern Italy town of Cassano, Avilino, arrived in Denver from Pittsburgh, Pennsylvania, in 1891. From the beginning, rumors followed Father Lepore, partially fueled by Italian husbands who distrusted the popular priest, but the rumors about the priest and women in his congregations were given some credibility when in 1895 an ecclesiastical court found the priest guilty of "undue familiarity with women."[16]

Father Lepore proved to be an energetic leader. Early on he became a champion for the poor Italian immigrants, many of whom were called "WOPS" which meant "without passports" The priest also founded a newspaper for the Italian community, *La Mazione*. One of his more notable achievements was the formation of the Mt. Carmel Society, with the support of North Denver business leader Michael Notary. The Mt. Carmel Society, with direction from Father Lepore, purchased seven lots for a new church. On Palm Sunday, March 18, 1894, Bishop Matz dedicated the original Our Lady of Mount Carmel Italian Catholic Church, a small frame structure. Unfortunately, this first Italian Catholic church in Denver burned four years later from an arson-caused fire. The *Denver Times* issue of August 17, 1898, reported that the fire left all of "Little Italy" in mourning.

Father Lepore, along with the Mt. Carmel Society, immediately began the construction of a new church. However, a rival Italian group, the St. Rocco Society, also had plans for an Italian church in the same area. Soon, an Italian Catholic rivalry was underway. Bishop Matz, who found himself caught in the middle of this rivalry, eventually refused to to consecrate the Chapel of Saint Rocco. Instead, he sided with Father Lepore, whom he had brought to Denver.

In late 1899, Bishop Matz consecrated the ground for the new church, located at the corner of West 36th Avenue and Navajo Street, with Father Lepore placing the cornerstone of the foundation for the new Our Lady of Mount Carmel Italian Catholic Church. It was an impressive structure. Built in the Romanesque style, it towered an astonishing one hundred feet, and stretched an entire block. Father Lepore became quite popular in North Denver and attendance rolls at the new Italian Catholic parish grew at a steady rate. The *Denver Times* issue of April 28, 1901, reported that there were 6,000 communicants at Mount Carmel.

Father Lepore was also a genius, creating scientific inventions years before other inventors. The Denver priest patented several inventions between the years of 1892 and 1903. The United States Naval Department even honored him for his ingenious "lifesaver." This apparatus was a rubber suit resembling a coffin, with a helmet for the head and a tube around the chest. The helmet visor could be raised and lowered after the suit was pulled on. Inside recesses in the suit stored fresh water, food and a light for a beacon. The wearer could float on his back inside the suit, eat lunch and clearly see around him. The person inside could also float upright by pumping air into chambers running up and down the sides of the legs.[17]

Another of the ingenious inventions of the priest was his fire escape, widely lauded in contemporary newspapers. This device was an endless ladder on a drum near a window. The weight of even a child descending the ladder kept the drum turning, and a wire on the ladder within easy reach operated a brake.[18]

Father Lepore's life's work remained his parish at the Our Lady of Mount Carmel Catholic Church. In 1902, learning of Mother Frances Xavier Cabrini's miraculous abilities in mission building and charity work with few resources, he suggested to Bishop Matz that Mother Cabrini would be a tremendous asset to the parishioners in North Denver. Bishop Matz agreed and urged Father Lepore to invite her to Denver. At the request of Father Lepore, Mother Frances Xavier Cabrini arrived in North Denver on October 24, 1902. One of her first acts was to bless the Mount Carmel parish. During her stay, Michael Notary, the co-founder of the Mt. Carmel Society, offered his home at the corner of Navajo Street and North 34th Avenue.[19]

Father Lepore delighted in escorting Mother Cabrini during tours of North Denver's "Little Italy," as well as various areas around the state. Mother Cabrini wrote of the tour with Father Lepore:

"Seated in a comfortable carriage of the Santa Fe Railway, my glance swept across those immense plains which, around Denver, are dotted with the cottages of our Italian agriculturists. Here, the hardest work is reserved for the Italian worker. There are few who regard him with a sympathetic eye, who care for him or remember him that he has a heart and soul: they merely look upon him as an ingenious machine for work. I saw these dear fellows of ours engaged on construction of railways in the most intricate mountain gorges."[20]

Father Lepore thoroughly enjoyed his association with Mother Cabrini, who did indeed made a difference in the Italian Catholic community. Mother Frances Xavier Cabrini did indeed provide miracles, for in 1946 she was canonized as a Saint, America's first official saint in the Catholic Church.[21]

However, dark days were to come for the good father.

In October 1903, two men, Joseph Guiseppe Sorice and Pasqual Gondosso, arrived in Denver with evil intentions. Sorice grew up in Cassano, Avilino, the same southern Italian town as Lepore and had followed the priest to New York and Pittsburgh, Pennsylvania. Lepore had been president of a bank which failed in New York State and many Italians had consequently lost their savings. The presumption has always been that Sorice was a depositor in the bank and never forgave Lepore for the loss of his savings. Lepore also had engaged in business and banking in Pittsburgh. Evidently, the two met at this Pittsburgh bank and an argument ensued concerning the losses incurred when the bank in New York failed, but information on the two men who followed the priest to Denver is very scarce.

After Sorice and Gondosso arrived in Denver, Lepore confided to friends that they had tried to blackmail him and that they frightened him. In an attempt to defuse their anger, the priest gave them free rent in one of the residences he owned in the Italian community, fed them at his table and located a job for Gondosso.[22]

On the evening of November 18, 1903, Sorice, quite drunk, left a card game at a north Denver grocery store and entered the priest's study at Our Lady of Mount Carmel Catholic Church. Two other men were also in the church, Mario Capanello, the cook, and Lepore's nephew Frank Lepore, who was in his room above the study. The two men heard a few shouts followed by four gunshots.

Father Lepore had been shot three times. Somehow, he managed to wrest the gun from his assailant's hand. He then shot Sorice in the abdomen. Sorice fell to the bottom of the cellar stairs with his head resting on a step. Father Lepore was able to stagger to the altar where he laid his head on a pillow, perhaps for comfort, perhaps for spiritual guidance.

Both men lingered between life and death until the following morning when authorities were called to the scene. Sorice remained as silent while dying as he had alive. The priest, however, muttering and gasping, was able to converse with the detectives. In a report of the incident, given to the district attorney's office, the report read in part:

He believed his assailant had been sent out to Denver for the purpose of killing him. Since his first conversation with him [Sorice] when he came to Denver about a month ago, he said he had feared the man and thought his life was in danger.

Lepore never revealed why he had been afraid of Sorice or why the assailant shot him. The police prepared his dying statement and he signed it.[23] Father Felice Mariano Lepore died a few days later. He was thirty-five years old.

At the time of his death, Father Lepore held fifteen patents, including one for his flying machine. Lepore's plans for a flying machine were drawn two years before the Wright brothers flew at Kitty Hawk.[24] A British company, Metta of London, had sponsored a worldwide aircraft design contest with a prize of $250,000. Three designs were selected with the Denver priest's being one. Lepore had created two models of his flying machine, sending the second one to the U. S. Patent Office in Washington D. C. Eastern capitalists eagerly advanced the $20,000 Lepore needed for construction of the 'machine', and he predicted that, "For use in war, there will be nothing to compare with it." For his part, Lepore promised his plane would be bulletproof and claimed the propellers could be either lengthened or shortened at the will of the operator. A few of Father Lepore's patented designs had provided a tidy side income for the priest. It would become a subject of contention following his death.

Speculation about the priest's estate occupied the gossip circles of North Denver for weeks. Then a bombshell revelation came when Evelyn Bennis (born in 1880 in Wyoming) asked the probate judge for the estate of her husband, Father Felice Mariano Lepore. According to Evelyn, she had married the priest in a ceremony he conducted in his study at the church on July 1, 1898, both kneeling before a crucifix and whispering their vows. At that time Evelyn lived next door with her widowed mother and had faithfully tidied the priest's house each day for years because he was too thrifty to hire a housekeeper. Evelyn then revealed that she bore Father Lepore a son, Victor Mariano, on September 15, 1898, and that he was the spitting image of his father. She further claimed that she and the priest together had constructed many of the models for his inventions in her small North Denver cottage. Because the patents were continuing to earn money for the estate, she wanted to be declared his common-law wife and the mother of his son.[25]

Then in what appeared to be an attempt to shield the church from scandal, church officials sidestepped the issue of the priest's marriage by suggesting he was never really ordained. They even went so far as to discredit the seminary he attended in southern Italy, suggesting it was an "educate you while you wait" institution. Claims were also made that he had only spent six months at the seminary and a course of study was a full five years. None of Father Lepore's charitable deeds were mentioned. Nothing was mentioned of his work in the Mt. Carmel Society, leading to the Our Lady of Mount Carmel Italian parish.

All the church's sputtering had no influence on the Colorado judicial system. In 1907 a civil court declared Evelyn the legal widow and gave her the name of the dead priest; she became Mrs. Evelyn Lepore. She found work in a cigar-box factory in Denver, happy that Victor now carried his father's name legally.

Beginning in 1920, census records report Evelyn and Victor were living together in Los Angeles and Victor was employed as a "postal worker" until his death on August 5, 1967.

In death, it seems Father Felice Mariano Lepore did indeed leave a legacy, just not the one his Church had in mind.

Murder at the Altar
"Death to the priests!"

Even in our cynical age it is difficult to imagine a more heinous murder than shooting a priest serving holy communion. The *Denver Post* was only too happy to feed its readers the details of the crime. From February 24 to February 28, 1908, the newspaper dedicated many of its front pages to the cold-blooded murder of a man of the cloth.

At the behest of Bishop Nicholas C. Matz, Franciscan fathers had agreed to handle the duties of the parish of St. Elizabeth Catholic Church. Father Leo Heinrichs, of the Roman Catholic Franciscan Order, arrived in Denver on September 23, 1907. With Bishop Matz' approval, the new Franciscan pastor became the leader of the second oldest Catholic parish in Denver. He would hold this position for five months before he would be murdered at the altar of the historic church.

St. Elizabeth Catholic Church, built of native stone, was erected at 1060 11th Street, in one of Denver's oldest neighborhoods, Auraria, in 1878. The German congregation, welcoming Russian Roman Catholics, in time became the largest Catholic congregation in Denver. It was not long before it became one of only three Catholic churches in all of Colorado to be debt-free at that time and therefore officially consecrated.[26]

Bishop Matz had long admired the spiritual dedication of Father Leo Heinrichs. Joseph Heinrichs was born August 15, 1867, in Oestrich, Germany. It was an area under the horrific religious persecution of Otto von Bismarck. In time, Heinrichs and his family were able to escape the region, making their way to the Franciscan Chapter of St. Elizabeth of Hungary. Here, young Heinrichs began his studies in minor seminary. During this time, several members of this parish chose to immigrate to America. Joseph Heinrichs was invited to join them.

Arriving in America, the Franciscan group settled at St. Bonaventure's Friary in Paterson, New Jersey. Here, Heinrichs continued with his seminary studies. On December 4, 1886, Joseph Heinrichs received the Franciscan habit, as well as the monastic name, "Brother Leo." Heinrichs took his final vows on December 8, 1890.

A month before his twenty-fourth birthday, Father Leo Heinrichs was ordained to the priesthood on July 26, 1891.

For the next eleven years, Father Leo Heinrichs served in various positions in New Jersey and New York, including pastor at Holy Angels parish in Little Falls, New Jersey, and St. Stephen's parish in Croghan, New York. Father Heinrichs demonstrated such remarkable character and devotion to his pastoral work that he was made Vicar of St. Bonaventure's and Director of the Third Order of St. Francis. Later, during a smallpox epidemic in New Jersey, Father Heinrichs spent untold hours at a

Denver Public Library, Western History Dept.

Father Leo Heinrichs was murdered at the alter of Denver's St. Elizabeth Catholic Church while celebrating early morning Mass.

nearby "pest house" ministering to the sick and the dying.[27] In 1902, following a fire that destroyed St. Stephen's in Croghan, New York, Father Heinrichs was asked to oversee the rebuilding of the church, which he did through charitable donations. Consequently, under Father Heinrichs' leadership, the new St. Stephen's parish was debt-free within two years.

This success led to the father's appointment to the new St. Elizabeth parish in Denver, in the summer of 1907. With such devotion, Bishop Matz felt he had made a divine choice in arranging for Father Heinrichs to be assigned to lead the congregation of the Franciscan parish in Denver.

It was not long, given Father Heinrichs' cheerful disposition and open care toward children and the elderly, that he had endeared himself to those of his parishioners, as well as the citizens of Denver, as a tireless champion of the poor. He was renowned for his accessibility to all.

Every Sunday, Father Heinrichs conducted the 8 a.m. mass. However, on that Sunday morning of February 23, 1908, due to a meeting hastily scheduled for later in the morning, Father Heinrichs arranged to switch the Mass duties with Father Wulstan Workman, who normally conducted the 6 a.m. Mass, fondly referred to as the "Workingman's Mass." This particular mass was very popular as it had a short sermon so that the men attending could arrive at their various places of employment on time.

Forty-year-old Father Heinrichs stood at the altar railing offering the wafers and wine to the parishioners at the early morning hour. One of those parishioners was Giuseppe Alia.

Giuseppe Alia was a fifty-year-old unemployed shoemaker and a known anarchist. He later revealed that he went to the stately church in the historic Auraria district that day with one purpose: "to kill a priest."

Alia, born in Sicily in 1857, was raised in the Catholic religion and married a Catholic. Until he was thirty-eight years old, he lived a quiet, unremarkable life. But on Easter Sunday in 1895, he later said, he lost his faith. That very Sunday, he participated in riots against the Church and allied with a socialist society, which caused him to gradually become separated from his wife and family. For the rest of his life he would blame the Church for the estrangement.

In 1895, he fled to Buenos Ayres, as it was then spelled, and worked as a shoemaker. There he purchased an American gun and ammunition and began target shooting. He emigrated to New York in 1907, but he lost his job there due to his ravings about religion. He drifted next to Ellis, Kansas, working for the railroad for forty-three days. When he was laid off by the railroad, he came to Denver. Gaining employment, which he soon lost, due to his anarchist actions, he was forced to eat at the Salvation Army soup kitchen. Despite his homeless situation, Alia had the funds to purchase a gun and ammunition. In his obvious free time, Alia honed his marksmanship so he could kill a priest because, he later said, "They always prey upon the poor."

On that peaceful Sunday morning of February 23, 1908, Giuseppe Alia arrived before the first early morning Mass, seating himself in the third row, and directly in front of the pulpit. In his confession, Alia would state he had never been to St. Elizabeth before, but the bells woke him that morning and he followed the sound to the sanctuary. He carried his revolver tucked into his belt; he always carried it, ready to "get a priest."

As Alia moved to the altar for communion "to get close to that

St. Elizabeth's Church on 11th Street in Denver's Auraria neighborhood, once the scene of murder, is the area's oldest church.

priest," as he later confessed, Alia spat the wafer into his hand and threw it in Father Heinrichs' face.

The angry Italian then pulled his gun and fired once. The bullet pierced the left ventricle of Heinrichs' heart.

One of the altar boys saw the revolver and cried out "Look out, Father!" Turning toward the boy, he asked "What is it?" As the bullet entered his chest, Father Leo Heinrichs staggered, dropping two wafers, then straightened, realizing instantly he was fatally shot. His last thought was for the sacred vessel which held the wafers,

Denver police officer Daniel Cronin was attending mass at St. Elizabeth Catholic Church when Father Leo Heinrichs was shot at the altar. Officer Cronin captured the assailant as he attempted to escape.

the ciborium, which he laid carefully on the altar step. Then he fell over, saying "Call Father Eusebius" to the altar boy, as this priest was the only person allowed to pick up the dropped wafers. As the mortally wounded priest fell to the floor, the altar boy remembered the Father exclaimed, "My God, my God." Father Wulstan Workman was summoned to the scene, where he could do nothing but administer the Last Rites.

Father Workman who had switched services with Father Heinrichs that Sunday morning, was interviewed by the *Denver Post*. The paper printed his reaction to the horrific murder in the the February 24, 1908, issue: *"I would have been killed and he would be alive now. There is one way to solve the affair that I can see, and that is that God chose the better man."*

One of the early morning parishioners, Rose Fisher, told the authorities Father Leo Heinrichs died with a smile, at the foot of the statue of the Blessed Virgin.

Another early worshiper that tragic Sunday was E. J. Quigley, a conductor for the Denver & Rio Grande Railroad. As Alia turned from the altar and began to make his escape down the church aisle, Quigley jumped forward and managed to trip Alia. Denver police patrolman, Daniel Cronin, also attending the early morning Mass, jumped over three pews in an attempt to reach the escaping assailant. Cronin finally caught him at the vestibule just as Alia reached to open the door. Alia turned his gun on the patrolman but the quick-thinking officer inserted his thumb under the trigger. Still he could not subdue the small Italian — Alia weighed only 122 pounds — until four men joined him.

Immediately a crowd, estimated in the newspapers at a thousand, gathered and managed to surround the assailant outside the church. Many in the crowd cried out to lynch the murderer. Father Eusebius saved the perpetrator by appearing at the church entrance calling for silence. In the hush he reminded the infuriated crowd that vengeance is the Lord's, and while the priest held their attention, Officer Cronin pushed his prisoner into a carriage standing nearby and the driver galloped to city hall. To those in the crowd, it seemed quite ironic that a Catholic priest saved the life of the murderer who had just killed a Catholic priest.

The *Denver Post* ran the following headline in the February 23, 1908, afternoon issue:

Anarchist Glories in Crime committed in View of Denver Congregation

CAPTURED AT CHURCH DOOR

The *Rocky Mountain News* ran a similar headline in their February 23, 1908, afternoon issue:

Assassin 'Hates All Priests'

Father Leo Heinrichs, pastor of St. Elizabeth's Catholic Church, was shot and killed at the altar this morning by Giuseppe Guarnacoto Alia an Italian Anarchist, who entered the church ostensibly to take the sacrament.

Following interrogation by police detectives, Giuseppe Alia freely confessed to the murder of the priest. All five of Denver's newspapers printed Alia's chilling words in their articles under banner headlines.

"I went over there because I have a grudge against all priests in general. They are all against the workingman. I went to the communion rail because I could get a better shot. I did not care whether he was a German priest or any other kind of priest. They are all in the same class. I am an Anarchist, [sic] and I am proud of it.

"I shot him, and my only regret is that I could not shoot the whole bunch of priests in the church."[28]

The following day, February 24, 1908, the story of the murder of a Denver priest was carried in newspapers across the country, including the *New York Times*, which ran the story under the headline:

PRIEST SHOT DEAD AT COMMUNION RAIL; Anarchist Glories in Crime[28]

Denver citizens were enraged by Alia's cold confession and again, crowds formed at the Denver City Jail with intentions of storming the facility and lynching the murderer. Sensing the unrest in the crowd, the Denver police chief quickly shepherded the prisoner to a train station in Littleton and transported him to Colorado Springs to thwart the lynch mob.[29] With further investigation, including the coronor's report, eyewitness accounts and Alia's own confession, Giuseppe Alia was charged with first-degree murder.

The *Denver Post* ran an interesting editorial regarding the actions of an anarchist which, in Alia's case, resulted in murder. The editorial appeared in the February 25, 1908, issue:

> *A student of the hand will recognize in Alia's hand a modified type of what is classified as an elementary hand, topped off with what is known as the 'murder's thumb'. The palm is thick and hard, rather than merely firm. The fingers are stiff and heavy and the tips rounded and shapeless..Possessed of a certain low cunning born of animal instinct, not of reason, and with very little mental capacity, are people with hands like those of this self-confessed anarchist. They represent the very lowest type of humanity.*

St. Elizabeth Church was immediately closed after the cold-blooded murder. The remaining Sunday Masses were transferred to St. Mary's Catholic Church. Bishop Nicholas Matz ordered St. Elizabeth reconsecrated the next day so that a proper memorial and traditional wake honoring Father Leo Heinrichs could take place.

The memorial was held on Wednesday, February 26, 1908. Nearly every priest in Denver attended the service and the Knights of St. John served as the escort of honor, with the Knights of Columbus also in line. Following the memorial, the body of Father Leo Heinrichs

Denver Public Library, Western History Department
The *Denver Times* covered the unthinkable murder of a priest.

was taken by train back to Paterson, New Jersey, for burial. The wake and requiem Mass were held at St. Bonaventure's Monastery, where he had been ordained. The body was then entombed in Totowa, New Jersey, in a vault at the Holy Sepulcher Roman Catholic Cemetery.

In Denver, the dead priest's legend had begun to take on a life of its own. Witnesses at the murder scene claimed that no blood ever oozed from the wound to stain Father Heinrichs' white priestly garments. When the coroner revealed that he had cut "penance chains" from the popular priest's body, Denver citizens could talk of little else. This almost forgotten ritual of earlier Franciscans consisted of wearing steel wire spiked every half-inch. Father Heinrichs' arms and waist were scarred from years of wearing these chains and the spikes were rusted with his blood. (The health risk was the primary reason the order had begun discouraging the practice years before.)[30]

Denver Public Library, Western History Dept. Giuseppe Alia was convicted of the murder of Father Leo Heinrichs.

The Denver court system moved rapidly to bring the "People of Colorado vs. Giuseppe Alia" murder case to trial. The trial was set for March 9, 1908, just two weeks to the day following the murder.

The prosecutors had a solid case against Giuseppe Alia. They had eye-witnesses, motive, and they had Alia's confession. The only strategy the court-appointed defense lawyers had was the insanity plea. Jury selection and opening remarks took up the first day. The second day the prosecution team laid out their case before the jurors. After calling several expert witnesses, as well as witnesses to the cold-blooded murder, the prosecution rested their case.

The defense had very little to work with in refuting the prosecutor's case. They had no character witnesses and no defense for their client, save the insanity defense. The defense called four experts in the field to the stand. But during cross examination of the defense "experts," the prosecution was able get them to admit there was no medical evidence of insanity.

The *Associated Press* picked up the story of the trial and it was carried across the nation, including the *New York Times*. In a March 15, 1908, interview with a reporter for the paper, the Italian consul, Baron Gustavo Tosti, declared: *"I have no intention of appealing to the Italian Government, or of trying to make this an international affair. It is purely a local case."*

Following the short and swift murder trial, Giuseppe Alia was convicted of first degree murder. The sentence was death by hanging. When the judge pronounced the death penalty, Alia replied:

> *"Provided he who died was a priest, anything else matters little."* [31]

Giuseppe Alia was incarcerated at the Colorado State Penitentiary and placed on death row. Alia tried to escape twice. In the first attempt, Alia pulled a knife on prison trustee. The trustee was severely wounded before guards could apprehend Alia. Following this first escape attempt by Alia, the Italian consul expressed his belief that Alia's actions proved to him that Alia must be mentally deranged. Nevertheless, the baron refused to get involved.

The second escape attempt also involved a knife, this time pulled on the prison's deputy warden. Alia was quickly overpowered. The officers believed local anarchists smuggled the knives into the Colorado State Penitentiary.

Despite the pleas for clemency by the Franciscans, who opposed the death penalty, Giuseppe Alia was hanged on July 15, 1908, at the Colorado State Penitentiary in Canon City. Defiant to the end, when the noose was fitted about his neck at the penitentiary in Canon City, the fifty-one year old murderer's last words were, *"Death to the priests!"*

Newspapers across Colorado and around the country carried the story. The *Washington Herald's* coverage in the July 16, 1908, issue:

He went to the gallows fighting, biting, and snarling. The night noises of the penitentiary had died away, when Warden Cleghorn summoned the murderer from his cell, and through an interpreter, told him that the hour of his death had arrived. Alia stood for just a moment glaring at the warden and the attendants. Then he raised his head, uttered a string of oaths, and offered his best physical resistance to accompanying the guards to the gallows. The murderer was held by the warden's assistants until he had exhausted himself; then he was supported to the trap, where the noose was adjusted and he was hanged.

As his body dropped the rope slipped and it took the small Italian anarchist nineteen long minutes to strangle to death.

In 1938, Father Leo Heinrich's cause for beatification was opened. The proposal noted his charity, piety and spiritual leadership. The lengthy process was never completed, although attempts have been made throughout the decades, the latest being in 2010.

Murder at the Brown Palace
What a Tangled Web We Weave

Mystery, mystique and murder haunt the famed Brown Palace Hotel. A torrid triangle love affair ended in murder at the "gentlemen's bar" of the Brown Palace Hotel on May 24, 1911. The Denver papers sensationalized the scandal and subsequent murder trials in the style of "yellow journalism" never seen before in Denver media. The May 26 front page editorial of the *Denver Post* read:

> *This gun-toting habit is getting to be such a fierce and uncontrollable proposition that the police do not seem able to cope with it. (If) this indiscriminate mowing down of human beings continues something may happen that Denver will regret far more than a murder or two.*

To fully understand this tangled love tryst that went horribly wrong, we must explore the very strange and even nefarious actions of Isabel Patterson "Sassy" Springer.[32]

Isabel Patterson grew up in the suburbs of St. Louis, Missouri, where during her high school years and later as a young woman, she was known as a social butterfly. She soon married John E. Folck, a traveling shoe salesman. However the marriage did not hold the interest of the young free-wheeling Isabel. During one of her many travels, this time to Denver in the summer of 1906, she met a lonely, quite wealthy and prominent widower by the name of John Wallace Springer.

Springer, an Illinois native, practiced law in that state for ten years before moving west. He settled in Texas, where in June 1891, he married Eliza Clifton Hughes, the daughter of a well respected cattleman in the Dallas area, Colonel William E. Hughes. Springer handled the financial interests of his father-in-law's cattle enterprise and eventually became an influential member of the Texas cattle industry in his own right. Meanwhile, Eliza gave birth to two daughters, Annie Clifton and Sarah Elizabeth, who sadly died in the first year of her life.

In 1897, in an effort to relieve Eliza's severe tuberculosis, Springer relocated his family to the Denver area. He became the director of Denver's Capitol Bank, served as the president of the National

Cattlemen's Association, and even ran for mayor of Denver against Robert Speer in the election of 1904. In 1898, through a series of land purchases, Springer acquired more than 12,000 acres of land south of the city in today's Douglas County. In 1901, along with his father-in-law, who also moved to Colorado from Texas, Springer started a pedigree horse ranch he called the Cross Country Horse and Cattle Ranch. The ranch soon became one of the top horse ranches in the state and home to prize winning show horses both locally and around the world. As the ranch gained in prominence and wealth for Springer, he built a fine German baron-style mansion. However, tragedy struck in the spring of 1904. His beloved wife, Eliza, died on May 22, from her long illness. Following the death of his wife, Springer continued his business enterprises under a suffocating cloud of misery and loneliness.

It was during this dark time of bereavement that Springer, searching for a brighter light, met the irresistible Isabel Patterson Folck. During that summer of 1906, the two soon began a more than cordial relationship. Springer would later testify, "I was smitten." By the end of summer, Isabel returned to St. Louis where she obtained a divorce and married the forty-seven-year-old Springer three weeks later in a lavish ceremony in that city, in April 1907. The bride was twenty-seven years old.

Meanwhile, even before the marriage, Colonel Hughes, Springer's father-in-law, disapproved of the relationship. As whispers of indiscretion and promiscuity on the part of Isabel Patterson Folck increased in Denver circles, the colonel obtained legal custody of his granddaughter, Springer's only living child, Annie.

Following the St. Louis wedding, the couple returned to Denver, first setting up housekeeping at 930 Washington Street, a home Springer had purchased in 1903. The Springers also spent considerable time at the horse ranch. Springer even renamed his mansion in honor of his bride, "Castle Isabel." As Springer went back to the management of his ranch and his beloved horses, it wasn't long before Isabel became bored at the ranch and yearned for the night life she left behind when she became Mrs. John W. Springer.

Evidently, Springer didn't mind. Ever the adoring husband, he granted his wife's every wish and even rented a suite at the Brown Palace Hotel in downtown Denver, where she could stay after late night parties with friends. Whether Springer was too busy with his considerable business affairs, or he simply turned a blind eye to the actions of his new bride, his former father-in-law and business partner, Colonel Hughes, did take notice and action. In 1909, Hughes sold his interests in every company associated with his former son-in-law.

During one of her many independent travels to St. Louis to visit friends, Isabel met an adventurous thirty-two-year-old entrepreneur by the name of Sylvester Louis Von Phul. Known as Tony to his friends, he was an avid balloonist. He and Isabel began an intimate relationship that would be an on-again off-again tryst Isabel would play at for the next few years. In January 1911, Isabel rekindled the relationship with Von Phul through a series of love letters. The two renewed their love affair in Hot Springs, Arkansas, where they were observed as a couple at several parties.[33]

Following this trip, in March 1911, during a visit to her husband's office in downtown Denver, Isabel Springer met a client of her husband's, Mr. Harold Francis (Frank) Henwood, an adventurous businessman in his own right. The Springers enjoyed Henwood's company and often invited him to their home and to social events. It wasn't long before Henwood began spending considerable time, including overnight stays, at the Springer ranch when Mr. Springer was out of town on business. Housemaids would later testify to finding two champagne or whiskey glasses in Isabel's room and strange requests such as moving a larger bed into the room.

All of this led to Isabel's strange behavior of a love letter campaign between herself and the two men (neither of whom were her husband) vying for her affections. Isabel continued to write love letters to Von Phul while carrying on with Henwood in her husband's mansion which he had renamed for her. The letters to Von Phul escalated in a feverish tone in May 1911. Meanwhile, Henwood had discovered evidence of Isabel's other love interest, Von Phul. In a heated confrontation, Isabel tearfully confessed, explaining that the relationship was over in her mind. She further told Henwood that Von Phul had several "silly" love letters she had written, and that Von Phul was threatening to send the letters to her husband.

Of course, none of this was true, for Von Phul had no idea of another lover in Isabel's life and believed, through her own love letters, he was the true object of her affections and therefore, had no reason to alert

The white marble bar in the Brown Palace Hotel. It was in this room that murder occurred.

Mr. Springer. Isabel, in a frantic state of mind, wrote more letters to Von Phul, including the final letter dated May 20, 1911, in which she insisted he come to Denver immediately, that everything was fine and she had "quite a surprise in store" for him. In the meantime, she was also placating Henwood, insisting the affair with Von Phul was over and asking his help in stopping Von Phul from revealing the affair via the love letters to her husband.

This cat and mouse game came to a deadly end when Isabel instructed Von Phul to meet her at the Brown Palace Hotel in downtown Denver. It can never be known what the true intentions of Isabel Patterson Springer were, for her testimony at the subsequent murder trial revealed nothing but denials and self-perceived innocence. For instance, Isabel claimed on the witness stand that she never told Von Phul about her relationship with Henwood, however, the final letter from Von Phul to Isabel, admitted into the court record, reads:

If you are too busy to write me a letter, just say so and I won't expect them. I have not heard from you for three days. I leave here about the 23rd for Denver, if father does not die, but I am afraid the old man is in pretty bad condition and am holding myself in readiness for a quick trip home. The least I expect from you is for you to behave yourself while I am under this terrific strain, and have nothing to do with that double-crosser. No, you don't have to take him out to the ranch or have anything to do with him — just show him where he gets off or I will. [34]

While it appears that Von Phul did know of Henwood's presence in Isabel's life, he nevertheless made the requested trip to Denver, checking into the Brown Palace Hotel on May 23, 1911. Expecting to meet with Isabel at the Springer's sixth floor suite, Von Phul was instead handed a note at the check-in desk, which read:

This is just to let you know that someone knows a great deal. Therefore, under no circumstances, telephone me or try to communicate with me in any way. Everything is finally and absolutely off and if you wish to save yourself serious trouble with someone and his friends you will forget that you ever knew me. Personally my future is of too much consequence and I'll never risk it again. I will send someone to you to have a final talk with you, and you must be guided by what they say. I have been forbidden to see you or hear from you in the future and I have given my word, which I propose to keep, not to see you again. I have taken this means to let you know.

Although the note was unsigned, there was no doubt who wrote it. Perhaps this was the surprise Isabel had in store for Von Phul. Instead, now that the two lovers knew of each other, a strange rivalry ensued, bested only by the goading of Mrs. Springer.

The two men met face-to-face for the first time in the lobby of the hotel later that afternoon. Henwood introduced himself as the "party referred to in the letter." The men agreed to meet later that evening to "talk things over." However just minutes before that scheduled meeting, each man, apparently unknown to the other, rushed to the Daniels & Fisher department store, where each knew Isabel Springer was. Henwood arrived first, confronting Isabel of going against his wishes by agreeing to see Von Phul. As Isabel stumbled in a startled response by saying she had not, Von Phul disrupted the scene by demanding an explanation from Isabel. A heated exchange between the now crossed lovers ensued.

Following this nasty encounter, Henwood met with Von Phul in his hotel room at the Brown Palace. Again a heated argument ensued, this time coming to blows between the men. According to trial testimony, while Von Phul had a gun, he never used it, instead he struck Henwood not once, but twice.

Immediately after this encounter, Von Phul stormed into the private hotel suite of the Springer couple. Finding Isabel alone, he flew into another rage, demanding that Isabel end her relationship with Henwood. A frantic Isabel then pleaded with Henwood to end the matter with Von Phul. Henwood refused.

Later that evening, in the hotel dining room, Henwood was dining alone. Nearby was Von Phul, dining with a friend. While the two men glared at each other, at another table were Mr. and Mrs. John Springer. It must have been a nervous and strained time for all three principals in this love saga, while the fourth person, Mr. Springer, astonishingly seemed unaware.

The following day, as Isabel left her suite, she was confronted by Von Phul in the hallway and more heated words and threats were exchanged. A shaken Isabel retreated back into her suite and immediately tried to contact Henwood to warn him. She sent a note to his office, via her maid, pleading with him to again drop the matter with Von Phul. Now Von Phul enters the note writing foray by sending a nasty note of his own to Henwood. Included in the envelope were pieces of a torn picture of Henwood that Von Phul had destroyed the day earlier in the Springer suite. Henwood left his office for a stop at a gun shop nearby where he purchased a .38 caliber Smith & Wesson revolver.

The evening of May 24, 1911, Henwood escorted his guests, Mr. and Mrs. Springer, to the Orpheum Theatre where he had box seats for the evening vaudeville performance by Russian dancer Mademoiselle Bianci Froehlich. Meanwhile Von Phul and a group of friends took in the Florenz Ziegfeld show, Follies of 1910, at the Broadway Theater, across from the Brown Palace Hotel. Following the performance, at approximately 11:30 p.m., Von Phul and his friends went across the street to the Brown Palace Hotel for drinks.

The Marble Bar at the Brown Palace Hotel, located next to the Broadway Street entrance to the hotel, typically enjoyed a large crowd of customers following the end of the theater performance. The crowd included a large group of businessmen from the Colorado Springs area, as well as Cripple Creek and Victor mining executives.

Already at the bar with a drink of his own was Frank Henwood, who had joined the group of men which included A. C. Rollestone, vice president of the Victor Bank; Charles Shilling, a dry goods merchant in Victor; and retired Judge James Owen, of Colorado Springs.

As Von Phul and his friend, Edward Rosenbaum, the manager of the Follies touring company, approached the bar, Rosenbaum took a place at the bar between Von Phul and Henwood. While eye-witnesses all agreed words were exchanged between the two rivals, no one agreed on what exactly was said. In any case, Von Phul moved next to Henwood and threw a punch, which landed on Henwood's jaw. Henwood went down on all fours.

As Henwood slowly regained his composure, he pulled his new gun. In an awkward rising motion, he began firing his weapon in Von Phul's direction. He didn't stop until all six chambers of the pistol were emptied.

Bar patrons took cover. When the shooting stopped, two wounded men lay on the bar room floor. Henwood yielded to a hotel employee who had grabbed his gun. Von Phul, with three bullets in his body, managed to make his way to the doorway of the bar. As for Henwood, he was immediately arrested and taken to the city jail for interrogation.

Meanwhile, the police took control of the crime scene, and the gunshot victims were taken by ambulance to St. Luke's Hospital (Von Phul insisted on a taxi.) James W. Atkinson, a businessman from Colorado Springs caught in the cross-fire, received a bullet from Henwood's gun in the left thigh, an injury that would plague him the rest of his life. The other innocent bystander, forty-three-year-old George E. Copeland of Victor, Colorado, was less fortunate. He received two bullets, one in the right hip and the other in the left thigh, which cut a major artery.

Although Von Phul's injuries did not immediately seem serious, given his alert state of mind and command of the situation following the shooting, the physicians at the hospital had a different outlook. The doctors removed two bullets from Von Phul; one from his upper right shoulder, and the other from the groin area. However, the damage to his vital organs was too extensive. Sylvester Louis Von Phul died of the bullet wounds of Henwood's gun at 11:20 a.m. the following morning, May 25, 1911.

The next day, a coroner's inquest quickly delivered the following opinion:

Sylvester L. Von Phul came to his death by gunshot wounds having been fired by Frank H. Henwood in the City and County of Denver in the state of Colorado about 11:35 P.M. on Wednesday, May 24, 1911, in the barroom of the Brown Palace Hotel at Seventeenth and Broadway; and we further find the said Sylvester L. Von Phul died at St. Luke's Hospital about 11:30 A.M. May 25, 1911, and we further find that said shots were fired with felonious intent.

Harold Francis Henwood was formally charged with the murder of Sylvester Louis Von Phul on May 31, 1911. At his arraignment, held on the morning of June 1, 1911, Denver District Attorney Willis V. Elliott submitted the charge before the court as "...the willful, deliberate and premeditated murder..." As a matter of course, Henwood's attorney, John T. Bottom, entered a plea on behalf of his client as "not guilty." However, the attorney claimed, on his client's behalf, that the killing of Von Phul was self-defense. A request for bond was denied.

The next day George Copeland died at St. Luke's Hospital following an operation to his bullet-wounded leg. In an attempt by the doctors to remove the gangrene that had set in, Copeland began to hemorrhage profusely and ultimately bled to death.

On June 2, Henwood was again in court. Charged with the murder of Copeland, he left court as an accused double murderer. The trial date was set for June 20, 1911.

As the trial date approached, all four Denver newspapers had daily coverage, stories, rumors and scandalous quotes from several eyewitnesses and other parties with "close ties" to the principals involved. Henwood, surprisingly enough, became somewhat of a darling to the press. Ever ready for an interview, he only added to the wild speculation of the feeding frenzy in the "yellow journalism" that spilled over the pages of the Denver newspapers. The focal point of the sensational torrid love affair that ended in murder was referred to in the press as "a Denver society woman."

The June 5, 1911 issue of the *Denver Post* printed an article with the headline:

Denver Public Library, Western History Department
A heavily veiled Isabel Springer is escorted to the courthouse by her husband. Her testimony was one of the highlights of Denver's most scandalous murder trial.

Von Phul Shot in Row Over Mrs. Springer, Friends Say.

The article went on to detail the love tryst between the accused murderer, Henwood, the victim, Von Phul and "the woman." The reporter also mentioned eight "love" letters found in Von Phul's hotel room, concluding, "Mrs. Springer enjoyed the most friendly relations with Von Phul." The article not only named Mrs. Isabel Springer, but also featured her photo.

It would only be speculation as to the cause or final straw as it were, but the fact is that the next day John Springer filed for divorce from "the woman" now named in the center of Denver's most sensational murder trial.

The trial began promptly at 10 a.m. on June 20, 1911. Opening for the prosecution, the district attorney, Willis V. Elliott, chose to present the Copeland murder charge first, rather than the Von Phul murder charge. This was a very unusual decision for the prosecution as Copeland was the innocent bystander, therefore intent would be a heavy burden for the prosecution to prove. Coupled with disagreeing eyewitness accounts, and Henwood's ever-changing accounts of the night of May 24, 1911, it would take two trials to convict Henwood of murder.

On the third day of the trial, the soon-to-be ex-Mrs. Isabel Springer took the witness stand for the defense. Arriving at the courthouse, Mrs. Springer was seen (and photographed, which later appeared in the newspapers) being escorted by her brother Mr. Arthur Patterson.

Once on the witness stand, Mrs. Springer seemed quite nervous, unsteady and even incoherent. Unable to follow or understand attorney Bottom's questions, a sidebar was called by both the prosecution and defense attorneys as to the admissibility of the witness' testimony. The presiding judge, Greeley W. Whitford, ruled in regard to Mrs. Isabel Springer's testimony: "In the present state of the record we will not receive the testimony."

Next to take the stand in his own defense was Henwood. He answered his attorney's questions in a straight-forward manner and to the point. However, on cross-examination by the district attorney, Henwood stumbled on several key points brought out by the prosecution. Henwood was asked about a particular conversation with the chief of police regarding his run-ins with Von Phul. When pressed about his threat to kill Von Phul during this conversation, Henwood deflected, saying he thought Mr. Springer would do the killing and he simply wanted to save the married man the trouble it would bring him by doing it himself.

When Henwood was asked about his stay at Springer's Cross Country Horse and Cattle Ranch the week prior to the shooting, Henwood became increasingly uncomfortable. Asked to explain the housemaid's testimony regarding the wine glasses and the moving of a larger bed, he maintained nothing improper had transpired. He further stated that he did not drink while he was there. On recross by the defense, Henwood was pressed on the events during the night of the shooting. Henwood fought to remain calm. He finally asked the judge for a short recess. Later, Henwood simply ended his testimony stating that he drew his gun and shot Von Phul in self-defense.

In the jury instructions, the judge added the provision, "There is no manslaughter in this case." This would later become part of Colorado legislative history. In any case, the following afternoon, the jury returned a verdict of "guilty of murder in the second degree." A stunned Henwood was led back to his jail cell to await sentencing.

On July 26, 1911, two days before Judge Whitford was set to pronounce the defendant's sentence, Henwood's attorney filed an appeal, stating among many factors, that the judge's jury instruction regarding "no manslaughter" was an incorrect fact of law, and that his client's subsequent trial for the murder of Von Phul would be considered "former jeopardy" under the law as the shooting deaths of both Copeland and Von Phul were of one and the same incident.

As Henwood's attorney, John T. Bottom, listed the nearly one hundred errors he felt the judge had made, the attorney further made allegations of misconduct by the judge himself. A verbal onslaught ensued between the lawyer and judge, all of which was admitted into the court record. In the end, the judge admonished the attorney for "scandalous and unprofessional conduct" of a lawyer. Two days later, on July 28, Judge Whitford was set to pronounce his sentence, which could have ranged from ten years to life at the state penitentiary. The judge asked the defendant if he had anything to say in his defense.

Henwood addressed the judge with no regard or respect for his position. He accused the judge of being prejudiced, of holding a preconceived attitude, and believing he was guilty before the trial began. He further stated he did not receive a fair trial and pointed out that Mrs. Springer's testimony was not allowed into the record. He ended by saying he was ready for the "prosecuting judge's" sentence.

Judge Whitford sentenced Henwood to "life imprisonment to begin at once."

Henwood's attorney immediately filed a series of appeals that went all the way to the Colorado Supreme Court. During the appeal process, Henwood remained incarcerated at the Denver County jail.

Meanwhile the divorce between Mr. and Mrs. Springer became final. As part of the divorce settlement, the ex-Mrs. Springer was to leave Denver and never return. She did; on the very next eastbound train.[35]

Finally on February 3, 1913, the Colorado Supreme Court handed down its ruling on the Henwood case. By reversing the verdict of murder in the second degree, the Court cited state law, and wrote in part:

> *The statutory provisions are a recognition of the frailty of human nature, the purpose of which is to reduce a homicide committed in the circumstances therein contemplated to the*

grade of manslaughter, either voluntary or involuntary, as the facts may warrant. It appears from the statutes that the unlawful killing of a human being, without malice and deliberation upon a sudden heat of passion, caused by a provocation apparently sufficient to excite an irresistible passion in a reasonable person, constitutes manslaughter.

Thus, Judge Whitford's jury instruction regarding manslaughter was ruled incorrect and Henwood received a new trial. The new district attorney, John A. Rush, refiled a murder charge against Henwood for the death of Sylvester Louis Von Phul. During the pretrial motions, there were several heated arguments between the prosecution and defense attorneys which were caricatured in the local papers. Presiding Judge Charles C. Butler eventually ruled the Von Phul murder charge would not be heard by the court. However he did order Henwood to again stand trial for the shooting death of the innocent bystander, George E. Copeland.

The trial began on May 28, 1913. Many of the witnesses who testified at the first trial were again called, including the Springer employees. However the star witness was James W. Atkinson, the other innocent bystander who was caught in the cross-fire that night of May 24, 1911. The gunshot wound which had shattered his left leg left him disabled for life. When he took the stand, aided by crutches, the permanent disability was visible to the jurors. He recounted the events of that night, stating that he saw Von Phul return to the bar after he struck Henwood, knocking him to the ground. He further stated that he was a few feet from the bar when he felt a pain in his leg and fell to the floor. He recounted the exchange between himself and Henwood following the shooting. Henwood walked over to him and asked if he had shot him. Atkinson replied he had and asked him to leave, as he had done enough damage.

This testimony was a blow to the defense. One of the defense attorneys, Henry Lubers, in a desperate move to sway the judge and jury and discredit the prosecuting attorney, produced the previous day's issue of the *Denver Post*. Dated June 8, 1913, the issue included an article regarding the trial, in which the prosecuter alluded to new "surprise" witnesses coming forth. As the defense team had not been told of these witnesses, Lubers cried foul. The prosecuting attorney, Rush, exploded with a few accusations of his own. As the two opposing attorneys traded barbs, it seemed as if Judge Butler lost control of his courtroom. The newspapers were full of cartoon depictions of the attorneys even calling each other out to a physical confrontation.

The judge spent considerable time and patience in restoring calm to the courtroom, while chastising the attorneys for their unprofessionalism in a court of law. As the proceedings continued, Henwood testified in his own defense. His testimony, basically the same as in the first trial, reiterated that he shot Von Phul in self-defense, fearing for his life.

The defense wisely chose not to call Isabel Springer as a witness, given her previous incoherent testimony. However, the prosecution was allowed, despite protests from the defense, to have Mrs. Springer's previous testimony read into the court record.

As the trial was coming to an end, the defense, which had previously objected to the possibility of surprise witnesses by the prosecution, suddenly produced one of their own.

On June 15, 1913, John Springer took the stand. He testified that Henwood was a business associate as well as a friend and that during his association with Henwood, he was the consummate gentleman.

Closing arguments were heard and the judge instructed the jury on the law. On June 17, 1913, at the late hour of 10:30 p.m, the jury retired behind closed doors. The following afternoon, the jury returned with a verdict. "Guilty of murder in the first degree." The penalty was set as death for the convicted murderer.

On July 19, defense attorney Bottom filed a motion for a new trial, which Judge Butler immediately denied. A week later, the judge formally sentenced Henwood to death by hanging.

Bottom again filed motions for appeal with the Colorado Supreme Court. The court denied the motion on July 14, 1914. A second appeal was also denied in October of the same year. Finally Bottom pleaded his case to Governor Elias Ammons, who eventually commuted Henwood's death sentence to life imprisonment.

Henwood was sent to the state penitentiary on October 18, 1914. He served ten years and was paroled in 1924. He eventually made his way to Mexico, where he attempted to rebuild his life. Unfortunately for Henwood, he ran afoul of the law when he became the focal point of a sexual assault case. As this was a clear violation of his parole,

Henwood was extradited back to Colorado and the state penitentiary. He died in prison in 1929.

Glamour, Greed & A Gun
Malicious Melodrama

Just four months after the murder trial involving Isabel Springer ended in appeal, another woman of Denver's high society set, Gertrude Gibson Patterson, was accused of murder. According to Frances Wayne, a reporter for the *Denver Post*, who covered the Patterson murder trial:

Blaring headlines informed the citizenry of the circus potentialities of the deed. Here were all the elements of sizzling, thrilling melodrama.

Newspaper publishers gave a go-the-limit order to editors, reporters, artists, cartoonists and special writers, to fill, not paragraphs, not columns, but entire pages of every edition of Denver's five daily newspapers, and warned that that the punishment for being scooped would be unlimited leisure. This order held for almost two months, as church clubs and organizations such as the Women's Christian Temperance Union and the Women's Citizen's League adopted resolutions denouncing the publication of 'sordid nauseous details' of this latest 'crime passionel.'

A voice howling into an empty barrel would have been as effective. The public demanded how 'Gertie did it,' even to the smallest detail, and who and what Gertie was and had been.[36]

"Gertie" was thirty-year-old Gertrude Gibson Patterson, accused of the murder of her husband, Charles A. Patterson, on September 25, 1911.

From an early age, the lovely Gertrude Gibson had been aware of her power over any male in her orbit. Born in the small town of Sandoval, in south-central Illinois, Gertrude had been removed from school at the age of thirteen for "conduct pertaining to morality." She promptly eloped to Chicago with a saloonkeeper. Her distraught father, a man of modest means, persuaded the town marshal to bring his daughter back. Shortly after the marshal returned young Gertrude to her family, she again took her leave, this time on a trip to visit her sister in St. Louis, Missouri. From there, she drifted to Chicago, where she was introduced to Emil W. Strouss, a wealthy clothing manufacturer, "old enough to be her grandfather."[37]

Strouss quickly became her benefactor. With her parents' consent, Strouss took Gertrude to Europe to further her education. For the next four years, the teenager lived in Paris, where she supposedly attended a convent school. She mastered French and the social graces and "enhanced her natural charm, beauty, intelligence and style." With Strouss as her escort, Gertrude was able to travel extensively throughout Europe, acquiring jewels and expensive clothing, which Strouss was happy to buy.

After four years of European living, Gertrude returned with Strouss to Chicago, where they resided in the finest hotel in the city, the Auditorium Hotel, near the fashionable Standard Country Club, which they often frequented. One day her life changed completely when she drove her electric car to the amusement area known as Sans Souci Park. There, at the skating rink, Gertrude met a man decades younger than Strouss and nearly two years younger than herself, Charles A. Patterson. In her reporting of the subsequent murder trial, Frances Wayne wrote:

> *Charles A. Patterson was little more than twenty years of age. He was the son of Mrs. Mary K. Patterson, for many years a teacher in Chicago public schools. He had left school to become a clerk for a printing firm. He was poor, had no social prestige, nothing but youth, health, and capacity for loving.*[38]

The two began to meet frequently at the park. Patterson was captivated by the beautiful Gertrude Gibson. And Gibson seemed to enjoy her time with him, at least for the time being. During one of their meetings, Gertrude explained her relationship with the much older Emil Strouss and of her plans to break off with the man. Frances Wayne reported:

> *One afternoon she told him she was going to California. She slipped a hundred-dollar bill and a railroad ticket into his hand and asked him to follow her there and they would be married. She had previously told him of her relations with Strouss and when she promised they would end, the youth agreed to forgive*

Denver Public Library, Western Histroy Dept.
Despite strong forensic evidence, a jury of twelve men acquitted Gertrude Gibson Patterson of murder.

and forget. Bygones would be bygones.

At enchanting Carmel-by-the-Sea, Charles A. Patterson and Gertrude Gibson were married by a justice of the peace.

He had written her impassioned letters in the brief interval of separation, in one of which he declared. 'Rain, snow, sunshine, I shall always love you and only you.'[39]

Following a brief honeymoon, the newlyweds returned to Chicago where they first lived with Charles' mother. Not happy with this arrangement, Gertrude rented a fully furnished apartment, apparently on funds provided by Strouss. The couple had lived in the apartment for three months when Gertrude told her husband she was leaving for a visit with her sister in St. Louis, Missouri. Charles seemed to be acquiring a healthy skepticism; he asked his wife how it was possible that they could afford for her to take a train trip to St. Louis, and how was she getting the money to pay the apartment rent? Gertrude finally admitted that she had been receiving the money from Strouss, and, indebted to him, she had agreed to accompany him on a business trip to Europe, strictly as an interpreter, she told Charles. Charles voiced his displeasure and asked his wife not to go. Gertrude insisted that she must go, to repay the debt.

Charles, seething with rage, managed to procure the passenger list of the ocean liner and saw that his wife and Strouss had registered as Mr. and Mrs. and were staying in the same cabin. He cabled her to return at once and followed up with a letter stating that if she didn't, he would come to Europe and kill both of them. Gertrude returned.

Fate intervened in the form of pneumonia, which left Charles with tuberculosis. He and his mother moved to Denver, where Charles entered the Agnes Memorial Sanitarium, commonly called

Phipps Sanitarium, in East Denver. Gertrude soon followed them, renting a home at 1008 Steele Street. Gertrude faithfully visited her ailing husband daily. Sadly, Charles continued to grow weaker. The handsome man she had married was now a sickly shadow of his former self; he weighed only 116 pounds.

Gertrude soon grew weary of the hospital visits and realizing her husband would never fully recover, Gertrude filed for divorce. When Charles received the divorce papers, he too filed a lawsuit; against Emil W. Strouss. Charles sought $25,000 for alienation of affections of his wife. When Gertrude learned of this lawsuit against her benefactor, she was enraged.

Gertrude had a gun. And she had a plan. She was given the gun by her neighbor, George W. Strain, while visiting at her home. During this visit, she tearfully told Strain a tall tale of physical abuse by her husband and that she feared for her life. Thus, concerned for his neighbor's safety, Strain left his neighbor, wishing her well, and giving her his gun.

Two days after procuring the weapon, on September 25, 1911, Gertrude telephoned Charles, asking him to meet her near the sanitarium, as he was now too weak to walk to her home on Steele Street. They agreed to meet by the stone wall of the nearby Richthofen Castle. Built in 1887, by the German Baron Walter Von Richthofen, at this time it was owned by the Edwin Hendrie family.

After a brief argument about the lawsuit, Gertrude pulled her gun from her purse and shot four times. Two of the shots hit Charles. Gertrude told the Hendrie maids Charles had beaten her and then committed suicide, but the maids later testified at the trial that they saw no marks or bruises on her or signs of tears.

The police were called to the scene by an eye-witness, George Schramm, caretaker of the landmark Von Richthofen Castle. Denver Police Surgeon Mudd, in examining the dead body, discovered a gun under the corpse. It would later be determined that the gun belonged to George W. Strain. Sergeant McIntyre interviewed Mrs. Patterson who admitted that she had the gun with her and after being slapped, beaten and spat upon, she pulled the gun from her purse and fired.

The body was taken to the the city morgue, and Gertrude was arrested and taken to the Denver County jail.

After a six-man coroner's jury had convened, a criminal complaint of murder was filed with the Denver District Attorney's office. Gertrude was charged with first degree murder. The charge read in part that the accused had "willfully, unlawfully, feloniously, with malice aforethought, shot and killed her husband thereby violating the peace, dignity, security of the people of the State of Colorado." If convicted, Gertrude Gibson Patterson faced up to thirty years in prison.

Horace V. Benson was selected to prosecute the case as leading prosecutor, Willis V. Elliott, had recused himself. Shortly before Mrs. Patterson had filed for divorce, she had consulted with Elliott in the matter of her divorce case. For her defense, Gertrude hired a well-known attorney in the city, O. N. Hilton.

The murder trial of *The People of the State of Colorado vs. Gertrude Gibson Patterson*, with the honorable Judge George W. Allen presiding, began on the cold morning of November 20, 1911. Frances Wayne reported the court atmosphere for the *Denver Post*:

> *Order restored in the court of law. Silence prevailed.*
>
> *Counsel were seated at opposite sides of a long table, reference books piled high, brief cases spread. To the left of the room a door leading to a jail corridor opened. Standing there, her large brown eyes glowing in a face of childlike loveliness, her tiny hands clasped above her breast, her charming figure clothed in a blue tailleur suit, her sunny brown hair crowned by a blue-plumed turban, was the self-widowed defendant.* "[40]

Other reporters for the Denver newspapers wrote similarly of the murder defendant. For example, the *Denver Times* wrote in their November 20, 1911, issue of her "deep brown eyes and cameo-like complexion," and further stated that Mrs. Patterson was:

> *"The prettiest woman ever to stand trial for murder in Denver."*

The first two days of the trial were devoted to jury selection. Denver had recently 'modernized' its jury system and no longer used paid professional jurors. However, the Denver jury system did not allow women to serve, despite the fact that Colorado, the second state after Wyoming, granted women the right to vote in 1893. In Colorado, women weren't allowed on juries until 1944. The twelve selected jurors were: grocer Stafford E. Beckett, age 26; broker Harvey W. Bird, age 38; broker Charles Bosworth, age 27; salesman J. L. Brubacker, age

Along this pathway near the stone wall of the Richthofen Castle, Gertrude Gibson Patterson was alleged to have murdered her husband, Charles Patterson.

30; mining engineer Francis J. Crane, age 28; merchant John P. Doyle, age 33; barber, John Dunbar, age 29; business executive, James J. Flint, age 40; realtor William H, Gartner, age 39; grocer M. G. Kinkle, age 41; metal worker Charles G. Oppenlander age, 44; and an assayer, Fred S. Perry, age 30.

Frances Wayne, writing for the *Denver Post*, said of the jury:

Here were no youngsters to be swayed by chivalry, no elders to be moved by beauty in chains. Just a group of plain, healthy Americans, with family responsibilities, on the hunt for truth and justice.[41]

With the jury seated, the trial began. Gertrude was again brought into the courtroom through the side door of the courtroom. Horace V.

Benson, presenting the state's case against Mrs, Patterson, began his opening remarks which included the statement that: *"This woman sitting here did in cold blood and with malice aforethought shoot her husband in the back and killed him."*

Prosecuting attorney, Benson, presented the facts of the murder case to the jury, including producing the gun found at the scene of the crime, owed by the defendant's neighbor, and thereby linked to Patterson. Benson called several witnesses to the stand, the most powerful being George Schramm, caretaker of the Von Richthofen Castle.

Schramm testified to what he had witnessed that day from his vantage point (the door of the tool shed adjacent to the brick wall of the castle grounds). Schramm said he watched a man and woman arguing. He saw the woman give a piece of paper to the man. The man read it and handed it back to the woman. Then he saw the woman shoot the man four times.

With this damning testimony, newspaper reporters dashed from the courthouse to make their deadlines. "It's thirty for Gertie," became the common phrase among the reporters in the newsroom of the *Denver Post*.

However, when the newspapers were dropped along the streets of Denver the following day, reports of the trial were all about the defendant's demeanor and appearance. Several reporters for the local newspapers seemed to be infatuated with the beautiful accused murderous. For example, the *Denver Times* wrote paragraphs describing her clothing, including the following printed in the November 23, 1911, issue:

She was gowned in a blue serge suit, with black satin bands. She wore a smart toque with Oriental colorings...Mrs. Patterson chatted with the deputy sheriff, George McLaughlin, who sat beside her, for half an hour before court opened.

Frances Wayne of the *Denver Post*, did not hold to the glowing admiration the other reporters had for the "lovely" murder defendant. Wayne wrote:

She drew such a vivid picture of innocence and beauty betrayed as to wring the heart of the most cynical rail bird at trial. As Ella Wheeler Wilcox, famed poet, might put it, leave her to Karma which knows only truth and justice.[42]

Defense attorney, O. N. Hilton, presented his case, first calling Gertrude's mother and sister to the stand, who both testified to the good and sweet nature of the defendant. Then, in the deafening silence of the courtroom, all eyes were on Gertrude Gibson Patterson as she made her way to the witness stand. Frances Wayne reported:

> *She went on the witness stand, fragile, sweet, appealing as a frightened lonely little girl. Her voice had the timbre of a ten year old's. Her eyes were wide and wondering.*[43]

Wayne's account continued with some of Gertrude's testimony:

> *I loved my husband very much. He told me again and again that since I was pretty it would be easy for me to get money for both of us. He insisted that I should sell my electric car for six hundred dollars so he could buy an interest in a printing shop. I sold the car and gave him the money.*
>
> *He consented to my accompanying Mr. Strouss to Europe when I put fifteen hundred dollars in his hands — my sale price.*[44]

With this astonishing statement, the prosecuting attorney, Horace V. Benson, turned toward the jurors and thundered, "Her innocence and purity were the price."

Gertrude was on the witness stand for two long days. The second day of her testimony was, in Frances Wayne's words, "a dolorous litany." Wayne wrote:

> *In a dull, monotonous voice she recited, On that day he beat me...On that day he slapped my face...On that day he bit me on the arm...On that day he he struck me in the face...On that day he struck me in the mouth and spat upon me...On that day he twisted my arm and knocked me down...On that day he struck me and ordered me to go out and get money or he would kill Mr. Strouss. On that day...'*
>
> *On and on she droned the story of indignities and humiliations.*[45]

However, on cross-examination of the witness, prosecuting attorney Benson had a series of questions for the lovely, yet broken defendant, who barely whispered her answers. In his closing arguments, Benson reminded the jury of the events of September 25, 1911. He told them of the phone call she had made to her husband, arranging for a meeting; of the gun she had received from her neighbor for protection after her tearful tale of fear; and of the news that her husband was suing her benefactor.

Benson went on to describe the crime scene, the body of her husband and the gun found underneath, linked to her. Benson recalled for the jury the defendant's own testimony regarding the events of that fateful day; that when her husband returned the piece of paper to her, he struck her in the face, spat on her, and hit her again, knocking her down to the ground.

Then Benson, with a pointed finger at Gertrude Gibson Patterson, shouted: *"And you, down on the ground, as you claim, opened your purse, took out Strain's gun and with it shot your sick husband in the back."*[46]

The defense team had been struck with a great blow. O. N. Hilton resorted to the cunning strategy he was famous for. On the final day of the trial, November 30, 1911, and just before closing arguments by the defense, Hilton called a mystery witness, Francis J. Easton, to the stand. Frances Wayne reported:

> *Everybody in the crowded court room looked at everybody else. Benson stiffened.*

Even Gertrude Gibson Patterson leaned toward her attorney and asked, "Who?" The prosecution objected as Mr. Easton was not on the witness list. Nevertheless, Judge Allen allowed the witness to testify.

Easton stated that he had arrived in Denver from Tacoma, Washington, on business on the day before the murder. He testified that on September 25 he rode the east-bound streetcar on Colfax, then began walking south toward the towers of the landmark Richthofen Castle to see the imposing building. There, he said he was about three hundred yards away when he saw the couple arguing near the Castle. Easton said that he knew the woman was in danger. He then repeated the same story Gertrude had steadfastly told; that Charles began hitting her and she shot him in self-defense.

On cross-examination, Benson asked a few direct questions as to why Easton didn't intervene during the argument and more importantly, why he didn't go to the woman's aid when he felt she was in danger. When Easton replied that he did not want to get involved, Benson asked the witness, "So you turned and walked away?" Not waiting for an answer, Benson whirled around to face the jury box and nearly shouted: *"No coincidence this, from a man who failed to give aid to the woman he had seen from afar — three hundred feet and no nearer."*[47]

With this final testimony from the defense, both sides rested their cases. After juror instructions from Judge Allen, the judge then reviewed for the jury, the options of a not guilty or guilty verdict. Should there be a guilty verdict, the jury had four options: First degree murder, with death or life imprisonment; second degree murder, life imprisonment to thirty years; manslaughter, ten to twenty years; or involuntary manslaughter, two years in the county jail. With these stipulations, the jury began their deliberations.

Gertrude was taken from the courtroom to the matron's room in the adjoining jail. *Denver Post* reporter, Frances Wayne was waiting and took the occasion ask the defendant, "What do you think of this experience and your chances?" Wayne reported the defendant's arrogant reply:

> *Sitting back in a deep rocking chair, her head leaning against the top ledge, her eyes closed as though to shut out all the horrors of the last ten days, she finally said, "What do I think of things now? I am sure that never has a woman been subjected to such persecution. As a woman of the world, I thought I knew the meaning of the rules which make for decency and kindness and truth. I find that one's mistakes, even those made in thoughtless youth, are used as instruments of torture by those in power to insist the mistake was a crime. Those mistakes are tossed into the balance against life and death. So I have learned more during these days than I could have learned in ten lives such as I have lived. Almost, I do not care what happens." She opened her eyes and sighed.*[49]

The other local newspapers took a different approach in their coverage of the last day of the murder trial. These publications lavished

Denver Public Library, Western History Dept.
The *Denver Times* covered the sensational murder trial of Gertrude Gibson Patterson.

ink on "this woman possessed of a face and figure attractive to men." Headlines referred to Gertrude Gibson Patterson as the "Dresden doll."

The next day, just after noon, the jury sent word to Judge Allen that a verdict had been reached. The courtroom was filled to capacity with newspaper reporters, photographers, and the curious public. All eyes turned toward the side door as it opened. The "Dresden doll" entered, dressed in a crisp black dress and a matching wide-brimmed black hat. Her attorney left his chair and escorted her to the defense table. With hands folded in her lap, she awaited her fate.

The judge asked the jury foreman for the verdict. As the bailiff handed the folded slip of paper to the judge, the courtroom fell into complete silence. Judge Allen read the verdict and then, in a state of dismay, announced the verdict: "Not guilty."

Reporter Frances Wayne asked prosecutor Horace V. Benson if he had a comment. Benson did. He bellowed: *"My God! If we couldn't convict a murderer on the evidence we presented, what is required in the way of truth and fact to convict?"*[50]

On the other side of the courtroom, a grateful Gertrude Gibson Patterson had thanked her attorney O. N. Hilton. Following their embrace, they were interrupted by four jurors, F. J. Crane, J. P. Doyle, J. J. Flint, and C. G. Oppenlander, who rushed from the jury box to offer their congratulations. Overwhelmed, Gertrude thanked them again and again. C. G. Oppenlander eagerly responded: *"Don't thank us, thank that fellow Easton. Before he came there was but one verdict. He took the rope from off your neck!"*[51]

Gertrude Gibson Patterson left the courthouse a free woman. Frances Wayne managed to ask her one question. Slyly, she asked, "Do you expect to meet Strouss now that you are acquitted?" Gertrude quickly replied, "I never want to meet or see him again."

As she walked away and into the streets of Denver, the first time in two months, she was met with jeers and taunts from the public. She spent her time in a hotel room away from the citizens who were outraged that she got away with murder. Gertrude had pawned $2,000 worth of diamonds to pay for her defense. She quickly redeemed these, and returned to seclusion in her hotel room.

Meanwhile, Horace V. Benson, believing the outcome of the murder trial was a mockery of the judicial system, filed a complaint with the Colorado Bar Association, regarding the sudden appearance of the "witness," Francis J. Easton. Where had this mystery witness come from and where did he go after the trial? The Colorado Bar Association agreed with Benson's concerns and elicited the services of the William Burns Detective Agency to track the surprise witness. but there were no clues. A fellow lodger at his hotel, on Larimer Street, told detectives he saw Easton leave "with a fat wad of bills." There were no other clues. Easton had vanished.

Soon the weary defendant returned to her parents' home for much needed support. She wrote the *Rocky Mountain News* that she was writing a book and planning to write a second. Neither of her novels sold well. Even so, Denver newspapers seemed eager for any scrap of gossip they could print about the sensational young beauty.

Then the tale became even stranger when the acquitted murderess was reported to have tragically drowned with the sinking of the *RMS Titanic* in April of 1912 — or was that a red herring promoted by the leading Denver newspaper, the *Denver Post*? The *Rocky Mountain News* accused the *Denver Post* of deliberately faking stories that Patterson had perished with the *Titanic*. (Neither she nor Emil Strouss were listed as *RMS Titanic* passengers on the official passenger list.) The *Rocky Mountain News* further reported that Gertrude Gibson Patterson was living in splendor in a fashionable section of Chicago under an assumed name, and that Strouss was supporting her still; she also allegedly lived in a villa in France with a French maid.

The known facts about Gertrude's life end in 1912.

Mystery & Murder
A Real 'Who Done It?'

The following story of greed and murder is largely retold through the newspaper accounts as the events unfolded. The reporters of the era left little to the imagination.

Denver residents were shocked when they opened their morning *Denver Post*. The bold front-page headline dated November 28, 1910, read:

Mysterious Foe Blindfolds, Gags and Kills Mrs.Cellanto

The body of Mrs. Dorinda Cellanto was discovered on a Sunday afternoon, six miles north of Denver, on the ranch property of Newton Bowles. A follow-up story appeared on the front page the following day, November 29, 1910:

Band of Cutthroats Blamed for Murders

The only result of the investigation into the murder of Mrs. Dorinda Cellanto, whose body was found Sunday in a ditch on a ranch six miles north of Denver, is a growing feeling, divined rather than ascertained that an organized band of murderers is responsible for the crime. Shortly after noon today, Chief of Police Armstrong issued orders to all patrolmen to arrest and bring before him Clemente Cellanto, husband of the woman whose body was found Sunday in a ravine about a mile beyond Globeville, in Adams county. The chief did not announce that any charge would be preferred against the husband, but directed his arrest and detention on the ground of 'investigation.'"

The November 30 evening issue of the *Post* (the paper printed two editions daily) updated the murder case:

Fear Lurks Close to All Who Could Solve Cellanto Murder

In the office of Chief Armstrong accusation followed accusation. The chief had arrested Mrs. Angelina Garramone, from whose home Mrs. Cellanto disappeared two weeks ago and who was the last person who was seen with Mrs. Mary

175

LaGuardia, the old woman who vanished from sight three months ago. With her, he arrested Salvatore Giaccolo, who is alleged to have been a sort of secretary to the Garramone woman in her [real] *estate dealings, and Clemente Cellanto, husband of the murdered woman.*

Then as now, journalists were often incorrect or just plain sloppy in their early reporting of a story. This report clearly states "Clemente Cellanto, husband of the murdered woman," yet names the murdered woman as "Mrs. Mary LaGuardia." The paper would make the clarification in subsequent articles regarding the murder case, as one of the suspects in the Dorinda Cellanto murder case would also come under suspicion for the disappearance of a Mrs. Maria LaGuardia.

The morning following his arrest, Clemente Cellanto was taken to the morgue at 1402 West 38th Avenue to provide a positive identification of the deceased. Cellanto identified the corpse as that of his wife, Dorinda Cellanto. It must have been a ghastly sight, as her throat had been slashed and her face swollen and discolored from being gagged. Her entire body was ravaged by the elements, having been in the ravine for nearly two weeks.

Following the inquest, the family and friends of Dorinda Cellanto raised funds for her burial, which occurred in Riverside Cemetery.

The coroner's inquest was held on Thursday of that week. Coroner E. G. Jones presented his results to Police Chief Armstrong, who then interrogated the suspects. The *Denver Post* printed a portion of the interrogation in the December 6, 1910 issue:

"[You] *said, 'I warned you one month ago that if you did not give me the money you owed me I should tell what you know of the disappearance of Mrs. Cellanto,' 'What did you mean by that?' asked Chief Armstrong. Salvatore* [Giaccolo] *cried, 'I mean that she* [Mrs. Garramone] *lied to me about it and lied to police. I mean she never came home the night Mrs. Cellanto disappeared. I mean she knew where Mrs. Cellanto* [was.]*"*

It should be noted that all three suspects were Italian immigrants and their English was sparse. This may account for a possible translation problem in the above newspaper account.

After the extensive interrogation by Denver Police and following the coroner's inquest, the official coroner's report was issued:

We the jury find from the evidence in the case that Mrs. Dorinda Labate Cellanto came to her death by a blow inflicted above the right eye, throat cut and other wounds inflicted by a person or persons unknown to this jury.[52]

While the mystery as to who murdered Dorinda Labate Cellanto seemed to be at a standstill, quite a bit is known as to who Dorinda Labate Cellanto was.

She was born Giuseppa Dorinda Labate on March 19, 1864, in Italy to Gemma and Carmine diCianno Labate. At the age of twenty-two, she married Felicito Frazzini, a deaf mute, on September 10, 1886. The couple had one child, Francesco Frazzini, born the following year. Felicito Frazzini emigrated to America with his uncle, Antonio Frazzini, arriving on May 11, 1898.

His wife, Dorinda, as she was commonly known, and their infant son arrived on December 6, 1898, on the *Hesperia*. The *Hesperia* manifest originally listed her reason for passage as "going to husband Felice Frazzini." However, the line is crossed out. While Dorinda was able to make passage to America, she and her husband later divorced - perhaps the reason for the crossed out reference. It seems as if Felicito Frazzini must have been fairly successful as his divorce garnered a headline and story in the *Denver Post* issue of April 19, 1899:

Unhappy Filicito
Felicito Frazzini divorces Dorinda

Dorinda next married Domenico Labate (no relation). Two children were born to this union, William in 1900, and Joseph, in 1901. But this marriage also ended in divorce. The *Denver Post* reported the court proceedings in the June 8, 1905 issue of the paper:

She Defied the Judge
Italian Woman Objects to Interpreter and Makes a Scene

The article described, as best as possible, given the broken English, the interaction in the courtroom:

"Datta man he noa treata me righta. He againa me. I noa

leta him talka to me. Oha, helpa! Helpa! Me bea killta! Me bea killta!"

With a shriek that went through the corridors of the court house, Mrs. Dorinda Labate, applicant for a divorce in the county court, refused to obey Judge Henry V. Johnson's order to 'stand up and be sworn' because of her objections to the selection of Henry Sphigetta as interpreter.

The Labate divorce case was replete with charges and countercharges. Mrs. Labate asked for a legal separation based on the grounds of desertion. Mr. Labate countered with a monetary demand, asserting that strange men had been in "the habit of making his home their home."

The divorce was finally granted on June 17, 1905. The *Denver Post*, issued the same day, gave the story a splashy headline:

No Alimony for Her

Judge Henry V. Johnson in the county court today refused the application of Mrs. Dorinda Labate for permanent alimony from Dominick Labate. The family troubles of the Labates have been occupying considerable time in the county courts recently.

Just five months later, Dorinda Labate Frazzini Labate married Clemente Cellanto. The marriage was performed by Justice of the Peace Benjamin F. Harrington on November 27, 1905.[53]

Nearly two years later, Dorinda was in the court system again, and again, the subject of newspaper articles. Her ex-husband, Domenico Labate, had filed for full custody of their children. The *Denver Post* covered the trial proceedings in the issue dated January 9, 1907:

Says Wife Drinks and Calls Children Names

"Of course she drinks," asserted Domenick [sic] Labate violently, on the witness stand. Domenick [sic] Labate is a railway foreman of the Southern Pacific road, and has asked the court to allow him the care of his two children, William, aged 7, and Joseph, aged 6. For two years, he has [paid] $12 a month to keep them in St. Vincent's orphan asylum. He claims that his former wife, now Mrs. Dorinda Frazzini-Labate-Cellanto is unfit to have charge of the boys.

The case was continued until further evidence could be procured. Investigators visited the home of Mrs. Dorinda Cellanto at 3433 Justina Street, an area known as the Italian Colony. Eventually, Domenico Labate was granted full custody of the children.

Sometime in 1908 or early 1909, Dorinda Cellanto entered into some sort of real estate partnership with Angelina Garramone. The Denver Post of July 30, 1909, ran a short article with the following statement, "Real Estate Transfer Angela Garramone to Dorinda Labate and Clemente Cellanto." Another transaction between the two women made a curious headline in the September 26, 1909 issue of the Denver Post:

Protecting Victims of Get Rich Quick Schemes
Property transfer from Angelina Garramone to Dorinda Labate and Clemente Cellanto, $1,800.

The article went on to describe how Angelina Garramone worked her real estate scam. She would find an Italian family living in a little home which they had paid for, in the lower portion of the city, the Italian Colony. She would befriend them and through conversation, ask what they thought their property was worth. Gaining their trust, she would then tell them that she would pay them a price which was a few hundred dollars in excess of their estimate, if they would sign the property over to her. Several property owners jumped at the proposition, and for a time, Garramone and Mrs. Dorinda Cellanto were making good money.

Angelina Garramone's name and activities were often covered by the Denver Post following the uncovering of the real estate scheme. One such article appeared in the December 11, 1910 issue:

Mrs. Angelina Garramone who has duped, with her 'real estate' transactions, practically every Italian property owner in the lower section of the city, has entered into a new line of business, which promises not quite so great a degree of success for her. She now deals in pianos. Within the last month or more, she has rented three pianos, each one from a different firm, and after paying the rent for the space of a few weeks on the three instruments, sold them. One she disposed of to the Ward Auction company, and upon the discovery of the fraud which the woman had practiced the company caused her to be brought before Justice Gavin, where her case was set for hearing Monday morning. The Italian woman conducts her operations under four names, her own, Angelina Garramone, Angelina Sericia, Marie Brown and Rose Wortley.

Evidently, Angelina Garramone and Dorinda Cellanto had a falling out and Cellanto chose to dissolve the partnership.

Police Chief Armstrong began to methodically piece together the clues of the mystery murder following another interrogation of the victim's husband. Clemente Cellanto explained to the chief that the day his wife disappeared Angelina Garramone was at his home, visiting with his wife. Cellanto left the home to run an errand and when he returned, his wife was not there.

Armstrong again questioned Garramone about the sudden disappearance of Mrs. Cellanto, as she seemed to be the last to see her alive. Garramone told the police chief that after she and Dorinda Cellanto concluded their business, Mrs. Cellanto said she was going to North Denver to visit a friend, and the two women parted company.

While Armstrong was quietly working the case, the *Denver Post* reported what they had learned in the August 2, 1911 issue:

Cellanto Murder Mystery is Fast Being Unraveled

> *Sheriff Herman J. Schloo of Adams county has turned over to Chief of Police Armstrong evidence which he has secured tending to connect Mrs. Angelina Garramone and Clemente Cellante with the murder of the latter's wife, Mrs. Dorinta [sic] Labate Cellante.*

Through earlier interrogation, and with the cooperation of Salvatore Giaccolo, a partner in Garramone's real estate scheme, Armstrong was able to arrest Angelina Garramone on charges of forgery.

Mrs. Garramone to be Tried Next Week for Forgery
This was the headline in the August 5, 1911 issue of the *Denver Post.* The article went on to report:

> *Angelina Garramone will hold the boards at the criminal court next week. She goes to trial charged with forgery and kindred offenses, all of which grew out of her desire to sustain*

her Chadwickian reputation in the Italian colony in North Denver.

Angelina Garramone, thirty-five years of age, was convicted of the forgery charges and sent to the Colorado State Penitentiary to serve a sentence of five to eight years.

Then the body of fifty-nine-year-old Maria LaGuardia, who had been missing for nearly a year, was found. The horrific details were recounted in the *Denver Post* issue of August 5, 1911:

> *Dismembered Corpse Found on Ranch is of American Woman*
>
> *Theory Body was that of Mrs. Laguardia Displayed by Size of Shoe*
>
> *No tangible clew to the identity of the woman whose dismembered corpse was found Friday on the Johnson ranch, twelve miles north of Denver, in Jefferson county, has been secured, but the police have started a systematic investigation of the women reported missing in Denver during the past two years, and it is expected when the work is completed the identity of the body will have been fixed if the woman was a resident of the city, as the police and authorities of Jefferson county are inclined to believe.*

Two days later, on August 7, 1911, the authorities released the news that they had indeed positively identified the body as that of Maria LaGuardia. That same day, the *Denver Post* rushed to print the gruesome details:

> *Body of Slain Woman is Identified as that of Maria LaGuardia.*
>
> *Her niece recognizes clothing, the stockings and even the skull. Holding her baby in one arm and the bleached skull of her dead aunt in the other hand, Mrs. Annie Dimotta this morning positively identified the remains of a woman found last Friday on the J. N. Johnson ranch, in Jefferson county, as those of Mrs. Maria Laguardia, who disappeared from Denver on Sept. 3, 1910. The baby reached out and patted the skull playfully.*

Another article in the same issue of the paper appeared:

Cellanto Turned over to Sheriff

Patrolman Percy Smith brought Clemente Cellanto, husband of Mrs. Dorinda Cellanto, whose dead body was discovered Nov 27, 1910, on an Adams county ranch. Mrs. Cellanto was a business associate of Mrs. Angela Garramone. Her body was wrapped in burlap after the same manner employed with the remains of Mrs. LaGuardia. The police say Mrs. Cellanto was killed to prevent her telling what she knew of the shooting of one of her relatives, but they never made any arrests. The body of Mrs. Cellante was found on the Bowles ranch, near Globeville Nov 27 of last year. The throat of the woman had been cut either with a sharp butcher knife or a razor and was nearly severed from the head. At that time, it was supposed that the murder had been committed in the vicinity of the spot where the body was found, but later developments have caused the police to believe that Mrs. Cellante was murdered in the Garramone home at 1230 West Thirty-eighth Ave.

Then, Chief Armstrong got a tip which ultimately led to a confession by accomplices to the murder of Maria LaGuardia. Again, the *Denver Post* broke the story on August 12, 1911:

Mrs. Garramone named as Mrs. Laguardia's Slayer

Mrs. Concetta Forgione and her daughter, Stella, 18 years old, confessed at Golden last night that they stood by while Mrs. Angelina Garramone cut the throat of Mrs. Marie Laguardia and robbed her of $320. Mrs. Forgione said she held Mrs. Garramone's 4-year-old baby in her arms while Mrs. Garramone committed the murder. The blood from the wound, Mrs. Forgione said, covered Mrs. Garramone's hands and she sucked it from her fingers with her lips. The killing was done with a butcher knife, according to Mrs. Forgione and her daughter, and of the money taken from the murdered woman Mrs. Forgione said she received $160. The murder occurred between 7 and 7:30 o'clock Saturday morning, August 13, 1910, after Mrs. Forgione, her daughter Stella and Mrs. Garramone had spent the night with Mrs. Laguardia in the open air near the tracks of the Intermountain railroad east of Golden.

Armstrong and his detectives interviewed many members of the North Denver Italian community. *The Denver Post* interviewed them as well as reported in the same August 12, 1911 issue:

Four Murder Farm Cases are Recalled

A merciless, cunning rogue, the Italians describe Mrs. Garramone, whom all feared and many followed. A dozen persons in Little Italy this morning repeat the same expressions. So they discuss Angelina Garramone, the plague of the settlement, mother of seven and one of the most remarkable women known in the state. 'Black Hand? No,' they say; 'only Angelina Garramone's black hand and black heart.'

Just three weeks after she was sent to prison for forgery, Angelina Garramone was arrested at the state penitentiary on charges of murder. Garramone's attorney, Edward L. Clover, immediately asked for a postponement, attempting to defer the trial until after his client had served her prison sentence for forgery. His request was denied. The murder trial was set for November 21, 1911.

The *Denver Post* was scooped on a major development. The August 10, 1911 issue of The *Weekly News*, printed the following article:

Garramone Slew Woman

Oh my God, will they never leave me alone? I didn't do it, I didn't do it,' sobbed Mrs. Angelina Garramone in the reception room in the woman's quarters in the penitentiary here tonight, when told that she had been charged with the murder of Marie LaGuardia.

Police soon learned more of Angelina Garramone and her background. Angelina Sassosa was the only daughter of E. Sassosa, a wealthy prosperous farmer living near Denver. When he died, Angelina was the sole heir, gaining some $20,000. It is with this new found fortune that she and her husband, Luigio Garramone, began their real estate business, which Angelina would later turn into a real estate scheme.

Meanwhile, detectives continued interrogating Concetta Forgione and her daughter, Stella, regarding their confession. The *Denver Post* put a new twist on their coverage in the August 13, 1911 issue:

To Burn LaGuardia's Body was Intention of Mrs. Garramone

Nothing in the stories of the Murders in the Rue Morgue of Paris by Poe, exceeds in horror the story of the murder of Mrs. Marie Laguardia as it was repeated yesterday by Mrs. Concetta Forgione at the Jefferson county jail at Golden.

More of the murder witnesses revelations appeared the next day in the *Denver Post*:

Confessed Accomplices Fear Mrs. Garramone's Mystic Power

Mrs. Concetta Forgione and her daughter, Stella, charged with being accessories to the murder of Mrs. Maria Laguardia, believe they are in danger of being stricken to death in their cells by a supernatural power. They believe that Mrs. Angelina Garramone, whom they accuse of having murdered Mrs. Maria Laguardia, has communed with the spirits of another world and that she has the ability to invoke the aid of evil spirits in punishing her enemies.

Angelina Garramone made her first court appearance facing a charge of murder on November 6, 1911. She pleaded not guilty, exclaiming, "No. I could not be guilty of such a crime as that."

Following two successful postponements by the defense attorney, Edward L. Clover, the murder trial finally began on December 17, 1911. The trial was held at the Jefferson County courthouse in Golden, the county where Maria LaGuardia's body was found.

Opening arguments, particularly by the defense, promised as strange a trial as the *Denver Post* recent coverage had been. Garramone's attorney, E. L. Clover, addressed the court in an effort to get the murder case against his client thrown out. His grounds for dismissal were that it had not been proven that the remains of Maria LaGuardia were actually human remains.

The *Denver Post* printed the attorney's words verbatim, the following day, which shocked the reading public: *"Why, how do we know but that Maria Laguardia is a race horse or someone's cow or something. There is nothing in the information to show that she is a human being."*

The judge overruled the motion for dismissal on the attorney's absurd grounds and the prosecution presented their case. Witnesses for the prosecution were Concetta and Stella Forgione, who were each given reduced prison sentences for being accomplices to murder. An interpreter, Frank Potestio, was used to translate. Both Concetta and her daughter Stella gave the same story to District Attorney Morgan as they had to the police.

The *Rocky Mountain News* gave the following courtroom description in its December 21, 1911 issue:

> *Mrs. Angelina Garramone...has had somewhat the same effect upon the Italian colony of Denver for years past as the hiss of a snake upon a band of monkeys.*

A separate article in the same issue of the *News* was equally unfavorable of the two accomplices, particularly Concetta Forgione:

> *[Her] shriveled, hard, cunning face, acrobatic with passionate Italian mobility, her beady black eyes restless and peering like a monkey's and her brittle, falsetto voice, working in time to her emotions, [as she] sat upon the witness stand in the district court at Golden yesterday and detailed the revolting murder of Mrs. Maria Laguardia on South Table mountain on the morning of August 20, 1910.*

The jurors were gripped by Concetta Forgione's vivid testimony, particularly the actual murder. On the witness stand, Forgione stated:

> *"She [Garramone] grabbed Mrs. Laguardia by the hair, pulled her head back and, as she said, 'Oh, godmother, you have a big worm on your throat,' she cut it with a butcher knife."*

With such horrific testimony, the judge wisely adjourned court for the day. Newspaper reporters clamored around Angelina Garramone for a statement. They got one and she had a great deal to say. The *Rocky Mountain News* printed an interview in the same issue as the trial coverage appeared:

> *"She [Forgione] lies. She lies. Just wait and you will see. She will be in hell before she gets through. She will think it over in Canon City — there is lots of time to think in the penitentiary. She won't look me in the eye when she lies. She is afraid."*

This last reference to the penitentiary is most likely due to the fact that if Garramone was found not guilty of murder, she would still return to prison to serve out her forgery sentence, and that Concetta and Stella Forgione would also serve time in the penitentiary for their roles in the murder. Angelina Garramone was indeed a calculating woman.

In court the following day, defense attorney Clover had the opportunity to cross examine the defense team's star witness. Through his questioning, Clover was able to bring up Concetta Forgione's sordid past, in an effort to discredit her testimony. Under sworn testimony, Forgione acknowledged that she was previously known as Mrs. Concetta Sabatina and had two children from that marriage, which ended in divorce. Showing the witness as well as the jurors numerous newspaper articles dating back to 1893, a shaken Concetta Forgione admitted to the horrible crime she had committed all those years ago. A few of the articles Clover presented for the jury included one from the *Rocky Mountain News*, dated March 5, 1893:

A Fiend Incarnate

A most inhuman and awful crime occurred in Highlands, suburb of Denver, to-day where the 6-year-old daughter of Mrs. Concetta Sabatina was discovered in a dying condition by the neighbors. The child was a mass of burns, but was able to tell that her mother had used hot flatirons on her and inserted burning sticks into her body, afterward hanging her to the bed-post, where she was found by the neighbors. She cannot recover. Mrs. Concetta and her 10-year-old nob, who is charged as an accessory, are in jail. No motive is known for the crime.

The *Denver Daily News* reported the outcome of Concetta Sabatina Forgione's trial in the March 7, 1893 issue:

Phenomenal Fiends
Sympathetic Women of all Classes Flock to see Concetta Sabatina

The largest crowd that ever filled Judge Landon's court room was the one that assembled yesterday to witness the trial of Concetta Sabatina and her 8-year-old son Nicholas for their unparalleled and atrocious treatment of the little baby girl,

In a confusing set of circumstances, Angelina Garramone was convicted of forgery and sent to the Colorado State Penitentiary. As evidence surfaced of the murder plot she was believed to have hatched, she was arrested at the prison. Garramone was convicted of murder and again sent to the prison to serve a life sentence.

Antonia. People came from all parts of the city and suburbs, some coming from Littleton, to get a glimpse of the inhuman mother and her fiendish offspring. Judge Landon sentenced the woman to three months on the charge of assault and battery, three months for cruelty to children, the sentences to be cumulative and bound her over the district court in the sum of $1,000 for assault to kill. The boy was sentenced to the reform school for three years. The little victim is at the county hospital and in such a critical condition that she could not be brought to court yesterday.

The prosecutor's next move in the trial was to introduce the evidence. A box containing skeletal remains, including a skull, were presented to the jury, one by one. Newspapers reported that Garramone smiled at the jury during the presentation and occasionally laughed.

Her demeanor became very stoic when the prosecution introduced a skeletal foot, with a shoe remaining.

District Attorney Morgan brought Maria LaGuardia's niece, Anne DeMotto to the stand. She testified that she recognized the shoe as she often tied the laces for her elderly aunt. She also testified that the blue calico material introduced into the evidence was the very fabric she had fashioned into a dress for her aunt.

Several witnesses for the prosecution testified that they believed Garramone also murdered Dorinda Cellanto, possibly, they said, because she knew about the LaGuardia murder. The *Denver Post* reported the court proceedings of the day in the December 22, 1911 edition:

> *Black Cat Startles Mrs. Garramone; Mrs. Cellanto's Murder Laid to Her*
>
> When Mrs. Maria Angelina Garramone walked through the corridor of the court house this morning under the guard of Deputy Warden James K. Dye of the penitentiary, a black cat ran in front of her.
>
> 'My God!' she exclaimed, and appeared to take this as a bad omen.
>
> Whether the fact of the black cat crossing her path has anything to do with it or not, Fate appears to have reserved a large share of trouble for the little Italian woman. Whether convicted or acquitted of the charge of killing Maria Laguardia, she will have to go back to Canon City.

The prosecution's next witness was another bombshell for the defense. Angelina Garramone's own son, Finobella Garramone, testified against his mother. He recounted in great detail how Angelina had defrauded many citizens in North Denver, including him and his father.

Police Chief Armstrong testified, recounting his many interrogations of the suspects in both the Cellanto and LaGuardia murder investigations, and the eventual confession which led to the evidence and arrest of Angelina Garramone.

As the prosecution rested its case, the flamboyant defense attorney, Edward L. Clover, did his best, in most unusual arguments, to save his client. Clover spent nearly two hours disputing the prosecution's case, primarily attacking the police department and accusing them of framing his client. In an about-face, he seemed to change his opening arguments regarding the "humanism" of the skeletal evidence and suggested that Maria LaGuardia's estranged husband, Michael LaGuardia, was actually the murderer.

The defense called one witness to the stand, the accused murderess, Angelina Garramone. She was on the witness stand for nearly two hours, questioned by her attorney, and then cross examined by District Attorney Morgan. Her attorney began his questioning by asking his client if she had committed the murder. Her reply was printed in the December 22, 1911, edition of the *Rocky Mountain News*:

> *Attorney Clover asked her if she had ever hurt anyone or whipped the children. 'That's why I left home,' she said, 'because I would not whip the children. I never could stay around when a chicken or a duck was killed.'*

Under direct questioning by her attorney, Garramone testified that she and various friends were with Maria LaGuardia at the tram depot at Eldorado Springs when Maria and her husband boarded the tramway. Garramone further testified that she was in Denver at the time of the LaGuardia murder and had attended her 10 a.m. court hearing on unrelated charges.

On cross examination, the prosecution asked Garramone several questions, including if she had actually been at the Eldorado Springs tram depot or the Golden depot. The defendant insisted it was the Eldorado Springs depot.

The prosecution recalled Police Chief Armstrong to the stand. Armstrong testified that during interrogations of Garramone, she originally said that she and Maria LaGuardia were at the Golden tram depot, where LaGuardia left to be reunited with her husband. Armstrong further testified that LaGuardia later changed her account, saying it was the Eldorado Springs depot.

With this strong refutation of the defendant's testimony, the prosecution presented a summation for the jury and asked for a verdict of guilty. In a surprise move for the era, District Attorney Morgan also asked for the death penalty.

After a long day of courtroom legalese, the jury was dismissed for deliberation at 8:30 p.m., on Saturday, December 23, 1911. After a little over an hour, the jury had a few questions for the judge and then returned to their deliberations.

Evidently, the Colorado Springs *Gazette Telegraph* issued a special edition of their paper, as the following article appeared in the paper dated December 23, 1911:

> *Garramone Jury Out*
>
> *The case of Mrs. Angelina Garramone, charged with the murder of Mrs. Maria Laguardia, August 10, 1910, went to the jury at 7 o'clock tonight. An hour later the jury reported there was no chance of an agreement tonight and was locked up. The court's instructions were either for a verdict in the first degree or acquittal.*

Early on Sunday morning, the jury reached a verdict. Attorneys and Angelina Garramone rushed to the courtroom along with the newspaper reporters.

For the first time since the trial began, the defiant defendant was solemn and stoic as the court clerk read the jury verdict: guilty of first degree murder. The sentence was life imprisonment. The *Denver Post* captured the scene in their coverage in the December 24, 1911, issue:

> *Angelina Garramone Sentenced to Life Imprisonment*
>
> *Guilty of murder in the first degree and fixing punishment at imprisonment for life, was the verdict returned by the jury in the case of Mrs. Angelina Garramone of Denver for the killing of Mrs. Maria Laguardia, whose throat she cut for the purpose of robbery, in the district court here this morning.*
>
> *The jury reached a verdict after taking two ballots - one last night and the other this morning.*

The *Rocky Mountain News* managed an interview with the convicted murderess shortly after the verdict. It appeared in the December 24, 1911, issue of the paper:

> *Mrs. Garramone's wonderful smile again came into evidence and she tossed her head and said: 'Well, you can tell them this one thing. My conscience is clear and that will keep me from being unhappy. I know I didn't kill her, no matter what*

the jury thought. Mr. Clover has asked the judge for a new trial, and maybe I will have better luck the next time. Maybe Mrs. LaGuardia will hear by that time and come and save me.'

This was followed by an interview with the *Denver Post,* printed the same day:

Life! Doom Haunts Mrs. Garramone

> *'Life! Life!' Angelina Garramone laughed bitterly. 'They give me life — but they let Patterson go and she commit murder.'*
>
> *'Don't you think they treated me fine,' she asked, and her mouth drew down sarcastically at the corners.*
>
> *'Bah! Don't talk to me about justice in this world. Only in heaven is there such a thing called justice, and sometimes we wonder if it is there also.'*

The Patterson name Garramone referenced was Gertrude Gibson Patterson who had been charged with the murder of her husband. She was acquitted of the murder in a highly publicized trial the month prior to Garromone's guilty verdict, despite her obvious guilt, perhaps Garramone was implying a double-standard.

Garramone's attorney, Edward L. Clover, immediately filed for a new trial. The court response was swift. Two weeks later, Clover's motion for a new trial was denied. The story was outlined in the January 13, 1912 issue of the *Denver Post:*

Mrs. Garramone Given Life Term: New Trial Denied

> *For the law — that magic word which rolls upon the professional tongue with all the mouthy majesty with which an actor pronounces 'Rome' - the law moved implacably yesterday in the district court at Golden and an ignorant foreign woman was sentenced to life imprisonment for murdering Maria Laguardia for money.*
>
> *On the ground that evidence important to the defense of Mrs. Angelina Garramone in her trial for the murder of Mrs. Maria Laguardia was hidden by the sheriff of Jefferson county, Attorney Edward L. Clover will file a motion for a new hearing in the supreme court.*
>
> *The newly discovered evidence is a man's coat in which part*

of the bones of Mrs. Laguardia were found wrapped. The coat was hidden by the sheriff and Mrs. Garramone's attorney did not learn of its existence until long after the trial which was held a year ago.

It's not clear from this newspaper report if the reporter contacted the sheriff's office for comment. There are no further articles regarding the discovery of "new" evidence. Regarding the "new" evidence, this is most likely a false statement by the defense attorney. Why would the sheriff hide incriminating evidence in a murder trial? It is also curious that the defense attorney, who originally claimed the remains of the body "may not" be human, now asserted the discovery of the "new" evidence claim into his motion for retrial before the Colorado Supreme Court. In any case, the court did not hear the case and Angelina Garramone remained behind bars at the Colorado State Penitentiary.

With no resolution to the murder of Dorinda Cellanto, local and county law enforcement continued to work the case. The *Denver Post* issue dated September 13, 1913, reported the latest twist in the murder mystery:

Italian May Clear Murder Mystery

Marco Cellanto, who shot Giacinto Decioci during a quarrel at the home of Mrs. Angelina Garramone on Nov. 6 1910 and who recently was captured at Pocatello, Idaho, arrived in Denver last night in custody of Deputy Sheriff Pollard. He will be tried on a charge of assault to kill.

The police hope to obtain information from Cellanto that will enable them to clear up the mystery surrounding the death of his sister-in-law, Mrs. Marie Dorinda Labate Cellanto, whose mutilated body was found on a ranch in Adams County several weeks after the shooting in which he was involved.

After further interrogation of Marco Cellanto, the detectives were unable to learn more as to the murder of Dorinda Cellanto. Although those working her murder case believed Angelina Garramone was the murderer, the case was never solved.

Angelina Garramone had served nearly eight years of her life sentence in prison when she went before the parole board seeking a pardon. The *Denver Post* printed the story in the August 18, 1920 issue:

Plea of Mrs. Garramone for Pardon Brings Storm of Protest from Italians

News that Mrs. Angelina Garramone, the 'Cassie Chadwick of Little Italy,' has applied for a pardon from the state prison has aroused a storm of protest among the Italian residents of Denver.

Perhaps due to the public outcry, Garramone's pardon request was denied.

Nearly two years later, Garramone again appeared before the prison parole board. The proceedings were kept out of the media until the decision was made; by all accounts a political decision. The *Rocky Mountain News* was the first to break the story on May 29, 1922:

Pardon of Angelina Garramone
Board Secretly Frees Denver Murderess

Mrs. Angelina Garramone, convicted Dec 23, 1911 of the brutal killing of Mrs. Maria Laguardia, a Denver Italian woman, near Golden, Aug 20, 1910 was discharged secretly about a month ago from the state prison at Canon City on a life parole, granted by the state board of pardons, according to a statement made by Thomas J. Tynan, warden of the penitentiary.

Notification of the action of the board of pardons in the Garramone case was never given to the public though it transpired some six months ago at a meeting held in Canon City, according to information given out at Canon City by F. E. Crawford, an attache at the prison, yesterday.

'Mrs. Garramone expressed a fear that she would be assaulted by the Italian 'blackhand' of Denver if news of her release became public,' Mr. Crawford explained. 'The case has been kept particularly quiet on that account.' Immediately upon her release Mrs. Garramone was spirited out of the state and is now in Youngstown, Ohio, according to a letter received by friends of the woman last week.

The news of the "secret" release of murderess Angelina Garramone, signed off by Governor Oliver Shoup, set off a firestorm among politicians, as well as the public. The *Rocky Mountain News* printed one such story of the injustice in May 30, 1922, issue:

> *There must be another motive behind this wholesale pardoning of criminals than just mercy,' declared Judge Samuel W. Johnson, who as former district attorney of the First Judicial District, prosecuted Frank H. Mulligan, one of the two convicts who tasted of gubernatorial clemency, declared yesterday.*

The *Rocky Mountain News* continued their coverage, reporting on June 4, 1922:

> *Shoup Sets More Criminals Free*
> *Irregularities Discovered in Release of Mrs. Garramone*
>
> *Two more paroles by Gov. Oliver H. Shoup and discovery of irregularities in the paroling of Mrs. Angelina Garramone last month were the developments yesterday in the chief executive's recent unparalleled releases from the state penitentiary. The releases by gubernatorial order yesterday brought the total of paroles for the last two months to twelve - eight murderers and four robbers.*
> *Regarding Angelina Garramone, the board feels that the recommendation of the board to the governor should stand, that the sentence be commuted from a term of twenty-six years to life imprisonment, which will permit of their release on parole, April 1926, which is ten years from the date she was discharged from the forgery charge.*

With this convoluted recommendation, forty-six year old Angelina Garramone was released from a life sentence of murder in the first degree.

The political decision did not sit well with the public. Governor Shoup was defeated in the next election and stricter laws were passed by both the Colorado House and Senate.

Rum Runners
Bootlegging Gets Ugly

The year 1916 began with a devastating blow to liquor establishments in Denver, as well as the state of Colorado. In the election of 1914 the voters of Colorado voted on a 129,589 to 118,017 margin to prohibit the sale of alcohol throughout the state, four years before Prohibition became national law under the Volstead Act. The voters of Denver actually voted 38,139 to 29,533 against the measure, yet because it was a statewide referendum, Denver businesses were forced to comply.[54] The law provided a grace period that ended at the stroke of midnight, December 31, 1915.

In Denver and all of Colorado, it was the beginning of a new wave of criminal activity, including murder the likes of which Denver had never before experienced. The front page of the January 1, 1916, edition of the *Rocky Mountain News* extolled the news that Prohibition had become law in Colorado:

DRY YEARS USHERED IN WITH MARKED QUIET AS BARS CLOSE EARLY[54]

> *Pueblo, Colorado Springs, Boulder, Cripple Creek and all the mountain and other Colorado towns went dry at midnight without ceremony. Most saloons closed doors before the final hour.*
>
> *A new era confronts Colorado today. The state is dry. The most conspicuous event in the common-wealth's history has taken place.*

Quite curious is that the editorial pages took no stance on the new law, and even more curious is that neither the headline nor the opening paragraph mention the city of Denver. Rather, walking a fine line with the voters of Denver, the article continues with a tone of gaiety, rushing in the New Year.

> *Toward midnight an immense throng gathered on Curtis street and other streets in the downtown business section, tooted horns and in other ways welcomed the New Year. At the stroke of 12, saloons emptied themselves of patrons, cafes and*

restaurants suspended their most lucrative activity, and 1916
was greeted by an orderly, if jovial throng.

A news article of innocence or naivete, the folks at the paper could not have known what that first day in January 1916 was about to bring to Denver and the state of Colorado.

When the law went into effect, it soon proved to be full of so many loopholes, that the bootleggers in Denver and around the state were able to drive their vehicles full of booze right through it. While churches were obviously immune from the law for religious purposes and ceremonies, the law also had a myriad of illogical provisions. For instance, the city of Denver issued over sixteen thousand permits to doctors, allowing them to prescribe a legal limit of four ounces of alcohol to their patients for medicinal purposes. The medicinal advantage didn't seem to be much of an advantage, as an exemption of sorts was also given to several citizens of Denver without the benefit of a doctor's prescription. Fred Stackhouse, Denver's city auditor, reported in an annual report issued in 1917, that the city had issued 59,339 liquor permits to local residents. Of note, that figure is twenty thousand more than those who voted against the prohibition measure the previous year!

However, the biggest loophole in the law which created the bootlegger enterprise was the provision allowing alcohol, including beer, to be transported across the state line for private use in the state of Colorado.

Within months, the bootlegging trade was in full force, transporting an estimated five thousand dollars' worth of liquor per month across the state lines into Colorado. There was limited law enforcement across the state to catch the bootleggers, let alone stop them, and many who attempted were bought off, creating corruption, more crime, and even murder.

Denver's newly elected mayor, Dewey Bailey, was rather lax when it came to crime enforcement regarding the illegal liquor trade. Soon, he found himself and his administration mired in controversy and alleged corruption in the Denver Police Department. Following a grand jury investigation, which found several instances of police corruption involving bootlegging and gambling, Mayor Bailey was finally forced to make changes in enforcing the law.

A veteran of the Denver Police Department, Detective George

Klein, was put in charge of the newly-formed bootleg task force. The task force was charged with enforcing the anti-liquor laws and made routine visits to various establishments.

On a routine inspection in May 1919, the task force suspected illegal liquor activity in the back of a soda parlor in North Denver. After a few weeks of surveillance, the suspicions proved to be correct. Well past the closing hour, the establishment was raided, with Detective Klein in the lead. As the task force rushed through the door of the soda parlor, pandemonium broke out. The few people inside the building scattered when they heard the warning, "Police!" One of the fellows managed to escape out the back door. Detective Klein followed in hot pursuit. Klein shouted for the man to stop as he ran after him in the back alley. The man continued to run and Klein fired a warning shot and again shouted for the man to halt. Continuing his pursuit, Klein fell and his drawn gun discharged, hitting his suspect in the back.

The man, who later died, was identified as Jerome Corbetta, a military veteran who had recently returned from service in World War I. While it was never proven he was involved in the illegal liquor activity, a firestorm erupted in the community over his death. Several residents of North Denver waged a campaign demanding Klein be immediately fired. The detective was placed on leave and testified at the coroner's hearing that the gunshot was accidental. He was later exonerated from any wrongdoing in the shooting of Corbetta. However, due to the public outcry, Klein was assigned to another position in the police department, which did not require a firearm.

Shortly after one in the morning of August 29, 1919, Officer Klein returned to his home at 1438 Newton Street, from his overnight shift. As he got out of his car, three shotgun blasts in rapid order shattered the silence of the night. Klein fell to the ground with severe wounds from all three shots. Because he didn't have a gun, he never stood a chance against his assailant. His wife ran screaming from the house to his side but it was too late. Buckshot had ripped into Klein's body. As he lay dying on the cold ground, the *Denver Post* of August 29, 1919, reported that the last words said to his wife were: *"They got me at last, dearie! Call the boys at the station and say 'Goodbye' to the kiddies for me."*

With that, Denver police detective, thirty-four-year-old George

Klein, died from a slug that had passed through his lungs and severed his spinal cord.

The August 29, 1919, morning edition of the *Denver Post* ran the story under the headline:

Detective Klein Killed from Ambush
Body of Officer Riddled by Buckshot

The same issue of the paper ran an editorial on the front page expressing their position in no uncertain terms:

COWARD

In all the putrid category of crime, there is nothing lower, nothing more dastardly than the man-animal would be the better word-who, slinking in the shadows, his own craven body protected by concealment, kills a fellow human being from ambush. But no matter who killed George Klein, that man was a coward.

Despite the best efforts of law enforcement, no arrests were ever made in the brutal murder of the police officer. There were suspicions. They were sure it was related to the bootlegging element that Klein was devoted to fighting against. Yet they weren't sure if it was not also in retaliation for the killing of Jerome Corbetta.

What Colorado's law enforcement also could not have known was that the murder of one of their own was the beginning of a thirteen-year span of crime and violence spawned by greed and power. Bootlegging in Denver and across the state would prove to be quite lucrative for some and deadly for others.

Before the end of Prohibition, thirty-three known murders related to bootlegging, would occur in Denver and throughout Colorado. It would prove to be a decade of violence, crime and murder.

1900 - 1919

Notes to Part III

1. Resolution 962-63. 9th Legislature of Colorado 1893.
2. The bill was signed on March 29, 1897, Colorado State Archives.
3. Governor Alva Adams' annual State of the State message, 1899.
4. The Rocky Mountain News, January 27, 1900.
5. Colorado State Archives also shows he was denied early parole in 1899.
6. See Part II.
7. *The Canon City Times.*
8. Colorado Territorial Prison archives and records. Many writers have incorrectly stated that Reynolds was hung from the same light pole as was Charles Witherill in 1888.
9. *The Canon City Clipper,* February 1, 1901.
10. Colorado Territorial Prison Museum archives.
11. "Dungeon treatment" was also known as "the hole," or solitary confinement.
12. *Denver Times,* January 3, 1902.
13. *Denver Times,* April 16, 1902.
14. ibid.
15. *Denver Times,* June 5, 1902.
16. The Archdiocese of Denver.
17. ibid.
18. *Rocky Mountain News,* December 15, 1901.
19 This large brick home is now a registered Denver landmark.
20. Archdiocese of Colorado, History of Our Lady of Mt. Carmel.
21. ibid.
22. *Rocky Mountain News,* November 20, 1903.
23. *The Denver Post,* November 20, 1903.
24. William Wise scrapbook, Denver Public Library Western History Collection.
25. *The Denver Post,* November 13, 1905.
26. *Denver Catholic Register,* January 30, 1958.
27. Memorial Booklet for Father Leo Heinrichs, Denver Public Library Western History Department.
28. Five Franciscan Martyrs Region, Secular Franciscan Order.
29. *The New York Times,* February 24, 1908.
30. ibid.
31. Denver's Pioneer Academy, and Sister Lilliana Owens, St. Mary's, published in 1940.
32. Owens, St. Mary's.
33. Memorial Booklet for Father Leo Heinrichs, Denver Public Library Western History Department.
34. No relation to Mrs. Gertrude Gibson Patterson.
35. Kreck, *Murder at the Brown Palace,* pg. 5.
36. Halliday, Brett, *Denver Murders,* pg.86.
37. Thereafter, Isabel's life was a downward spiral. She became addicted to morphine and opium and died in the charity ward of the Metropolitan Hospital in New York City on March 28, 1917. She was thirty-seven years old.
38. *Denver Murders,* Gertrude Gibson Patterson, by Frances Wayne.
39. Wayne, *Denver Murders.*
40. ibid.
41. ibid.
42. ibid.
43. ibid.
44. ibid.
45. ibid.
46. ibid.
47. ibid.
48. ibid.
49. ibid.

50. *The Denver Post*, December 1, 1911.
51. *The Denver Post*, December 2, 1911.
52. A reflective piece by Bob Ewegen, printed in the November 29, 2003 issue of the *Denver Post*.
53. *The Rocky Mountain News*, November 10, 1912.
54. *The Denver Post*, December 9, 1910.
55. State of Colorado, Division of Vital Statistics. Marriage Record #37166.
56. Noel, *The City and the Saloon*, pg. 109.

Part IV

1920 - 1939

The era of the 1920s in America is legendary for its speakeasies and backwoods stills, mobsters and gang killings. This was the Prohibition Era, when the newly-adopted Eighteenth Amendment to the United States Constitution prohibited the manufacture, transportation and/or sale of alcohol and was the law of the land from January 16, 1920 through December 5, 1933. The amendment, ratified by Congress on January 16, 1919, read in part:

> *After one year from the ratification of this article the manufacture, the sale, or transportation of intoxicating liquors within, the importation thereof into, or the exportation thereof from the United States and all territory subject to the jurisdiction thereof for beverage purposes is hereby prohibited.*

The majority of Americans were not about to give up their fondness for alcohol and merriment. Thus, the banishment of alcohol created an underworld network to supply the demand, despite the law. And despite the law, the demand created lawlessness, greed, and a massive crime wave across the country that spawned the likes of Al Capone, Lucky Luciano, Bugsy Moran, and the Gambino crime mob.

Denver's population soared past 260,000 in the 1920s. Denver was perhaps more chaotic than other large cities at that time because local politics had previously been tightly controlled by Mayor Robert W. Speer. After his death there seemed to be no one in charge. Historian Lyle Dorsett states that Mayor Speer had always run the city efficiently and profitably for everyone in Denver, and after his demise, business leaders were stunned when, on August 5, 1920, a violent mob destroyed the Tramway Company streetcars manned by armed strikebreakers and followed that by occupying the *Denver Post* building.[1]

The 1920s are remembered for flagrant flaunting of the new Prohibition law, but there were other social disruptions after World War I. Three respected Colorado historians lament in their textbook that "The emphasis of the age [the Twenties] was derived from attention to material gain and personal well-being."[2] When the war ended, discharged servicemen joined displaced miners and agricultural workers to glut the labor market, while foreign competition increased and foreign workers flooded our land, further disenfranchising working men.

Adding to the chaos in Denver was the eradication of its underworld kingpin. The Lou Blonger gang had controlled vice in Denver for twenty years after the beginning of the twentieth century before a huge raid in 1922 caught thirty-three gang members. That raid was engineered when the crusading District Attorney Philip Van Cise was elected. He had publicly stated his top priority was to stop the Blonger gang and he did just that in one well-planned move, trapping not only the thirty-three gang members but Blonger himself. The philosophical Van Cise knew that he hadn't ended organized crime. He predicted in his biographical book that:

> *Fighting the underworld is like fighting a forest fire. Let a small or un-co-ordinated* [sic] *force attack a huge blaze, it stops it in one place only to have it break out on a score of fronts. Fighting the underworld is a local problem, a State problem, a national problem. Fighting the underworld* [is] *the problem of Society.*[3]

In the roiling cauldron of the 1920s, the Ku Klux Klan's promise of law and order was appealing to men across America and particularly in Colorado's capital city. Colorado welcomed the Klan when they arrived here in 1921 and the white-hooded organization gained a strong foothold in the mid-1920s. Under Grand Ruler Dr. John Galen Locke of Denver, the Klan rose rapidly. Beginning in 1924, Clarence J. Morley was elected governor; Rice Means, U.S. senator; and Benjamin Stapleton, Denver mayor. The Klan controlled the new Colorado House of Representatives also, but as quickly as the Klan rose to power in Colorado, it fell. When Grand Dragon Locke resigned in the summer of 1925, the Klan era in Colorado politics thankfully ended.

Although the Klan was virulently anti-foreign and anti-Catholic, as well as anti-black and anti-Jewish, Clyde Smaldone always maintained he operated more or less openly beside the Klan in the 1920s and they never bothered the Smaldone brothers.[4]

With the new federal prohibition law now in full force, the state received additional help in enforcing the liquor ban, as well as fighting the crime the very law created. Federal Prohibition director E. H. McClenahan was brought in to oversee the enforcement in Colorado. Yet even with the additional aid of the federal government, the crime and the murders continued. The following example is not only indicative of the rising crime rate, but illustrates the brazen act of cold-blooded murder.

Denver police patrolman Richard Rose joined the force in 1921 specifically to make a difference and fight the crime element he saw permeating his city.[5] As a street patrolman, his beat was the North Denver area bordering West 38th Avenue and Kalamath Street. After a morning coffee break, on October 21, 1922, Rose made his routine stop at the police call box at the corner of West 38th Avenue and Lipan Street. As he was placing the call, a sudden barrage of gunfire erupted. Patrolman Rose was dead before he hit the ground. He was thirty-two years old. The autopsy report revealed twenty-one gun shots to his body, all at point-blank range. Eyewitnesses later reported the shots came from a dark-colored Ford vehicle parked nearby. His murderers were never apprehended. Investigators were confident that the murder was gang related, as it was an obvious "hit."

However, the crime wave in the city of Denver began to skyrocket nearly out of control. The criminal acts of bootlegging, and the smuggling of illegal alcohol, spawned more criminals, more crime and more murder.

* * *

Jealously Turns to Murder
Affair of the Heart

The people of Denver welcomed the 1920s with optimism. It was a gay time for those of wealth and opportunity. After all, it was the beginning of the fabulous "Roaring Twenties." For those who could afford it, life was grand, filled with merriment and social parties.

While the newspapers covered the social parties, charity events and otherwise positive aspects of society in the new decade, crime and even murder were often underreported by the press.

The New Year celebrations were a distant memory on the cold morning of February 23, 1920, when gunshots rang out at the Waldorf Hotel, 1757 Stout Street, in downtown Denver. When the Denver police arrived at the hotel and entered room 8, the scene was unusual to say the least. And when the local reporters barged into the room with their own set of questions, the murder scene became one of confusion and chaos.

Charles T. Brown, a brakeman for the Union Pacific Railroad, lived in room 8, at the Waldorf Hotel. The hotel manager, Mrs. Williamson, assumed that the lady living with Brown was his wife. That is, until the murder in room 8 of her hotel.

It was a strange scene when the young lady opened the door of room 8 to allow Mrs. Williamson and the police into the room. Just inside the room, not far from the door entrance, lay the corpse of a man, face up. At the finger tips of his cold right hand rested a pearl-handed Colt single-action revolver.

Sitting up in the bed, pillow behind his head and the bed covers up to waist, was a young man, with a Colt single-action revolver laying near his right hand.

Denver police detective Frank McCabe addressed the man lying in the bed, first inquiring as to his identity, and then asking for the events leading up to the dead man on the floor. In a calm manner, Brown replied: *"He came here to kill me. He went to pull his gun and I just got him first. That's all there is to it."*[6]

Then, investigators were stunned when the woman they presumed to be Mrs. Brown, suddenly rushed to the dead man, crying out, "Oh, my poor dead husband."[7]

This revelation brought a whole new set of questions by both the

A night scene on Denver's Curtis Street, circa 1910. Notice the trolley rails in the center of the street.

police detectives and the reporters. As the woman did her best to answer the questions, Detective McCabe made his way around the room, studying the scene and gathering evidence.

As he carefully examined the Colt revolver laying on the bed, he noticed that the cylinder contained only two of the six bullets. He addressed Mr. Brown with a single question, "How many times did you shoot?" Brown replied that he wasn't sure, but that it was more than once.

At this point, McCabe advised Brown of his rights under the law and placed him under arrest for murder. The reporters were stunned. All agreed it looked like a clear-cut case of self defense.

The coroner arrived to remove the body and the police removed Brown and the woman, for good measure, to new accommodations at the city jail.

Formally booked into jail were the accused murderer, Charles T. Brown, and Jessie Rodgers who had identified the deceased man as Edward Bell Rodgers, her estranged husband. During the interrogation sessions conducted by Detective McCabe, a sordid tale of domestic abuse, jealousy and good old-fashioned chivalry slowly emerged.

Mrs. Rodgers eventually got her story out through many tears and sobs, as a patient McCabe took it all down in his notes, asking an occasional question or two. During her married life, she claimed Mr. Rodgers often beat her and threatened to kill her on many occasions. She said she knew he had a gun, but never actually saw it. She said that finally she left him and their home in Green River, Wyoming, and came to Denver. She said that happened two years previous to the shooting at the Waldorf Hotel. She said shortly after that, she met Brown.

In questioning Brown of the events leading up to the shooting, McCabe learned even more regarding the now-widowed Mrs. Rodgers and her present relationship with Brown. He readily admitted that he and Mrs. Rodgers had been living together at the hotel for quite some time. (Although he said he did not know she was married.) He explained the events of the morning leading up to the shooting in room 8 of the hotel. He said he had taken ill a few days previously and been in bed since. He said that on the morning of the shooting, Jessie (Mrs. Rodgers) had returned to the room from a shopping trip, in an agitated state. Brown related for McCabe the series of events as Jessie had told him.

As she was returning to the hotel, she was confronted by her estranged husband at the corner of 18th and Champa streets. Stunned, Jessie stood in terror as Rodgers told her he knew about her affair with the man in the hotel, as he had been spying on her for months. He had a few more choice words for her and threatened her and Brown, as well. Jessie went on to explain her married status to Brown and that she was afraid to tell him because she thought he would leave her.

Brown told Detective McCabe that as he reassured Jessie of his love and calmed her down, he checked his revolver for ammunition and placed it within reach. McCabe asked about the gun. Brown said he bought it for protection against the thieves and hoboes along the rail lines. Brown continued with his version of the events. He said that shortly after he and Jessie finished lunch, there was a knock on the door. He said Jessie answered the door and in walked her estranged husband. He said Rodgers pushed Jessie aside and addressed him as a "son-of-a-bitch."

Words were exchanged between the two men, Brown said, which boiled down to the fact that Rodgers wanted his wife back. Brown said that was fine, it was up to Jessie, at which point, Jessie began sobbing, saying she would never leave Brown. An infuriated Rodgers allegedly continued shouting at his wife and Brown, calling Jessie foul names. Brown said he tried to reason with Rodgers and asked him to leave. Suddenly Rodgers reached inside his coat. Brown instantly reacted, he said. He pulled his revolver and shot. Brown again asked how many times Brown fired his revolver. Again, Brown replied, "more than once."[8]

This was enough for McCabe to take the case to the district attorney. Brown was indicted on the charge of murder, and the widowed Mrs. Rodgers was charged as an accessory to murder. District Attorney Foley personally prosecuted the case. The defense team, claiming self-defense, was led by Charles E. Friend.

The murder trial began in the criminal court of downtown Denver on May 12, 1920. The prosecution presented a very weak case, claiming that Brown had fired the first shot at Rodgers from under the blanket which covered him in his sick bed. The defense team quickly shot holes through that thin-blanketed assertion, as did a witness who happened to be an acquaintance of the deceased. That witness testified that Rodgers did indeed own a pearl-handled Colt single-action revolver, and was known to have used it.

Brown then took the witness stand in his own defense. His testimony was nearly verbatim as that told to Detective McCabe in the jail cell nearly three months previous. He recounted the events that led to the shooting in a calm clear manner. He explained for the jury the sudden appearance of Rodgers in room 8 of the Waldorf Hotel, and the threats made against him. He then described the scene when Rodgers reached in his coat and Brown fired.

It was a devastating recounting of events as far as the prosecution was concerned. District Attorney Foley tried to poke holes in Brown's testimony, but Brown was steadfast in his answers. After two days of testimony, the case was given to the jury. At 10:30 on the night of May

14, 1920, the jury returned a verdict of "not guilty." Following this verdict, the charges against the widowed Mrs. Rodgers were dropped.

Detective McCabe remained convinced there was more than "self-defense" to the events of that day in room 8 of the Waldorf Hotel. His hunch may have been right, as the trial transcripts mysteriously disappeared from the Colorado District Court records shortly after the trial.[9]

Gangland Shootout
Dog Day Afternoon

On a cold crisp December day in 1922, a classic 1920s gangster-style robbery was carried out in broad daylight on the streets of Denver. Although well planned and the timing was perfect, it would end in murder. Newspaper accounts, as well as many historians, dubbed the incident the "Great Mint Robbery."

With vast amounts of gold pouring from the Colorado Rockies during the gold rush of the early 1860s, the bustling new town of Denver City needed the services of a reputable assayer, not to mention a trusted bank. Brothers Austin M. and Milton E. Clark soon arrived to provide those needs and more. Arriving from Leavenworth, Kansas, in January 1860, the Clark brothers' reputation as honorable bankers was well received. The brothers, along with partner Emanuel H. Gruber, were given the deeds to three town lots, for six hundred dollars, by the Denver Town Company on January 18, 1860.[10] The partners erected a building, at the southwest corner of "G" and McGaa streets, the corner later known as Sixteenth and Market streets. The two-story building was one of the first brick structures in the new town. With a wide sign on the top which read "Bank & Mint," Clark, Gruber & Company opened for business on July 10, 1860. Business was so brisk that George T. Clark (no relation) soon joined in partnership. When the Territory of Colorado was created on February 26, 1861, George T. Clark was appointed Treasurer of the Territory by Governor William Gilpin. In 1863 he was appointed as Treasurer of the newly-created Arapahoe County and the City of Denver.[11]

The U.S. government purchased the Clark, Gruber & Company banking and minting establishment in 1863 for the stated reason of producing a standard value of coin, although rumors persisted that the government was unhappy, even jealous, of the company because the private mint's coins contained more gold and therefore were more prized than the government's coinage. With the purchase of the private facility, the federal government was able to enter this market.

The new federal mint, operating in the original brick building, became the victim of its first robbery in 1864. It was an inside job. James D. Clarke, age twenty-one, a former accountant for the *Rocky Mountain News,* gained a position as pay clerk at the Denver Mint, on December 30, 1863. Through his trusted position, Clarke managed to embezzle over $37,000 in gold and treasury notes. The theft was noticed on February 13, 1864. The *Rocky Mountain News* reported the event as:

> One of the most serious, strange events that have [has] occured [sic] in in our country's history. The little bookkeeper [is] galloping into the grim abyss of infamy eternal.[12]

Clarke escaped on his newly-purchased horse, but the poor beast was greatly overburdened carrying the man and the gold bars. Six days later Clarke was captured on foot south of Colorado Springs, already short $4,419.90 of the stolen amount. Clarke was brought back to Denver and incarcerated in the Denver jail but soon escaped. Clarke was quickly apprehended, tried and convicted of theft. Clarke was then ordered by the People's Court to leave Colorado Territory.[13]

In 1904, the Mint moved to the impressive building, built by the federal government, on West Colfax Avenue.[14] This new facility also was robbed. Again, it, was an inside job.

A Mint employee, Orville Harrington had a wooden leg. One evening, in 1921, at the end of Harrington's shift, a few of his fellow employees realized several gold bars were missing. They immediately notified the authorities who then followed Harrington home. After questioning Harrington, Denver detectives, led by Rowland Goddard, discovered Harrington had buried forty gold bars in his back yard and another fifty in his basement. For decades the rumor has persisted that Harrington smuggled out the gold bars in his wooden leg. Harrington was convicted of larceny and sentenced to the Colorado State Penitentiary. His wife, Lydia, dutifully stood by his side while he served his sentence and was overjoyed when he was paroled after three years, but the cad left her and their children stranded and headed for Florida.[15]

Less than a year later, on December 18, 1922, another robbery took place at the Mint. While the heist took place outside the walls of building, this too would eventually prove to be an inside job. Tragically, in this robbery, a brave veteran of the Denver Police Department, Charles T. Linton, was killed.

At approximately 10:30 a.m., an armored Federal Reserve truck pulled up to the front entrance of the Denver Mint, as scheduled, for the transfer of $200,000 — all in five dollar bills — to the Federal Reserve branch bank in Denver. Just as two guards were carrying the money from the mint building to the unlocked wire cage of the armored car, a Buick touring car roared to a stop close by and a voice called out, "Hands up."

Four men, wearing kerchiefs around their faces, jumped from the car with guns drawn, demanding the guards turn over the money. In his hurry to draw his revolver, one guard lost his weapon and ducked behind a parked car. The second guard, Charles T. Linton, a veteran cop of thirty years, heroically attempted to lock the cage door. Although the 64-year-old officer was shot and mortally wounded, he returned fire as he fell.

Linton had captured notice once before in the press. On May 18, 1882, Deputies Charles Linton and Barney Cutler had arrested the notorious John Henry "Doc" Holliday on an Arizona warrant for the murder of Frank Stillwell. This incident was just seven months after the famous OK Corral shoot-out involving the Earp Brothers, and history would eventually finger Wyatt Earp as the killer of Stillwell. But the arrest made the two deputies famous in Colorado. At the time of the arrest, Linton was an Arapahoe County deputy, assigned to the city of Denver. A friend of Wyatt Earp's, Bat Masterson, famed lawman, then serving as city marshal in Trinidad, filed a fictitious gambling charge against Holliday. Masterson then traveled to Denver to take charge of his "prisoner." Eventually all charges were dropped. Linton remained a deputy for the city and county of Denver after the new entity was created. Linton served in that capacity for twenty-six years before changing jobs, becoming a guard for the Federal Reserve.

As news of the robbery and murder of a guard reached the

Denver Public Library, Western History Department
The Denver Mint crime scene where Denver police officer Charles T. Linton was killed in the line of duty.

newsroom of the *Rocky Mountain News*, reporter Lee Casey rushed to the scene. Casey later wrote of what he saw when he arrived:

> *On the lawn in front of the mint was the body of a guard, killed either by a stray shot by the infantry on his side or by a bullet from the enemy. Nobody ever found out which.* [16]

As the veteran officer lay on the ground, mortally wounded, the masked bandits carried on with their heist. While one bandit tossed packets of money into the touring car, the other three blasted the building entrance as two additional Mint guards fired back and a third set off an alarm inside. Joseph Olson, the Federal Reserve Bank cashier, was caught in the crossfire but managed to scramble into the building where he was seized by guards who thought he was one of the robbers.

The whole episode played out in ninety seconds. It was clear that one bandit was hit because he dropped his shotgun and was seen climbing very slowly back into the getaway car. A second outlaw grabbed packets totaling $100,000 while his hand dripped blood. The Buick touring car then sped off heading east on Colfax Avenue. Within a half-block of the Mint, however, the getaway driver sideswiped a car, forcing it into a fire hydrant which broke and created a geyser of water, further confusing the scene. The robbers continued speeding east and disappeared. Chief Rugg Williams of the Denver police ordered an intensive search for the car, and all hospitals and doctors' offices were checked for treatment of gunshot victims, to no avail.

The following day, the December 19, 1922, issue of the *Rocky Mountain News* ran a large print headline on the front page:

ALL CLEWS FAIL IN $200,000 MINT HOLDUP
  Outlaws cover up trail in dash for open country with fortune in plunder.
  Bloody fingerprints on stock of shotgun have no duplicates in records of the Police Department.

Another sidebar article reported the actions of local and federal officers:

While federal and county officers watched all roads throughout Colorado and neighboring states and officers of the law were sharpening their wits in effort to checkmate the fugitives, the four bandits who robbed a United States mint at 10:30 o'clock yesterday morning and killed Charles T. Linton, a guard, were still at liberty late last night, and the searchers frankly admitted that they were without clews.

According to the *Rocky Mountain News* report of the incident, over one hundred shots had been exchanged. Robert Grant, Superintendent of the Denver Mint, was quoted, saying:

"I heard a shot, then several. Then the general alarm going in the mint. Every man picked up a rifle and rushed to the door. I understand that the bandit car drove up just as our men had re-entered the mint. It was just nicely timed and the bandits evidently had followed the bank truck from Arapahoe street."

As reporters continued to press with questions. Three days after the heinous act, the staunch Superintendent of the Denver Mint, Robert Grant was quoted in the *Rocky Mountain News* of December 21, 1922:

"The fact that Federal Reserve messengers and guards were robbed of $200,000 in the street in front of the United States Mint in Denver has led to erroneous reports that the mint itself was robbed. United States mints are not robbed. Each is like a fortress and is so heavily guarded that bandits never invade them."

As Denver detectives worked to solve the murder of Linton and apprehend the thieves, photographs of the blood-smeared fingerprints found from a shotgun left at the scene were sent to police departments across the entire country. No matches were found. The Denver Police Department offered a $10,000 reward leading to the apprehension of the criminals. Local newspapers followed suit. The *Rocky Mountain News* and the *Denver Times* joined in advertising a $50 reward.

Meanwhile, Charles T. Linton's funeral was held with several fellow officers in attendance. He was buried with the honors due a veteran officer with thirty-six years of service.

A big break in the case finally occurred in January 1923, when the Buick touring car was found. It was sitting in a garage behind a residence at 1631 Gilpin Street. The double garage was rented to two tenants who didn't know each other or the renter of the house. A plumber rented one side of the garage and became curious about the big car stored in the other side with its curtains drawn and apparently never driven. He reported his suspicion to a policeman he knew and the police came to investigate.

Police detectives discovered one of the criminals dead, frozen stiff in the front seat, just as the bandit had fallen into the front passenger seat on Colfax twenty-seven days before. The corpse had a bullet hole through his heart and another through the left hand. A .45-caliber Colt revolver was in the dead man's hip pocket with all six chambers filled. Three caps and one hat were in the car.

The floor of the black Buick get-away car was covered with revolver shells, and a fully loaded 30-30 Winchester rifle was found on the back seat. Under the cushion was a pump shot gun, also fully loaded. The only money found in the Buick was two dollars in small change, which was in the dead man's pants pocket.

When interviewed by detectives, the tenant of the house could offer no information about the garage renters: when the owner of the property provided police with the name of the renter, it proved to be false.

In an interview given to the *Denver Post* and printed in the January 15, 1923, issue, Chief Williams spoke of the dead man found in the car, theorizing: *"The fellow is an ex-convict. His large hands don't go with his body. He's big and strong, while obviously not of a high mental caliber."*

The investigation continued, with no real leads. For months afterward, and particularly during the Christmas shopping season of 1922, Denver residents refused to use or accept a $5 bill for fear it might be one of the stolen bills.

Rowland Goddard, the detective who had been instrumental in the apprehension of Orville Harrington in the 1904 theft from the Denver Mint, had been working hard on the case. A long-time veteran himself, Goddard took a particular interest in solving the murder of one of his fellow officers.

Goddard felt all along that there was an insider connection, yet through his investigations, he could not find a telephone tap on either the Mint or the Federal Reserve Bank. Of the hundreds of tips given to the police, Goddard found two he considered worth following, and the seasoned investigator's instincts were right. Both concerned couples who had suddenly abandoned their Denver Capitol Hill apartments just prior to the crimes.

One couple left behind a steamer trunk with instructions to deliver it to a sleazy Curtis Street boarding house. Police didn't find either couple at that address but they did find two trunks with names - Sloan and Burns. Both couples had been living suspiciously well with no clear source of income, according to their neighbors. When the trunks were opened, Goddard and the police found snapshots of the Sloans and the Burns. Due to the photographs, the detectives were able to identify the body in the black get-away car as James Sloan, a known St. Paul mobster and triggerman. The detectives then discovered that Burns was wanted in Grand Rapids for bank robbery and murder. They were able to track his auto to a public garage in Denver, stored in the name of a Denver bootlegger named Otto Schulz. Schulz quickly "sang" and identified the "wives" of the men as Omaha prostitutes. Meanwhile some of the stolen $5 bills surfaced in St. Paul.

The next month, February 1923, a break in the case seemed possible. A Cincinnati banker confided he'd been offered the mint money for ninety cents on the dollar. Authorities laid a trap — or so they thought — while the banker haggled with the gang's representative and agreed to accept the money for far less. A meeting was arranged, where $80,000 was bought back for $13,000. The agents planned to move in at a second meeting, where $100,000 would be delivered, but the banker couldn't keep quiet. He bragged to the press about his importance as a go-between and the story was carried on front pages across the country. The banker had his brief taste of fame, but the meeting never happened,

Denver Public Library, Western History Dept.
A photo of the interior of the get-away car from the Mint robbery that ended in murder. The Buick touring car, owned by James S. Sloan, was found with Sloan's body inside.

of course, and the investigation completely stalled. Goddard was assigned to other cases and the murder of his fellow officer, Charles T. Linton, as well as those who committed the the 1922 Denver Mint robbery, remained unsolved.

More than a dozen years passed, when in December 1934, the Mint Robbery was again in the news. The Denver Police Department released the news that the case was solved with no one ever charged.

The police insisted that all the gangsters were accounted for, either dead or in prison for other crimes, but no one was ever charged with the murder or robbery. The police department revealed that two Denver detectives had quietly been working on the crime for the previous two years, and they implicated five men and two women: Harold Burns, the leader, now dead; Frank Farland, also dead; James Sloan, the frozen corpse in the Buick; Jim Franklin, serving a life sentence at Alcatraz for complicity in the kidnapping of Charles Urschel, a millionaire Oklahoma oilman; James Clark, serving a life sentence in Indiana State Penitentiary for a Clinton, Indiana, bank holdup. The two common-law "wives," Margaret Burns and Florence Sloan, had been found shot and burned together in a car near Red Wing, Minnesota, in 1932. There were doubts about the identity of the body identified to be Florence.[17]

Charles T. Linton is listed on the Denver Police Memorial at the Cherokee Street branch of the Denver Police Department.

* * *

When Edward "Little Eddie" Ives fired the bullets that took the life of of Denver police officer Harry Ohle and that of an innocent bystander, as well as injuring another Denver police officer, Robert Evans, a strange set of circumstances was set into motion. The following story of murder born from desperation and jealousy is that which the *Denver Post* phrased as "the tangled skein one bullet started."

A Scorned Woman's Revenge
The Original Fatal Attraction

Farice King hadn't seen her one-time lover in years and was engaged to another man, but when she glimpsed Robert "Bob" Evans again in Denver General Hospital, all her passion came flooding back, followed by vengeance.

Farice was one of nine children raised in Lincoln, Linn County, Kansas, by A. A. and Lucy King. Seven of the nine were boys: Leslie, Harry, Walter, Clyde, Wallace, Floyd and Ray, and the brothers doted on the twins, Clarice and Farice, born in 1892 and next to the youngest. The twins were often thought of as spoiled by relatives. Lucy particularly doted on baby Farice.

In 1912, the year the King family relocated to Denver, twenty-year-old Farice married Bert Hiner, on July 3. The marriage didn't last long, as the two were divorced on October 6, 1914. Farice King Hiner retained custody of their infant daughter.

Two years later Farice King Hiner met Robert "Bob" Evans, a

machinist. After a long courtship, the couple were engaged. During this time, Evans became quite fond of Farice's little girl. In time, the three became inseparable. When the child died, Evans grieved as much as the child's mother did and helped Farice cope with her loss.

When America entered World War I, Bob Evans quit his job, kissed Farice goodbye and joined the United States Navy. While Evans was away fighting the war overseas, Farice pined for him, writing to him nearly every day. She wrote of her love for him in her diary, almost daily, and pasted notes, crumpled yellow letters and photos of the two of them in a scrapbook. Farice treasured the two diamonds Evans had given her and read and reread the several hundred love letters he wrote to her during the war. It was during this time that Farice graduated from nursing school.

Denver Police Museum

Denver police officer Robert K. Evans was shot by Eddie Ives. While recovering in the hospital, he was murdered by a former lover, Farice King.

When the war was over, Farice counted the days until she would be reunited with the love of her life. But when Bob Evans finally came home, it wasn't long before Farice noticed a significant change in his demeanor toward her. Evans joined the Denver police force where the work demanded long hours. Soon, his ardor cooled and the couple's once close relationship suffered. Evans finally broke their engagement in 1922.

Less then a year later, on October 25, 1923, Bob Evans married Lillian Hirzel, a younger woman, and moved to 65 Logan Street.

When Farice King learned of her former fiance's marriage, she maintained an air of indifference to her friends and family. Privately, the scorned woman remained devoted to the man, pasting any print mention of Evans and accounts of her sightings of him in her scrapbook.

In time, Farice did try rebuild her life. Leaving her close-knit family in Denver, she moved to Texas. It wasn't long before Farice was yet again engaged to be married, this time to a young Dallas businessman.

In the summer of 1928, the poor health of Farice's mother and her repeated pleas brought Farice back to Denver. Lucy King, seventy-six years old, was widowed and living with two of her sons on Garfield Street. Farice spent pleasurable hours with her ailing mother. After many shopping trips for new treasures for the wedding trousseau, Farice would gaily lay out her purchases for her mother, who enjoyed sharing in the excitement of her daughter's upcoming wedding.

Finding work while she stayed in Denver was no problem for the bride-to-be, a graduate nurse. Farice was quickly hired at Denver General Hospital. Her skills were in demand on Thursday, November 22, 1928, when a Denver fireman, Lewis Smith, was hospitalized for an operation and needed round-the-clock care.

As luck would have it, the very night she was on duty, caring for Smith, two Denver policeman, Harry Ohle and Bob Evans, were involved in a shoot-out with Edward "Little Eddie" Ives in a rooming house on Curtis Street. Ohle was killed. Evans was shot in the arm and transported to Denver General Hospital. Following his surgery, Evans happened to be moved to a room across the hall from fireman Lewis Smith.

Later that night, Farice happened to check on the patient in the room across the hall from Lewis Smith. She was shocked when she realized it was her one-time lover, Bob Evans. Smith would later reveal that Farice spent hours every night sitting on Evan's bed and whispering with him until morning.

Despite their bedside whispering, Evans apparently intended to return home to his wife and let that be clearly known to Farice. Again scorned, Farice purchased a pistol from a pawnshop on the day before Evans was to be released from the hospital. Later that night, while Farice was on duty at the hospital, she found time to be with Evans.

At 5:40 a.m. on Wednesday, November 28, 1928, the injured fireman, Lewis Smith, woke with a start in his hospital bed when he heard three gunshots. Smith did the only thing that came to mind; he threw his call bell through the room's open doorway. A nurse, who had also heard the shots, logically assumed that whoever fired the gunshots was loose in the hospital. An alert was quickly sounded and the hospital went on a procedural shutdown, causing panic and chaos.

Doctors, nurses and law enforcement officers soon rushed into the room of Robert "Bob" Evans. Evans lay dead in his bed.[18] He had been shot in the head and blood oozing from the mid-section of his body led a doctor to discover a bullet lodged in his side. Not far from the bed lay Farice King. Doctors examined her and found that she too had been shot, the bullet lodging in her breast. Police officers did a preliminary check of the room before allowing the doctors to take the wounded nurse to the operating room. After the officers finished processing the crime scene, the Denver County coroner removed the body of Robert Evans, transporting the corpse to Rogers' Mortuary.

Following surgery to remove the bullet, Farice was taken to a private room in the hospital for care and recuperation. The nurse charged with the care of Farice was her brother Leslie's wife. Denver police detectives desperately wanted to speak with the wounded woman but were not immediately allowed to interview her. Whether this was the policy of Denver General Hospital or was the action of Farice's sister-in-law is not known. Nevertheless, reporters from the local newspapers, descended upon the hospital for any information they could get regarding the murder in the hospital.[19]

Meanwhile, Denver police detectives were hard at work on this murder mystery. During their investigation, detectives discovered what they considered to be a "suicide note" found on Farice King's desktop. The note was addressed to Farice's brother Floyd, who was the funeral director at Rogers' Mortuary. Then the detectives found another note. This one was addressed to the now-deceased Robert Evans. The detectives took the evidence to the Denver District Attorney's office.

Further investigation led to interviews with various members of Farice King's family, who confirmed a previous relationship between Farice and Robert Evans, and the fact that they were once engaged. In interviewing Farice's twin sister, Clarice, she explained, "..all of a sudden, he dropped her, without any reason or explanation, and married his present wife."[20]

The detectives now turned their attention to the manner in which Farice King received her wound, based on the now suspicious "suicide note." Interviewing the surgeon who removed the bullet, the officers were told that the wound was superficial and was in no way life-threatening.

With this information, the detectives now believed that Farice King killed her one-time lover out of revenge and then shot herself to make it look like a suicide attempt. The Denver District Attorney agreed and charged Farice King with first degree murder.

Both the prosecution and defense attorneys agreed that Farice King had murdered Robert Evans. It would be the prosecution's duty to prove "intent" on the part of the defendant.

Farice King, the thirty-eight-year-old spurned nurse sat silent at the defense table during her murder trial. The prosecution presented its case, first offering for the jury the dated receipt from the pawnshop, where the gun was purchased. The date, November 27, 1928, was the day before the defendant committed the murder. Next, they heard the testimony of the surgeon at Denver General Hospital, as well as the statements made by members of Farice King's family. The prosecuting attorneys then produced the blood-stained pajama top Robert Evans was wearing when he was murdered in his hospital bed.

In a riveting scene during the murder trial, Farice King ran across the courtroom to clutch the blood-stained pajama top Evans had worn on his last night on earth. She hugged it, crying "Oh, Bob, my Bob!"

Stunned silence descended upon the courtroom. The unnerved defense attorney gathered his client and did his best to regain his composure.

In summation, the prosecutor offered into evidence the supposed suicide note, written by the defendant. Then they presented for the jury's consideration the note Farice King wrote to Robert Evans before she murdered him, which was read to the jury:

> *Dearest Bob, you belong to me and I cannot go on any longer living without you and you shall not go on. I have waited over 5 years for this chance, and it came. I hope no one else will ever know the real cause for this. Only you and I. Farice*[21]

Given the defendant's emotional outburst earlier in the day, the prosecution rested their case. The day's courtroom drama was covered in all the newspapers, just the sort of sensationalism reporters loved.

The lead defense attorney argued that his client's actions were due to her obsession with Robert Evans, which the attorney called, "love-mania." This was the strategy employed in an effort to sway the jury away from first degree murder and render a verdict of manslaughter.

Principals in Triangle Love c

Fate put Patrolman Robert K. Evans in the same ward in which his former sweetheart, Farice King, was on duty as a nurse, and yesterday the nurse shot the wounded officer to death and then fired a bullet into her own breast.

Above left Mrs. Lillian F. Mrs. Evans to their home a

Denver Police Museum
Newspaper photos of Farice King and Robert K. Evans.
Local newspapers relished covering the case of a woman
who killed the lover who spurned her.

The defense council called very few witnesses on behalf of their client, although her twin sister, Clarice, did serve as a character witness. Before the day was over the defense team had rested their case. Later that afternoon the jury was given the case for deliberation.

It was not a surprise to either side when, early the following morning, the jury informed the judge that they had reached a verdict. The judge summoned all parties to the courtroom. The jury foreman announced the unanimous verdict of "guilty" of first degree murder.

On March 11, 1929, Farice King was sentenced to life imprisonment at the Colorado State Penitentiary at Canon City.

Not long after Robert Evans' murder, it was revealed that he had led somewhat of a double life. When Evans married Lillian Hirzel in October 1923, the marriage license was issued to "John C. Bobzine," Robert Evans' legal name. He also checked on this marriage license that he had never been married before.

However, since Evans was deceased by the time this information came to light, it was never known why he changed his name. Shortly after the death of Robert Evans/John C. Bobzine, a young man named Marion Bobzine, a student at the Capitol City Commercial College in Des Moines, Iowa, came to Denver with interesting information, which was reported in a lengthy interview in the *Rocky Mountain News*. It turned out that Marion was the oldest son of John C. and Emma Bobzine and was born in Gilman, Iowa. He said they were living there when his younger brother, Carl, was born two years later. Marion said his parents divorced when he and his brother were quite young, and had very little contact with their father, particularly after he moved to Denver, in 1915. Marion also told of a visit he had with his father in Denver, in 1927. The meeting, Marion said, was at the police headquarters in the basement of the city hall. It was during this meeting, according to Marion, that his father told him that he had taken out a life insurance policy naming Emma, Carl and Marion as beneficiaries.[22]

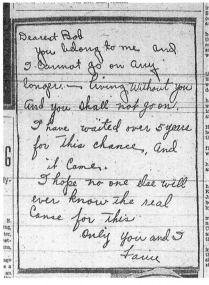

Denver Public Library, Western History Dept.
Local newspapers printed the love letter Farice King wrote after murdering her former lover, Robert Evans, and then shooting herself, in an effort to claim attempted suicide as a defense.

It is obvious that Marion Bobzine arrived in Denver to collect on the insurance policy. It was never known if he succeeded.

In 1931, an underground movement lobbied to have Farice King released from prison. Governor William H. Adams refused to grant clemency despite the *Denver Post* presenting him with a petition signed by 15,000 Coloradans. But the movement continued, aided by the *Post*.

Two years later, the *Denver Post* pressured Edwin C. Johnson, the newly-elected governor, through a series of editorials. Eventually,

Governor Johnson caved under the pressure. In 1934 he granted clemency to Farice King.

The final chapter of the sordid lover's tale which ended in murder was written on Valentines Day, of all days, in the pages of the *Rocky Mountain News*. The article described Farice King as the *"woman who had dedicated her training as a nurse to become an angel of mercy in the state penitentiary."*[23]

The Ultimate Wicked Stepmother
Mommy Dearest

The victim was a pretty young girl who attended parochial school. Her father was a Denver police detective with an unblemished career. The brutal methods the Denver Police Department used for five days to force a confession from the accused would result in a split decision when the murder case was appealed before the Colorado Supreme Court.

Leo O'Loughlin, a Denver police detective, married Pearl Millican in January 1928. He had a ten-year-old daughter, Leona, and Pearl had an eight-year-old son, Douglas. The melded family, along with Leo's brother, Frank, resided in Leo's house at 2320 Tremont Street. It was not a happy situation. The couple separated three times in the twenty months they had been married.

Pearl prepared all meals served in her home and on the evening of Tuesday, October 14, 1930, she served lamb chops, potatoes and rice. Leo later testified that, "When Douglas asked for rice, she told him no, he couldn't have any."[24] Leo had two helpings and Pearl entreated Leona to eat at least one tablespoonful. After dinner Leo returned to his office at the Central Headquarters of the Denver Detective Bureau. He had no idea he would never see his daughter, Leona, alive again.

About ten o'clock. that evening, Pearl appeared at the home of a friend, Mrs. Ethel Sparr, with a story about taking another friend, June Sorensen, to a doctor earlier, and later still she picked up Leo from work; they arrived home around midnight.

The following morning Leo O'Loughlin left for work promptly at 7 a.m., as was his routine. However, he returned home about 10:30 a.m., violently ill. Pearl then informed him that Leona was not in the home when she went to gather the children for school earlier that morning. Despite his ill condition, O'Loughlin called his partner, Detective Clarence Jones, asking him to put out a "missing persons" alert. Assured that the detective would handle the situation, O'Loughlin made an attempt to leave his home to assist, but collapsed to the floor in pain. Soon Leo's condition grew worse and he was confined to bed. With no improvement, two days later, on Friday, October 17, he was taken to St. Joseph's Hospital.

That same day Leo O'Loughlin was admitted to the hospital, a grocer on Denver's west side, William McLeod, discovered little Leona's body in Berkeley Lake. An ambulance, fire truck and Denver police squad cars raced to the scene. Captain Albert T. Clark of the Denver policewatched as the body, just a few feet from the shore, was retrieved from the lake. There was severe trauma to the girl's head, and by the clothing, a school uniform, Captain Clark was sure that the body was the daughter of his police officer, Leo O'Loughlin.

As the ambulance left the scene with the corpse of little Leona O'Loughlin, Clark ordered the county coroner, George Bostwick, to perform an autopsy. Detectives at the scene conducted a thorough search of the area for clues leading to how the little girl ended up in the lake. There were no tire tracks, the grassy shores appeared undisturbed, and no weapon. Chief investigator for the Denver District Attorney's Office, Ray Humphreys, later wrote:

> On the hunch that the lake itself might give up an answer or two, we sought to drain it. But the lake, we found, was fed by such large natural springs that the level was maintained, no matter how rapidly the water was taken out. So that plan was abandoned. We dragged the lake thoroughly, however. We found nothing. We thought the weapon that had been used to beat Leona about the head might be there. But the lake was large, deep, and bottomed with feet of mud and our hooks retrieved nothing we considered of importance.[25]

Back at police headquarters, Captain Clark's intuitive nature turned toward Mrs. Pearl O'Loughlin. Clark phoned Mrs. O'Loughlin, asking her to come to the police station. When Clark informed her that Leona had been found, his suspicions were greatly enhanced when Mrs. O'Loughlin replied, "Oh. Is she dead?" Clark answered in the affirmative to which the stepmother's only reply was, "Poor little dear."[26] Then Clark asked the same questions he had asked the morning the child was reported missing. Pearl O'Loughlin's answers were the same.

Denver papers rushed to report the news of the mysterious death of a local ten-year-old girl. Tender stories ran on the front pages of the *Denver Post* about the grieving of Pat, the Pekingese puppy, who would allow only Leona to feed and reprimand him, and heart-wrenching photos pictured the "orphaned" dolls left behind in the child's room.[27]

Not only were Denver citizens concerned, the entire state seemed to be captivated with the mystery surrounding the death of the young girl.

Meanwhile, Denver County Coroner Bostwick, along with Doctor B. B, Jaffa, manager of health, brought the autopsy report to Captain Clark. The autopsy revealed two scalp wounds, causing a concussion. It was their belief that Leona O'Loughlin was alive when she was thrown into the lake and died by drowning. A chemical analysis of the contents found in the stomach of the deceased revealed ground glass. The autopsy report included the written findings of Doctor Frances McConnell, expert toxicologist at Denver General Hospital. Dr. McConnell's findings indicated that the crushed glass, approximately a teaspoon and a half, had been ingested with her final meal. Based on the damage the crushed glass had caused and the remains of the food in her stomach, Dr. McConnell placed the time of death within two or three hours after the child's final meal. Finally, the report concluded that Leona O'Loughlin had first ingested the crushed glass, was later beaten, and then thrown into the lake.

With this stunning revelation, Captain Clark rushed to St. Joseph's Hospital. He asked the doctors caring for Leo O'Loughlin to pump the officer's stomach. After an agonizing wait, the doctors finally confirmed what the captain had suspected; crushed glass was found in his stomach.

Captain Clark asked for a search warrant and sent a squad car the O'Loughlin home. A search of the home produced nothing. However, in searching the family automobile, a blood smear was detected on the exterior. Inside the trunk, a tire iron with dark stains was found. Lab results would conclude the stain to be blood.

Captain Clark, who had informed Leo O'Loughlin of the death of his daughter, made regular visits to the hospital, keeping the man informed of the investigation. When Clark told O'Loughlin of the blood-stained tire iron, O'Loughlin insisted that another search be conducted. Ray Humphreys, chief investigator for the Denver District Attorney's Office, later wrote:

> *Under orders of District Attorney Wettengel, I took a squad of investigators to the O'Loughlin home. Detective O'Loughlin, from his sick bed [said] 'Tear the house down, if necessary.' In the kitchen, notably on the sink board and under the sink, under the floor, we found minute, shiny crystals. We gathered them up, one by one, with tweezers. We got a quarter of a teaspoonful. We surmised that these bits of glass — if they were glass, had been dropped while certain food or foods, under preparation in the O'Loughlin kitchen, had been sprinkled with the particles. In the basement, from the bottom of a washing machine, near which hung a pair of Pearl's stockings, we took a quantity of fine sand.[29]*

Detective Leo O'Loughlin was noticeably shocked when informed of the findings in his home. After some thought and reflection, he told his partners that he remembered that Pearl had done a load of wash the morning that she told him Leona was missing. O'Loughlin thought it was unusual as Pearl always did the laundry on Saturdays. Due to the concern over his missing daughter, and the onset of his severe illness, O'Loughlin didn't think to mention it at the time. Humphreys continued his account:

> *The laboratory confirmed our discoveries. The stuff we found in the sink and on the floor in the O'Loughlin kitchen was ground glass. And the silt we had taken from the washing machine, the experts said, was of the same type of sandy material that bordered Berkeley Lake. We concluded the sand had come from the stockings hung near by and that Pearl had been around Berkeley Lake.[30]*

Mrs. Pearl O'Loughlin was again brought into the Denver Police Department headquarters, this time for serious interrogation. Her accounts of events leading up to Leona's disappearance didn't change.

The night before she had visited her hairdresser. Leona was in bed. When asked about ground glass particles found in her home, Pearl replied she knew nothing of it. Asked about the blood on the tire iron found in her car, Pearl again replied she knew nothing of it. Despite her denials, Captain Clark held Pearl O'Loughlin on suspicion of murder. Denver District Attorney Earl Wettengel reviewed the evidence found at the O'Loughlin home as well as the autopsy and toxicology reports, and Pearl O'Loughlin's statements. Wettengel charged Pearl O'Loughlin with murder.

When arrested for the murder of her stepdaughter, Pearl exclaimed, "Why would I want to kill poor little Leona?"

The arrest of Pearl O'Loughlin caused a frenzy in the Denver media. Many of the local reporters and even some of the detectives thought she was innocent and refused to talk because she was shielding someone else. The two leading newspapers in Denver, the *Rocky Mountain News* and the *Denver Post,* had a field day with the case of "The Smiling Stepmother," as they called her.

The Denver Police Department quickly came under fire as public sentiment swelled in favor of the pretty red-headed stepmother whose picture appeared in all the local newspapers.

Detectives working the case, confident in their work, continued in an effort to discover anything they may have missed. Ray Humphreys later described the ongoing investigation:

> *So we started back over the murder trail, to try to find an answer as to why she would kill* [Leona,] *when the answer walked in on us! He was a kindly faced, quiet old gentleman from Fort Collins, Colorado. He was the father of of Detective Leo O'Loughlin, and the grandfather of Leona. He lived in Fort Collins for many years. He came in, volunteering an amazing story.*[31]

Denver District Attorney Earl Wettengel asked Captain Clark to sit in on the meeting with Dennis O'Loughlin. Humphreys, continuing with his account, recalled the conversation as O'Loughlin spoke:

> *Since I learned they had found ground glass in Leo's stomach, and in the poor little kid's body, I've been thinking hard. On Sunday, August twenty-fourth, Leo drove up to visit*

me, with his wife, Pearl, and Leona. My wife has been dead about twenty-five years.

Well, Leo and the folks came up. And there were some other people there. The women got the meal. I didn't feel like eating. But later that day, after everybody left, I went to the sugar bowl. Now I have a habit of eating sugar just like some folks eat candy. The family all knows that. I took two or three spoonfuls and I thought someone had put some sand in my sugar. I sat down to think about it. Then I looked in the sugar bowl again and there seemed to be about two ounces of sugar there. I took some out in a spoon and dissolved it in a cup of water. Some of it didn't dissolve and when I looked at this closely I saw it was glass — grounded up — not sand![32]

Captain Clark immediately dispatched two officers to Fort Collins to retrieve Dennis O'Loughlin's sugar bowl. Chemists in a Denver lab later confirmed O'Loughlin's discovery; traces of crushed glass were indeed present in his sugar bowl.

The local newspapers had trumpeted each new discovery in the murder case, including this new piece of evidence pointing to Pearl O'Loughlin. Still, several reporters claimed the evidence was merely circumstantial.

Then Denver police officers were again called to the neighborhood of the O'Loughlin home. Two dogs and a cat had died. The pet owners believed the deaths were caused by eating food scraps from the O'Loughlin's garbage. When this latest tidbit in the murder mystery ran in the newspapers, public sentiment toward Pearl O'Loughlin soured.

Meanwhile, Leo O'Loughlin, released from the hospital on October 21, immediately began plans for little Leona's funeral and burial.

Knowing that Leona's corpse would not remain long in the city morgue, Captain Clark tried a different tack to get his only suspect to crack. Clark and a few officers took Pearl to the city morgue for a last look at her stepdaughter. In the solemn moment, Pearl only stared. Clark asked her if she thought it was time to admit what she had done. Pearl remained silent. When the officers returned Pearl to her jail cell, she had a visitor. It was her husband Leo, who also asked her to tell the truth. Pearl tearfully told her husband she was innocent and walked away.

As the investigators with the District Attorney's office prepared their case for trial, they interviewed and reinterviewed witnesses. Ralph Santorno told the investigators that he was walking home after dark on the evening of October 14, 1930. He said he saw two woman come out of the O'Loughlin home carrying a "large bundle" which they put in the trunk of a car parked at the curb. Then, he said, the two women got into the car and drove away.

District Attorney Wettengel felt that Pearl's hairdresser had a shaky story. He ordered his investigators to reinterview her. Ray Humphreys was one of the investigators assigned. Humphreys later recounted the event:

> *I took an investigator and went out to the woman's home. She readily agreed to accompany us to the D. A.'s office. 'But I've told you all I know,' she insisted. And she stuck to that through some seven hours of questioning in our office. Wettengel, his assistant, Ralph Cummings, and myself took turns with her. But the hairdresser was adamant. Several times I caught her hesitating — but that was all. 'She's not telling the truth,' I told the district attorney, 'but I can't break her,' I said.*
>
> *We considered holding her but decided against it. After all, we had nothing definite against her. And putting a woman in jail just because you think she is lying isn't the wisest public policy. So I sent her home in the care of an investigator.*[33]

Humphreys and the others in the D. A.'s office were quite surprised when the hairdresser, accompanied by her attorney, appeared the following morning. The hairdresser, with her lawyer present, admitted she had lied. Humphreys recounted the admission:

> *Pearl rushed into my home the evening of October 14, greatly excited, in a house dress and without any stockings. She begged me to help her establish an alibi in case anyone wanted to know where she was that night. She told me she had been out with a Mrs. Sorenson and had been to see a certain doctor and that she didn't want Leo to know. So I agreed to help her. And that is why I lied.*[34]

With this new information, Wettengel sent his chief investigator, Ray Humphreys, to find and interview Mrs. Sorenson. Humphreys proved his skills, not only finding the woman, but the doctor as well. Humphreys recounted:

> *We located and grabbed Mrs. Sorenson. She admitted knowing Mrs. O'Loughlin but denied having been with her the evening of October 14 or any other evening when a doctor was visited. We picked up the doctor, who, in turn, proved to us that he hadn't seen either Mrs. Sorenson or Mrs. O'Loughlin that night.*[35]

Now armed with additional information, District Attorney Earl Wettengel went forward with the case, *The State of Colorado vs. Pearl O'Loughlin.* Under the law, the accused was not allowed bail, as Wettengel argued that, "certain statements she has made could be construed as elements of a confession." Those statements made during the various interrogations included, "I could tell you things, but I won't." "I alone am to blame. Why make any more suffer?" "I have done a great wrong. Let me atone for it the best I can."

Pearl's family obtained the services of two of the state's most noted defense attorneys, John M. Keating and J. W. Shireman. The attorneys' first act was to deny any sort of confession by their client. They further stated before the court, that any statement made by the defendant was made under duress. This was a point that would be included in the appeal.

Hundreds of spectators, primarily young women, gathered at the Denver West Side Courthouse for a chance to see the trial, or more importantly, Pearl O'Loughlin. With Judge Henley A. Calvert presiding, the trial began with jury selection on November 28, 1930.

Before the prosecution began its case, the defense attorneys asked the judge to rule against any portion of their client's statements presented by the prosecution that could be construed as a "confession." It was their contention, they told the judge, that any and all of such statements were obtained under duress. Judge H. A. Calvert agreed with the defense team and ruled that such statements would not be permissible by the prosecution.

In his opening statement, District Attorney Wettengel laid out the prosecution's case for the jurors and assured them that the evidence produced in the trial would lead to no other conclusion but that Pearl O'Loughlin was guilty of the murder of her ten year old stepdaughter.

The defense attorneys, in their opening statement, told the jury that Pearl's movements between 7 and 10 p.m. on the night in question would be explained to their satisfaction.

The prosecutors presented expert testimony supported by the bagged evidence they introduced for the jurors. Doctor W. S. Dennis, the city pathologist who had performed the autopsy on little Leona, was the first to appear on the stand. He testified that the child had died from drowning, and that two blows to the head, resulting in concussion, was a contributory cause. Then the prosecutors brought forth the tire iron found in the trunk of the O'Loughlin car with human blood on it. Doctor B. B. Jaffa, manager of health, testified that upon examination of the food content in the stomach of the dead girl, ground glass was found; approximately a half teaspoon. Doctor Frances McConnell, toxicologist, also present, concurred with Dr. Jaffa's testimony.

Next to testify were the detectives who found the multiple articles of evidence at the O'Loughlin home, thereby establishing control of such with no possibility of contamination. The prosecutors produced their next piece of evidence: the small particles of glass found under the sink board.

Leo O'Loughlin's father, Dennis O'Loughlin took the witness stand. He recounted for the jury the same story he had told the D. A. investigators regarding the ground glass in his sugar bowl. The prosecutors then placed the O'Loughlin sugar bowl, with trace particles of ground glass, into evidence. District Attorney Earl Wettengel then offered, for the jury, Pearl's motive: money. Her father-in-law, Dennis O'Loughlin, had a comfortable fortune, which would pass to his two sons if he died. Pearl's husband, Leo, owned his home and if he died, both his half of Dennis' money and Leo's own assets would go to Leo's only child, Leona. But if Leona died, then Pearl would receive her husband's estate. Thus the attempt to kill her father-in-law by placing ground glass in his sugar bowl.

Finally, Leo O'Loughlin took the stand. During his riveting testimony, he recounted the morning he had come home sick, only to learn his only child was missing. He told of how his condition worsened, and during his hospital stay crushed glass was found in his stomach. He told of his horror when evidence of ground glass was found in his home. At one point during his testimony, O'Loughlin looked at his wife, seated at the defense table and shouted, "You're as guilty as hell." O'Loughlin ended his testimony by recounting for the jury his profound grief when he learned the body of his only child had been found.

With that powerful testimony, the prosecution rested their case.

The defense attorneys called four character witnesses, all testifying to the kind nature of Pearl O'Loughlin and of the endearing relationship between the thirty-one year old stepmother and her ten -year-old stepdaughter. Conspicuously absent from the witness list was the hairdresser who originally provided Pearl's alibi for the night of October 14, 1930.

The defense was about to rest their case when Pearl, who had refused to take the stand in her own defense, now asked the judge for permission to speak to the jury, without being sworn by oath and with no cross-examination by the district attorney. This was highly irregular and illegal; Pearl's attorneys, shocked at such a request, remained silent. The prosecution team did not. They immediately voiced their objections to the judge. Judge Calvert denied the defendant's request on obvious legal grounds.

In closing arguments, the prosecution summed up their case and made much of the fact that the defense had failed to clear their client and in fact could not account for their client's three missing hours on the night of the murder. Defense attorney John M. Keating addressed the twelve men with perhaps the only appeal he could offer:

> *Everyone is prejudiced against a stepmother. There has been a mad rush to convict Pearl O'Loughlin. Everyone said: 'That stepmother did it. Get that stepmother.' And the police and everyone else went after the stepmother.*[36]

The judge gave the instructions to the jury. Should the jury find the defendant guilty of murder, the sentence would be life in prison. Colorado law, in 1930, did not allow for the death penalty in the case of murder, unless there was an eyewitness to the murder.

In less than two hours, the all-male jury had unanimously agreed that the defendant was guilty of murder in the first degree. Pearl O'Loughlin, seated at the defense table, was stunned. Her attorneys were not.

On December 10, 1930, Judge Calvert sentenced Pearl O'Loughlin to life imprisonment at hard labor. A reporter for the *Denver Post* was able to ask a question as Pearl left the Denver County Jail, on her way to the Colorado State Penitentiary. Pearl responded, "I haven't begun to fight. Justice will prevail in the end."

In the same issue of the *Denver Post*, Denver District Attorney Earl Wettengel was quoted as saying: *"I believe that the trial was fair from the standpoint of the defendant, and that justice was done."*[37]

Meanwhile, the defense attorneys, prepared their appeal of the guilty verdict. Their primary basis for appeal was that, in their estimation, the incriminating evidence produced by the district attorney was merely circumstantial. Not surprisingly, Judge Henley A. Calvert denied the appeal. Undaunted, the attorneys took their case to the Colorado Supreme Court. Included in this appeal was the accusation of "interrogation harassment." Incidents cited included,"long, grueling hours of questions through several days and nights," while the defendant was incarcerated in the Denver County Jail.[38]

The Colorado State Supreme Court ruled on the case of Pearl O'Loughlin in February 1932. In a 4-3 decision, the original murder trial, resulting in a "guilty" verdict, was upheld.

Incarcerated at the state penitentiary, Pearl was an exemplary prisoner, working first as a laundress, and then as a seamstress. She so impressed Warden Roy Best that he hired her as a housekeeper in his own home. For nearly twenty years, Pearl not only kept the Best home clean, she also cared for many ill members of the family. During that time, she cared for his small nephew, then a niece, next his dying mother-in-law and finally the warden's first wife before her death. Later she cared for his seven-year-old stepdaughter, Suzanne, his second wife's child.[39]

In 1949, nineteen years after her murder conviction, there was a new development in Pearl's case. Legal arguments had been made across the country regarding law enforcement interrogations, commonly known as "Third Degree" methods. In the spring of 1951, United States Attorney General George W. Wickersham, in a lengthy report, used the case of Pearl O'Loughlin as a prime example of police brutality. In his lengthy brief, Wickersham wrote:

Five days after her [Pearl's] arrest, this woman was given her first respite from almost continual grilling. By third-degree methods, a confession had been wrung from her tortured, thirsty lips.[40]

Wickersham's findings were instrumental in forcing the abandonment of third-degree methods throughout the nation. Eugene Cervi asserted in his Cervi's *Rocky Mountain Journal* of May 1951 that the local papers sensationalized the case so much that:

> *...it was impossible for her to have been tried in an atmosphere of calm deliberation..Justice and dignity - oh, them? They went that-away!*[41]

As a result of this change in legal jurisprudence, Governor Walter W. Johnson, in his last official act as governor, commuted the life sentence of Pearl O'Loughlin, in January 1951.

While not immediately free from incarceration, Pearl was now eligible for parole. In June 1951, the Colorado State Parole Board granted her appeal for parole, and granted an exception to their rule that parolees must leave Fremont County. This was in deference to prison warden Roy Best, who intended to retain the services of the now paroled murderess.

Reporters and photographers for the *Denver Post* were at the state prison when Pearl O'Loughlin was released, June 30, 1951. The following day, the paper published a photo of tearful females embracing after hearing the decision — Pearl, Mrs. Best and Suzanne.

Warden Best was quoted as saying, "She is a good woman and she will make good on parole."[42]

Pearl received the twenty-five dollars in cash and one civilian outfit. When she left the prison facility, Pearl went directly to Warden Best's Hitch Rack Ranch, where she continued her employment, caring for the warden's stepdaughter Suzanne. Pearl declared "It would break my heart to leave Suzanne."

After Suzanne no longer needed her 'nanny,' Pearl drifted to California, where she continued caring for the ill and elderly.

Leo O'Loughlin, a broken man after the murder of his daughter at the hand of his wife, tried to go on with his life. It was a sad existence. Leo O'Loughlin died alone in 1956 at the age of sixty-seven, having separated from his third wife. Because the marriage had not been terminated, the third Mrs. O'Loughlin inherited his estate of $2,800.

After all these years, the question as to how and why little Leona O'Loughlin was murdered still lingers.

* * *

During the decade of the 1930s — Colorado's busiest decade for executions — twenty-five hangings took place, seven in 1930 alone. With the hanging of Edward "Little Eddie" Ives, in January 1930, the Colorado legislature voiced their displeasure of the state's method of carrying out the death penalty. It would be a two-year debate.

Double Double Toil & Trouble
"You can't hang a man twice"

Edward Ives was commonly known as Little Eddie Ives, as his stature was the size of a jockey; at most he weighed ninety pounds. As such, "Little" Eddie didn't look intimidating, but his actions, including murder, would prove otherwise.

Little Eddie Ives had a troubled childhood and came from a dysfunctional family. At the age of eight he started his criminal career, crawling through small basement windows and unlocking doors to let his brothers into a targeted house. His brothers would then steal whatever they wanted. His first jail term was at the age of fourteen. Two of his brothers, also involved in crime, had been killed by law enforcement; one by officers in Oregon, and the other by Denver police officers in a fight at the Denver jail.

Most of Eddie Ives' life was spent behind bars in Colorado, Utah and Oregon. His record in Denver alone was lengthy — he had committed over a hundred burglaries in the city without ever carrying a gun.

Ives was just adjusting to normal civilian life after being recently released from prison when he and a compatriot, Henry Hill, held up a drug store in Denver on the night of November 22, 1928. Their timing was poor, and their luck couldn't have been worse.

A few hours after the drug store hold-up, two Denver police officers, Harry Ohle and Robert Evans, were patrolling the vicinity when they spotted a dark-colored sedan slowly driving northeast through the downtown area. The officers suspected the vehicle might be connected to a local group selling illegal liquor and the officers tailed the car.

As the midnight hour approached, the vehicle parked in front of a well-known brothel on Curtis Street, near the Five Points area; the epicenter of the city's black community. The patrol car eased to the curb, parking at a distance, while still being able to witness the activity. The officers observed the driver, an averaged-sized white man, exit the vehicle and enter the house with a gallon jug. Believing the container held bootleg booze, Officers Ohle and Evans stormed into the brothel.

The officers immediately grabbed the man and confiscated the jug of booze. Next they ordered the nearly dozen men and women in the house against the wall with their hands up. With the situation under control, Officer Ohle began a careful search of the house, accompanied by Mrs. Louvenia Reese, the owner of the house of ill-repute.

In a bedroom, Ohle found a man sitting on a bed. Checking him for weapons, Ohle ordered him to join the others in the custody of Officer Evans. Continuing his search of the room, Ohle stooped to look under the bed. Three shots rang out from that hidden space and Ohle fell to the floor, fatally wounded with a bullet to the head and another lodged in the shoulder. The third gunshot hit Louvenia Reese in the chest as she stood in the doorway. The bullet passed through Mrs. Reese and lodged in the right arm of Officer Evans who immediately spun around, thereby dodging a fourth bullet.[43] In the confusing moments following the gunfire the shooter under the bed managed to escape, via the backstairs of the home.

Evans, bleeding profusely from the bullet wound to his left arm, managed to get out of the house and find a phone to call for backup. Within minutes, several patrol cars, as well as an ambulance, were speeding to the Curtis Park dwelling. Mrs. Reese and Officer Evans were rushed to Denver General Hospital.[44]

Meanwhile, on Lawrence Street, just two blocks west of the crime scene, Chief R. F. Reed and Captain Albert Clark of the Denver police ran into a piece of good luck when they were vigorously flagged down by a black man. The man identified himself as Henry Hill, and told the police officers he had information about the shooting on Curtis Street. He said he had witnessed the entire episode.

The officers took the willing Henry Hill to police headquarters for further questioning. Hill said he was the man sitting on the bed, whom Officer Ohle encountered when he entered that bedroom just before the gunfire erupted. He further stated, "It was Eddie Ives who killed that copper."[45] Hill further told the officers he had met Ives in prison, and had recently reconnected with him in Denver. He told the officers he had invited Ives to the Reese house on Curtis Street for a "slug of mule," and Ives had accepted. Thus, the reason, he said, why he and Ives were at the scene of the crime.

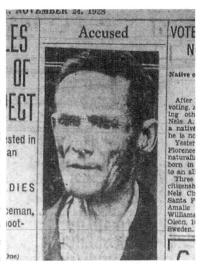

Denver Piblic Library, Western History Dept.

With this information, the officers quickly obtained the long rap sheet of Edward Ives and a previous mug shot, while holding Hill in the Denver County Jail pending charges. Meanwhile officers raced to the hospital to interview Mrs. Reese.

The *Rocky Mountain News* published this photo of Edward "Little" Eddie Ives, accused of murder, following his capture in 1928.

At the hospital, Louvenia Reese was in a grave condition but did manage to identify the mug shot of Ives as the man that Henry Hill had brought to her house. A few hours later, Mrs. Reese died from the result of the gunshot to her chest. The Denver police were now looking for a double murderer.

Back at the police station everyone arrested at the Curtis Street house had been questioned and released, with the exception of the suspected bootlegger that led Officers Ohle and Evans to the house originally. Identified as John Morrissey, the man emphatically denied knowing the man in the mug shot. Nevertheless, Morrissey was booked on charges of violating state and federal prohibition laws.

There were also more questions for Henry Hill. The majority of the Denver police force were in a foul mood, including Officer Ohle's brother and father-in-law, who were also police officers. They wanted answers from Hill. After a grueling interrogation, Hill finally cracked. He told the officers he and Ives had held up a drug store earlier that night and had gone to the Reese house on Curtis Street for entertainment afterward.

The officers worked on the theory that when the police raided the house, Ives must have thought they were after him for the drug store robbery, which would be why Ives hid under the bed. Hill further volunteered that Ives could probably be located at his mother's home. With this tip, finding Eddie Ives was easy — he was in bed in his mother's nearby home.

With a warrant in hand, the Denver police searched Mrs. Ives' home. Finding Eddie Ives in his bed, they also found a cache of weapons and evidence relative to various petty crimes, including burglary tools, an automatic rifle, and a .45 caliber revolver hidden under his pillow. Ives was immediately arrested and taken to the county jail, where he was held pending charges of first degree murder for the deaths of Officer Ohle and Mrs. Louvenia Reese.

Under interrogation, Ives first denied knowing Henry Hill. Then under pressure, in a convoluted explanation, he said the gun found at the Curtis Street house belonged to Hill. The Denver district attorney charged Edward Ives with two counts of first degree murder.

The murder trial of Edward Ives, held in Denver District Court in 1929, was short and swift. He was found guilty of first degree murder for the murders of Officer Harry Ohle and Louvenia Reese, and sentenced to be hanged by the neck until dead.

During his incarceration at the Colorado State Penitentiary at Canon City (inmate #12457) Ives cleverly plotted several postponements to his date with death, such as pretending to be insane before one scheduled hanging. He had been acting strangely for weeks, talking to himself and shouting at insects no one else saw. Moved to solitary confinement, he often dipped his food into the toilet before eating it.

Newspaper reporters traveling to the prison for the "last" interview before the hanging, came away with nothing but endless ramblings from the condemned man. Warden F. E. Crawford and the prosecuting attorney both agreed that the execution should be delayed until after a mental evaluation in Denver. After an extensive examination by psychiatrists, Ives was pronounced as quite sane.

Escorting the prisoner back to the state penitentiary, Warden F. E. Crawford had finally had enough of the constant gibberish from Ives, and told him the act wasn't working anymore. After a long silence,

Ives spoke. In the first coherent words he had spoken in nearly six months, Ives said simply, "For God's sake, give me a cigarette."[46]

Another postponement to Ives' execution resulted when the worst prison riot in Colorado history erupted on October 3, 1929. The prisoners involved in the riot, led by Albert A. Daniels, offered a hammer to Ives to entice him to join the rioters. Ives refused and the men bypassed his jail cell.[47] Eddie sided with the guards during the bloody, murderous riot.[48]

Because of Ives' stand against the rioters, Warden F. E. Crawford appeared before the prison board, as well as Governor William H. Adams, in an effort to commute Ives' sentence to life in prison. The *Rocky Mountain News* of January 9, 1930, reported the story under the headline, "Warden to Make Final Plea for Life of Ives." Evidently the prison warden's plea fell on deaf ears, as the following issue of the *Rocky Mountain News* carried this headline:

Last Hope of Eddie Ives Escaping Noose Vanishes

Ultimately the date of execution was set: January 10, 1930. On that fateful day, the noose was adjusted around Ives' neck and the executioner released the lever. A five-hundred-pound weight slid down a chute, springing the black steel plates. In theory the condemned man would be jerked upward and his neck would be broken by the violent jerk, but Ives was too light for the machinery to work properly.

The hanging gallows used at the Colorado State Penitentiary at the time were complicated contraptions involving high beams, weights, ropes and pulleys. Known as the "twitch-up" method, it was designed to break the neck of the condemned by jerking their body upward, as opposed to the nineteenth century method of the hanged man falling through a trap door.[49]

In "Little" Eddie Ives' case, the hanging rope jumped off the pulley and Ives flew up to the ceiling and dropped back down to the floor. As he lay there, Ives' mind was cleverly devising a way out of his prediciment. He squirmed and thrashed on the floor as the onlookers shrieked, and he announced over and over that he should be freed because, "You can't hang a man twice."

Eddie's pleas were ignored. The executioners made a second attempt and readjusted the weights and the rope. The lever was sprung precisely at 10:36 p.m. This time, the mechanism worked correctly, although it still failed to break Eddie Ives' neck. Witnesses watched in horror for twenty-three agonizing minutes as Ives slowly strangled to death.[50]

At 10:59 p.m., forty-six-year-old Edward Ives was pronounced dead. The two examining physicians determined he died of slow strangulation, not by a broken neck as the law assumed would be the cause of death.

In the days following his horrible death, Eddie's fellow inmates, in sympathy for their friend, took up a collection to purchase one of the few headstones in the prisoner's section of Greenwood Cemetery in Canon City, known as Woodpecker Hill.[51]

The horrific double hanging of Eddie Ives was front-page news in all the local papers. The *Rocky Mountain News* ran this headline the day after the hanging:

Eddie Ives Is Hanged at Canon City Prison:
Killer Goes to Gallows with Prayer on Lips

A second story appeared on the third page of the paper, with the following headline:

Eddie Ives Ends 40 Years of Crime in Three States on
Gallows at Canon City

The reporter concluded his article with this incredible statement, "Ives had spent all but eight of his 46 years doing time in one prison or another, including the penitentiaries of Colorado, Utah and Oregon."

While the debacle of the state's execution was closed to the press, the news of the horror of Ives' death eventually leaked out. It wasn't long before newspapers across the country picked up the Colorado story. Thus, the debate of humane executions gained national attention. "Little" Eddie Ives' "double dates" with death brought passion to those discussions.

The botched double-hanging of Eddie Ives became an embarrassment for the state of Colorado. Proponents of change included several state politicians, as well as F. E. Crawford. As the warden of the Colorado State Penitentiary, Crawford supervised a dozen hangings during his tenure as warden from 1927 to 1931. Crawford was against capital punishment and considered hangings "a form of punishment out of the Middle Ages."[52] Thomas J. Tynan, prison warden from 1909 to 1927, weighed in on the issue, saying in an interview with the *Rocky Mountain News:*

> Colorado has one of the most ghastly hanging machines possible.

Tynan went on to say that, "More than half of the men executed at Canon City have not been hanged at all. They have strangled."

In Colorado, the "twitch-up" execution mechanism never held up with the perfection advertised by the inventors. In his research of capital punishment in Colorado, Professor William M. King recounted that, "in forty of the forty-four instances where this

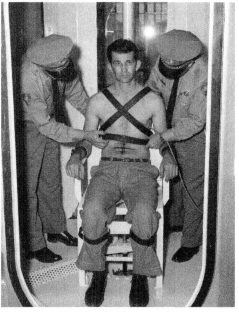

Denver Public Library, Western History Dept.

After the botched hanging of Edward "Little" Eddie Ives, the state of Colorado legally changed executions from hanging to lethal gas.

method was employed in Colorado between 1890 and 1933, death by strangulation was the result; in only four instances did the neck of the felon actually break."[52]

As the debate regarding capital punishment escalated, the Colorado legislature weighed in with their displeasure of the state's method of carrying out the death penalty. The politicians in both the Senate and the House argued back and forth for the next two years. In the meantime, fourteen more hangings in Colorado occurred and, unfortunately, fully half of those men died slowly, by strangulation.

Finally, in March 1933, the Colorado Senate passed a bill abolishing the death penalty by a vote of twenty to twelve. Both leading Denver papers, the *Denver Post* and the *Rocky Mountain News* respectively, carried the story in headline banners:

Death Penalty Bill May Save Doomed Men

Measure to Abolish Death Penalty Is Passed by State Senate and Sent to House

However, the bill later died in the state House of Representatives.[53] That same year, President Franklin D. Roosevelt called for a national end of the death penalty. While this action failed, several states, including Colorado (the second state to do so) did pass legislation formally changing the state's method of execution from "hanging to asphyxiation."[54]

On March 31, 1933 Colorado Governor Edwin C. Johnson signed the bill into law. Again, both papers heralded the news:

Denver Public Library, Western History Dept.
Warden Roy Best, left, shows Governor Thornton various jobs performed by the inmates at the Colorado State Penitentiary.

Colorado Senate Approves Lethal Gas for Executions

Governor Signs Lethal Gas Bill[55]

The new law did not go into effect until the following year. The last man hanged in Colorado was Walter Jones on December 1, 1933.

With Edward Ives' botched double-hanging still fresh in the minds of the state legislators, in May 1933, Warden Roy Best had been asked to procure the best gas chamber system in the country. After several visits across the country, Best turned to the Denver firm of Eaton Metal Products Co. The Colorado State Penitentiary used the three-seat gas chamber, nicknamed "Roy's Penthouse" in honor of Warden Roy Best, until 1955, when the state constructed a new, smaller execution chamber (just one seat) to fit into the remodeling of the prison and perhaps to appease the again growing outcry against capital punishment.

* * *

As the economy continued to weaken during the years of the Great Depression, bootlegging illegal booze became an added source of income for many. Mayor Benjamin Stapleton faced considerable pressure to clean up the illicit activity. He instructed the police force to conduct periodic raids, which occasionally resulted in arrests and the closing of a few speakeasies. Captain Albert T. Clark of the Denver police assured the public that the police department was indeed fighting against the increased crime in the city. In an interview in the January 28, 1931, issue of the *Denver Post*, Clark said:

"It's a fight to the finish. We will permit no liquor markets here, for once they gain a foothold, it is virtually impossible to stamp them out. Denver police are ready for you guntoters. You start anything and police will finish you with machine guns."

The following month, Clark led a raid through North Denver, hitting restaurants, pool halls and soft-drink parlors. Following the raid, several arrests were made, including three members of the notorious gang of the Carlino Brothers. The *Denver Post* covered the raid in their February 23, 1931, issue. Under the headline, "Score of North Denver Pool Halls Closed," Captain Clark was again quoted:

"Close those places and see that they stay closed. If members of these liquor gangs do not have a specific place to congregate, there will be less trouble."

Despite the effort, crime and murder continued. The Denver newspapers, particularly the *Denver Post*, ran articles and editorials against the Stapleton administration, dubbing it the "Do Nothing" administration. The paper seemed to ridicule the mayor at every turn, in one case referring to him as "the most incapable and utterly incompetent and extravagant mayor this city has ever had." As if that wasn't enough, their particular angst seemed to be with Chief of Police Robert F. Reed. Editorials portrayed him as weak on crime and in denial regarding the increase of gang-related crime. They referred to him as "Diamond Dick" for his lavish fashion jewelry, which also happened to be the moniker of a well-known gangster with ties to Al Capone who lived in Colorado's Garfield County at the time. In the May 10, 1931, issue of the *Denver Post*, Reed was mocked in a poem of sorts, the title being:

There Ain't No Crime In Denver

No racketeers in Denver
Where, Denver? Yes, Denver.
That we've heard, and here's why:
Of rackets we have no fear -
We just stuff cotton in our ears,
And silence them in Denver.
Chief Diamond Dick and I

As it turned out, there was more than a ring of truth to the many editorials printed in the *Denver Post*. Again, the paper was the first to report the news that the Denver Police Department had enlisted the assistance of federal law enforcement to help rein in the crime elements that were seemingly out of control. The article appeared in the March 19, 1931, issue under the headline, "Mayor and Reed Rush for U. S. Aid as Public Demands Protection." The article read in part that the Stapleton administration, "openly admitted, for the first time, that a gang situation actually exists here." U. S. Attorney Ralph Carr was sent to Denver to help stem the tide of crime and corruption. Carr would later become governor of Colorado in 1939. As for Mayor Stapleton, a former member of the Ku Klux Klan, the *Denver Post's* ongoing campaign to remove him from office, as well as his ineffective leadership in fighting crime, were undoubtedly the causes for his defeat in his re- election campaign of 1931. Stapleton lost the mayoral election to George D. Begole, the city auditor, by 990 votes. Begole promised to clean up the crime in Denver.

Gangster Violence & Murder
"A bloodbath raged"

Throughout the 1920s much of Denver's crime element controlled not only the city, but much of the state. Various members of the Ku Klux Klan had infiltrated into politics and held local and state-wide office. By the 1930s, during the Great Depression, bootlegging had also reached a new level in criminal activity: murder.

Gangs formed and competition led to such violence that historian Dick Kreck wrote:

The period from 1919 to 1933 was the most violent in modern Colorado history, a bloodbath that raged as mobs in the northern and southern halves of the state fought over the lucrative market.[56]

It was at this critical time in Denver's history that Philip Van Cise, a veteran of World War I, was elected to the office of Denver district attorney, in 1921. Gambling, prostitution and bootlegging flourished in the city's underworld. Politicians and policemen were bought off by the criminal kingpins. During his tenure, Van Cise was responsible for breaking up that crime element in Denver.

Van Cise was fearless. Not only did he refuse a $20,000 campaign contribution from Lou Blonger, Denver's underworld boss, one of his first acts as the new D. A. was to go after Blonger and his "Million-Dollar Bunco Ring." Van Cise later wrote:

As he [Blonger] *went away, I wondered how much of a boob Blonger thought I was.*[57]

Lou Blonger, an overweight elderly man, was shrewd and cunning, as he seemed to have had something on everyone. From street cops to legitimate business owners and from trial judges to politicians, many took payoffs to look the other way. Those who refused were often intimidated into silence. Van Cise used the latest technology, the dictaphone, which was secretly placed in Blonger's office. Van Cise eventually gathered enough evidence to arrest and successfully prosecute Blonger. Len Reamey, alias J. K. Ross, one of Blonger's top men and a known killer, cut a deal with Van Cise and turned against Blonger. In 1922, during Colorado's longest and most expensive trial at that time, Lou Blonger and twenty of his associates were convicted and sent to prison. Next, Van Cise took on the Ku Klux Klan.

With several members of the Klan holding city and state offices, it was a bold step for Van Cise. Governor Clarence J. Morley, elected in 1925, bowed to the Klan pressure, allowing Grand Dragon Dr. John Locke to hold tight control of Morley's politics and his government. Denver's mayor, Benjamin F. Stapleton, was also a Klan supporter. Several bills were introduced in the senate to abolish and recreate state agencies based on Klan motives. Van Cise eventually prosecuted Locke for tax evasion and sent him to prison in 1926. With the conviction of Colorado's leader of the Ku Klux Klan, Van Cise effectively caused the fall of Klan influence in the state, almost as suddenly as it had emerged. The political dominoes soon fell. Governor Morley's personal secretary was indicted for mail fraud, two of Locke's advisors went to prison for embezzlement, and Morley was defeated in the following election. Shortly thereafter, Morley was convicted of mail fraud and served five years at Leavenworth, the only governor of Colorado to be sent to prison.

Following the conviction and imprisonment of Lou Blonger, Giuseppe Joseph "Joe" Roma had successfully taken over the area's crime element, including bootlegging and vice. Gangsters instinctively knew there was big money in the making, transporting

Denver Public Library, Western History Dept. Philip Van Cise was instrumental in cleaning up Denver's gang-related crimes.

and selling of illicit booze after the passage of the Eighteenth Amendment prohibited such action. Therefore, bootlegging was more lucrative than ever in Denver, and Roma intended to corner the market.

Roma set up his bootlegging enterprise inside his grocery store located at 3420 Quivas Street in the Italian neighborhood of North Denver. The Denver Vice Squad quickly discovered that the grocery store was a front for his illegal booze running. In January 1933, Roma and his brother-in-law, Frank Greco, were arrested for operating an illegal alcohol still in Gilpin County. When the two were quickly convicted of the charge, the January 19, 1933, issue of the *Denver Post* ran the particulars under the headline:

Joe Roma Convicted as Liquor King, Claimed to be Grocer

Roma's response to the conviction was also printed in the article: *"This is terrible! This incident will ruin my grocery business."*

Many of the illegal stills were located in Gilpin County, in the mountains west of Denver, where law enforcement was nearly nonexistent, and where bubbling mountain streams reachable only by rough trails made detection difficult and abandoned mines made perfect 'coolers' for booze. Most of the ranchers in the valleys of east Gilpin County lived in harmony with the bootleggers; they appreciated the generous amounts of money the bootleggers left on their doorsteps after the rancher pulled their big car out of a deep mud puddle, and the miners in the southern half of the county depended on the payoffs they received for 'renting' their hidden mine to the bootleggers.[58] The bootleggers therefore thought they had the perfect setup, that is until Joe Roma was busted. Within weeks after the conviction, paying a hefty fine, Roma was back in business.

Roma, although small in stature, barely over five feet tall, was a ruthless gangster. His competitors neither respected him nor feared him. They hated him.

Gang rivalry soon erupted into deadly violence. It was not long before the "bloodbath" Kreck referenced raged in Denver. It would continue for years. Philip Van Cise, by this time out of office, later wrote of his profound disappointment that he was unable to stop the crime element in Denver.

The first death listed was the ambush of the chief of the Bootleg Squad, Detective George Klein, on August 29, 1919, killed on his lawn as he arrived home from a late shift. Of the nearly three dozen bootlegging deaths in Colorado over the next fifteen years, fourteen were in Denver, fifteen in Pueblo, the rest in other Colorado towns. Four of the victims included local policemen and federal agents.

Whether any of these murders were done on the orders of the new Denver crime boss, Joe Roma, is not known. Roma, known as "Little Caesar" both for his ruthlessness as well as his territorial hold in North Denver's Italian section, had joined forces for a time with Pete and Sam Carlino, crime bosses of southern Colorado, based in Pueblo. However, they became rivals following a dispute over territory when the Carlino brothers expanded into Denver.

In an attempt to stem the tide of violence, Roma decided to have a meeting with more than two dozen crime figures, including the Carlino brothers. The meeting, which occurred on the night of January 24, 1931, was held in a back room of his grocery store on Quivas Street. However the meeting was abruptly interrupted before the gangsters had reached any sort of agreement. The Denver Vice Squad broke down the door and raided the building, arresting several of the men present. Some historians believe that the police raid unwittingly, ignited the gang war to higher levels, at least in Denver. However, Joe Roma and the Carlino brothers formed a relationship, at least for a time.

When Sam Carlino was gunned down in the kitchen of his home in North Denver, on May 8, 1931, Roma was questioned by Denver police. Roma provided an alibi. A month later, June 19, 1931, Pete Carlino was arrested on a charge of conspiracy to commit arson. His five thousand dollar bail was posted by none other than Joe Roma on June 23, 1931.

Three months later, on September 13, 1931, the body of Pete Carlino was found near a bridge some twenty miles south of Pueblo. He had three .38 slugs in his body, two in the back and one in the head.

Once again, Roma became law enforcement's number one suspect. Although it was never been known if Roma was behind the murders of the Carlino brothers, he was never arrested for either murder.

What is known is that after the murders, Roma once again became the kingpin of North Denver's crime element. Thus, Roma continued to be hated and his enemy list only grew longer, including the Smaldone brothers of North Denver. It was only a matter of time before his enemies would react.

It happened on Saturday, February 18, 1933. Joe Roma was alone in his comfortable bungalow-style home on 3504 Vallejo Street in a quiet neighborhood in North Denver. Sometime around the noon hour, Joe Roma was shot to death in the living room. He was thirty-eight years old.

When Roma's wife, Nellie, returned home, following a visit with her mother, she discovered her husband slumped in his favorite chair. When she attempted to wake him, she realized he was badly hurt, if not dead. A pool of blood oozed from his body. Nellie Roma pulled him to the floor in an effort to revive him. With no result, she called the police.

While detectives were sent inside the home, other officers surveyed the exterior including doors, windows and the lawn for any signs of evidence of intrusion. Denver law enforcement soon came to a conclusion. Giuseppe Joseph "Joe" Roma was murdered by people he knew. Roma had been shot seven times; six of those bullets were to

Denver Public Library, Western History Department
Pete Carlino (shown) and his brother Sam were both crime partners and enemies
with Joe Roma. After Sam was murdered, some believe by Roma, Pete was arrested
on arson charges.

his head. Blood and brains were sprayed on the wall behind the chair.
Roma must have either been playing his beloved mandolin or holding
it, as it was laying haphazardly, in the chair, with a bullet hole in it.
Next to the chair was a toppled music stand which had held a copy of
"Singer's Complete Mandolin Methods." The detectives found shell
casings near the piano stool on one side of the chair where Nellie
Roma had found him. Shell casings were also found near a chair
located across from where Joe Roma had been shot. This indicated
that Roma was shot in a crossfire. The shell casings were of .38 and
.45 caliber.

The scene of the murder, coupled with no sign of forced entry, led
the police to believe that Roma was killed by men he not only knew,
but felt comfortable with in his home. This theory was reinforced by
Nellie Roma's statement to the officers, which was reported on the
front page of the February 19, 1933, issue of the *Rocky Mountain
News*:

*"No stranger could have got into the house. Joe wouldn't let a
stranger in. I don't know who did it. I don't know of anyone who was
coming to see him, or of anyone expected."*

The front page of that February 19, 1933 issue of the *Rocky*

Mountain News was devoted to articles covering the mob hit. One article described the widow, Nellie Roma:

...the beautiful head with its faultlessly-featured Madonna-face. Her hair is raven black and clusters in waves and curls about her brow, framing her face and emphasizing the clearness of her almond-toned complexion. Her figure is slight and girlish and her eyes black and velvet soft. The youthful widow sobbed, 'I loved him so much, so much.'

As Denver detectives worked the murder case, three names rose to the top of their list of suspects. They were James Spinelli, Eugene Smaldone and Louis Brendisi. The detectives conducted a series of interviews while the funeral of Joe Roma was being planned.

Services for Joe Roma were held on February 23, 1933. It was one of the finest funerals ever conducted in Denver. The *Rocky Mountain News* covered the elaborate affair in their issue of the following day:

The pageantry could rival the splendor attending the burial of gangland kings in Chicago.

The funeral was held in the Roma home on Vallejo Street and in the very room where Joe Roma was murdered. The casket, a $3,000 polished copper beauty, complete with a glass dome, lay in the center of the room. An array of extremely large flower arrangements were placed throughout the room, discreetly hiding the blood-stained walls. Two of these floral displays were courtesy of the Smaldone brothers.

Cars arriving to the house caused traffic jams in the neighborhood. More than two thousand mourners gathered. Because of the small room, Nellie opened her home for an hour before the service was to begin. Small groups of people filed into the room to view the body of Joe Roma through the glass dome. Once the service began at 2 p.m., only family and close friends were in attendance.

Following the funeral, a few of the known mob leaders, including Charley Blanda, Tom "Whiskers" Incerto and Joe "The Ram" Salardino, carried the coffin out of the home to the awaiting hearse. The funeral procession, nearly three blocks long, included two flatbed trucks that transported all the large flower arrangements to the cemetery.

The long stream of vehicles slowly wound their way through North

Joseph "Joe" Roma was murdered in his northwest Denver home. The police believed it was a mob hit job but were unable solve the murder.

Denver, finally arriving at Crown Hill Cemetery. After a short service at the cemetery, where a few people in attendance made appropriate remarks, Joe Roma's body was entombed in the cemetery's Tower of Memories.[59] Although Roma was Catholic, he been divorced from his first wife. Therefore, his body was laid to rest without the blessings of the church.

The following day, the *Rocky Mountain News* continued their coverage of the funeral and burial under the headline, "2,000 Thronged to Burial Services for 'Little Joe'"

Not to be outdone, the *Denver Post* printed an interview with one of the detectives who was working on the Roma murder case. The anonymous detective gave his impression of the now deceased gangster, Joe Roma, which was printed in the February 26, 1933, issue:

"He was just a little shrimp but he might as well have been of Herculean Stature. Those who first saw him laughed at the

idea of him being called a gangster. He looked more like an errand boy for a department store."

Meanwhile, Denver detectives continued their investigation of Roma's murder. Nellie Roma told the detectives that Louis Brendisi and James Spinelli, as well as Eugene "Checkers" Smaldone, all known criminals, had arrived a few hours before she left the house to visit her mother. The three men were brought into police headquarters for extensive questioning. All three provided alibis. The men admitted they were in the Roma home, visiting with Joe, but bid the man goodbye and left shortly after noon, to see a movie on Curtis Street. The three men even produced the ticket stubs. The detectives were never able to shake the men or disprove the alibi.

With no leads as to the murderer, the newspapers ran editorials demanding action. Under a headline which read, "That's That," the *Denver Post* wrote:

Joe Roma's assassination emphasizes that 'Crime Never Pays.' The 'big shot' of today in the gang world is the bullet-riddled target of tomorrow. Greed and envy flourish in gangland. Honor among crooks is an illusion. If they had any honor, they wouldn't be crooks.[60]

The February 26, 1933, issue of the *Rocky Mountain News* editorialized:

A single gangster is a greater peril to a community than all the Socialist and Communist spellbinders.

The obvious gang-style murder of Joe Roma was never solved. Many, including Denver's law enforcement, felt that Roma's death primarily benefited the Smaldone brothers. Denver District Attorney Earl Wettengal thought so. Under the headline, "Denver Gang Leaders Fight For Roma's Place," the December 22, 1933, issue of the *Denver Post* ran an interview with the D. A., where he said as much.

Wettengal was correct in his assessment. The Smaldone brothers rose to absolute control of the Denver gangster faction.

Sixty years after the fact, an elderly and ailing Smaldone brother, Clyde, was asked about the Roma murder by his son, Gene. Caught on tape, Clyde Smaldone, saying he was there, gave his recollection of the events of that day:

Somebody shot him in his house. [The police] *thought we did it because we left the house about two hours before he got shot. Well, they knew we didn't do it, but somebody shot him. It didn't bother me one way or the other. Mobs was always arguing and fighting amongst themselves about the business, and they weren't capable of handling business, to tell you the truth.*[61]

Denver Public Library, Western History Dept.
Clyde Smaldone, along with his brother, Eugene "Checkers," were heavily involved in North Denver's crime operations.

The gang violence continued. The last murder during the nearly fifteen-year period of mob violence, was August "Augie" Marino, on May 5, 1933. Marino had been shot in the neck and legs just five months earlier, in December 1932, and was still walking on crutches. He lingered in the Denver Physicians & Surgeons Hospital for weeks and had only recently been released. Marino had somehow been duped into taking a ride in a fellow gangster's automobile. His body was dumped in a remote area of North Denver. The fatal gunshot wound was in the exact spot where he'd been shot in the December gun battle.[62]

On May 6, 1933, the *Denver Post* headlined:

Thirty-three Die in Gang War over Colorado Liquor Trade

On December 5, 1933, The Twenty-first Amendment to the United States Constitution was ratified. This amendment effectively repealed the Eighteenth Amendment which had allowed for the Prohibition of alcohol, a federal law for the past thirteen years. The amendment read:

253

> Section 1. The eighteenth article of amendment to the Constitution of the United States is hereby repealed.
>
> Section 2. The transportation or importation into any State, Territory, or possession of the United States for delivery or use there in of intoxicating liquors, in violation of the laws thereof, is hereby repealed.
>
> Section 3. This article shall be inoperative unless it shall have been ratified as an amendment to the Constitution by conventions in the several States, as provided in the Constitution, within seven years from the date of the submission hereof to the States by the Congress.

A Senseless Murder
One of Denver's Finest

Any officer will say that a call of domestic violence is the most dangerous police will ever face. One such call proved to be tragic for Denver's police department. It was October 13, 1938, when Detective Fred Renovato responded to the call about a "crazed man" by the name of Joe Coats, who was dragging a woman named Virginia Garcia by the hair from her apartment.

When Renovato exited his patrol car in front of the home at 1221 22nd Street, Coats immediately opened fire. Detective Renovato was hit in the neck, shoulder, leg, and heart.

Coats then turned the gun on Virginia Garcia, pulling the trigger three times, but the weapon never discharged. Coats fled the scene on foot. Renovato managed to lift himself into position and fired toward Coats five times, but he missed.

The police department issued an "all points" bulletin. All available officers were called out to search for Coats and given orders to "shoot to kill."

Meanwhile, Detective Renovato, mortally wounded, was transported to Denver General Hospital but died enroute.

The *Rocky Mountain News* issue of October 15, 1938, reported the story of the search with the headline, *"Door-to-Door Manhunt Ordered"*.

The article went on to describe Coats as a "marijuana-crazed negro

Denver Police Museum
Denver detective Fred Renovato responded to a call at 1221 22nd Street. He was fatally shot four times by Joe Coats, who was high on narcotics and marijuana.

who shot and killed Detective Fred Renovato."

Following the apprehension of Coats and police interrogation, Denver District Attorney John A. Carroll filed a charge of first-degree murder. As the District Attorney's office was preparing for trial, the Federal Bureau of Narcotics became involved in the case.

Will S. Wood, of the Denver division of the Federal Bureau of Narcotics, wrote a letter of inquiry to Mrs. Elisabeth Bass, the Denver district supervisor. The letter, dated October 27, 1938, read:

Dear Mrs. Bass:

An article appeared in the News, Denver, Colorado, on October 15, 1938, under the heading "Door-to-Door Manhunt Ordered" relative to one Joe Coates, [sic] marihuana [sic} crazed negro who shot and killed Detective Fred Renovato.

Please submit a report to this office on the above matter.
Very truly yours,
Will S. Wood,
Acting Commissioner.
TREASURY DEPARTMENT
BUREAU OF NARCOTICS
DENVER, COLO.

Evidently the request was taken quite seriously, as it was forwarded on to John W. Marsh, commissioner of narcotics for District No. 13, which included the states of Arizona, Colorado, New Mexico, Utah and Wyoming. Mr. Marsh responded in a letter dated November 12, 1938, sent from his office in Washington D. C.

Dear Sir:

Reference is made to your request of October 27, 1938, that a report be submitted in the matter of an article in the Rocky Mountain News, *Denver, Colorado, on October 15, 1938, under the heading "Door-to-Door Manhunt Ordered" relative to one Joe Coates,* [sic] *marihuana-crazed* [sic] *negro who shot and killed Detective Fred Renovato.*

Please be advised that a complete investigation has been made in this matter and there appears to be no basis for the charge that Coates [sic] *was "Marihuana-crazed."* [sic] *None of the police reporters for the* Rocky Mountain News *will assume responsibility for the statements concerning marihuana [sic] in the article.*

Coates [sic] himself denies that he ever used marihuana [sic] *and in his statement to the District Attorney, he said that he was not drunk, had not been smoking "hey" and was not excited at the time he shot Detective Renovato.*

The chief witness in the case, Virginia Garcia, whom Coates [sic] *was dragging down the street when accosted by Renovato, states that as far as she knows, Coates* [sic] *was not smoking marihuana* [sic] *prior to the shooting and that she had made no such statement to the police or members of the District Attorney's office. I have interviewed John A. Carroll, the District Attorney for the county, Captain of Detectives James Childers, the City Editor of the* Rocky Mountain News *and several police reporters on that paper and I can find no foundation for the charge that Cotes* [sic] *had been using marihuana.* [sic] *In fact, one of the reporters stated that he believed whoever wrote the story dressed it up a bit.*

Investigation of the matter was commenced by this office at the time the above article appeared in the Rocky Mountain News, having in mind the requirements of Circular Letter No. 458, dated September 29, 1937.

However, no report was submitted at that time as nothing was found to indicate that marihuana [sic] was responsible in any way for the commission of this crime.

Very truly yours,
John W. Marsh,
Acting District Supervisor, District No. 13.

It is interesting that the Federal Bureau of Narcotics would even take the time to investigate the possibility of whether the murder suspect, Joseph Coats, was under the influence of narcotics at the time he shot and killed a Denver police officer. It is also interesting that the *Rocky Mountain News*, which reported the "marijuana-crazed" story, refused to back up the story. Nor was the story carried in any other newspaper.

After a lengthy trial, Joe Coats was found guilty of first-degree murder in the cold-blooded shooting of Detective Fred Renovato.

The conviction carried the death penalty. His punishment was swift. Joe Coats was executed on January 10, 1939, just three months after the murder.

Officer Down
A Few Good Men

During the 1930s it seemed as if the entire country was in the grip of a crime wave. Al Capone, John Dillinger, Pretty Boy Floyd, Bonnie and Clyde, are just a few of the bigger names in American crime during this decade.

While Denver County had its own share of crime and murder, a new element seemed to emerge as Denver policeman were being killed more frequently.

The following incidents are just a few of the many that caused policeman to relay the call: "Officer Down."[63]

* * *

Clarence W. Alston was a night patrolman for the Denver Police Department. On the night of March 24,1929, Alston was walking his beat shortly before 11 p.m. when he noticed two men pulling another man out of a car at the intersection of Broadway and Colfax. Officer Alston ran to the vehicle, and demanded to know what was going on. Suddenly two shots rang out and Alston fell to the street. He had been shot in the chest and the other bullet was lodged in his leg. He was quickly transported to Denver General Hospital where he died an hour later.

The police knew who they were after and soon arrested William Marshall, as he was attempting to board a streetcar. They later found their second suspect in his hotel room closet, where he had shot himself in the head.

* * *

During his early morning shift, at 4:30 a.m. on August 31, 1931, Officer William Keating was checking in with headquarters from the call box in front of the McCarty-Sherman auto dealership. During the call he heard a window break at the dealership and went to investigate. Finding the garage doors at the alley entrance unlocked, Keating entered the building and searched for intruders.

Two youths, Donald Ray and William Piskoty, had broken into the dealership to break open the safe. During their attempt, one of them happened to spot Officer Keating at the call box. Assuming the officer had seen them, the youths panicked, fleeing the dealership by breaking the window.

Meanwhile, Officer Keating carefully combed the building, looking for any unusual signs, when he spotted a set of keys. Keating continued to roam the building.

After about an hour, Ray and Piskoty figured it was safe to return to the dealership where they had mistakenly left their keys. Officer Keating was waiting patiently when he saw them enter. He ordered both young men to put up their hands and told them they were under arrest. The two told Keating that they were tourists, that their car had broken down, and they thought someone at the dealership could repair their car.

Officer Keating wasn't buying their story and marched them toward the call box, so he could call in the arrest. On the way, he asked Piskoty for a driver's license. At the same time, Ray dropped his hands and said he had one, but then turned around with a .38 automatic pistol and fired at Keating. The two ran off but not before Ray managed to get another shot off aimed at Keating.

Denver officers soon arrived at the scene and Keating was rushed to Denver General Hospital. Keating was able to give a description of the two assailants before he died.

Donald Ray and William Piskoty were quickly arrested and

confessed to the murder of Officer Keating. Following their murder trial they were each sentenced to sixty-five years to life imprisonment.

* * *

A normal business auction held on Sunday, February 11, 1933, at the Colorado Auction Company in downtown Denver, turned into a day of terror for the proprietors and their nearly one hundred customers.

Shortly after the auction opened, the owner, Henry Zelinger, received twenty dollars' worth of tools on consignment from Gay Rice. Suspicious about the tools, thinking they were possibly stolen property, Zelinger called the police. Presenting Rice with a receipt, he asked the man to return at 2 p.m. for the auction.

Precisely at 2 p.m. Rice returned. He was met by Detectives John F. Dea and George P. Schneider. The two detectives asked Rice to step into a separate room away from the auction gallery full of patrons. As Rice entered the room, he pulled a gun from his pocket and shot Detective Dea twice, dropping him immediately. He then turned and shot Schneider twice. After Schneider fell, Rice stood over him and fired five more rounds into his body.

Rice then ran through the auction gallery, firing at will toward people, walls and windows. He must have found a moment or two to reload as it was later ascertained that Rice fired nearly fifty rounds in the gallery. At some point, he moved back into the room where the two detectives lay mortally wounded. In a final act which would prove heroic, Detective Dea managed to to fire his weapon at Rice four times. While his first three shots missed, the fourth hit Rice square in the forehead. Rice died about an hour later.

Three of the gallery patrons were injured, with one later dying at a local hospital. Officer George P. Schneider was found dead at the scene. Officer John F. Dea was taken to the hospital where he managed to give a detailed account of the horrific incident before he died from his injuries at sic o'clock that evening. The *Rocky Mountain News,* in their coverage the next day, February 12, 1933, included a portion of Officer Dea's description of the murder spree:

> *We hadn't even started to talk to him* [Rice] *when he jerked out his gun. He shot me first and then shot Schneider, Schneider didn't stand a chance*

The same article went on to recount the horrendous scene and the heroic act of Officer John F. Dea:

Policeman dying upon floor fatally wounds his assailant. Bystanders struck by flying bullets. Crowd attending auction thrown into panic and scrambles frantically for exits. Pandemonium broke loose in the Colorado Auction Co, store, at 1456 Welton St., where the shooting occurred, as the nearly 100 men and women awaiting the auction dashed towards exits or sought shelter under furniture from the hail of bullets.

It was later learned that Gay Rice had previously been arrested for carrying concealed weapons and was regarded as a "mental defective" for threats he had made against the police.

* * *

Denver Detective Pasquale Marinaro and his partners were patrolling the downtown area along 23rd Street in search of Amos Hayhurst, who was wanted for the murder of Joseph Dicker. Shortly after 9 p.m. on April 17, 1936, Marinaro and his partners entered an apartment building at 335 23rd Street, where Hayhurst's ex-wife Edna, lived.

Entering the apartment, the detectives each searched a room looking for the murderer. As Marinaro walked into the kitchen, he was met with a barrage of gunfire. Hayhurst's first bullet caused a mortal wound, hitting the detective in the heart. Somehow, Marinaro managed to fire two shots, one of which hit Hayhurst in the hip.

Hayhurst knew he was caught. Perhaps out of desperation, he put his gun to his head and fired.

Officer Pasquale Marinaro died of a bullet wound to the heart in an ambulance on the route to Denver General Hospital.

* * *

Fred Stallings had been drinking all day. After a confrontation with his twin brother, whom he threatened to kill, he left his brother's house with his wife who insisted on driving. At a stoplight, an impatient Stallings told his wife to drive through the red light. When she refused,

Stallings pulled a gun and threatened to kill her. Instead, the couple switched places in the car and Stallings drove them home.

Finally home, Stallings called the local police station and requested policemen to come to his house and arrest him because, he said, he "was crazy." Officer Sawyer and his partner, a rookie named Carroll, responded to the call. It was March 8, 1937.

As the two policemen left their vehicle and approached the home, Stallings swung the door open and opened fire. He shot Sawyer near the heart and Carroll in the chest. Sawyer stumbled down the driveway, where he collapsed and died. Carroll managed to make his way to a gas station where he called for backup, relaying the report: "Officer down."

The sound of gunfire alerted the neighbors, and bystanders in the area were alarmed. It wasn't long before all heard another shot, this one from inside the Stallings home. Fred Stallings committed suicide.

* * *

The crime wave across the country and in Denver continued throughout the decade of the 1930s.

It would take America's involvement in World War II for the crime and murder rate to subside.

Notes to Part IV

1. Dorsett, The Queen City.
2. Ubbelohde, Benson and Smith, A Colorado History.
3. Van Cise, Fighting the Underworld.
4. Kreck, Smaldone, The Untold Story of an American Crime Family.
5. The Denver Police Department Pictorial Review and History, 1859-1985.
6. Kreck, Smaldone, pg. 58.
7. Clyde Brion Davis, Denver Murders, pg. 143.
8. ibid.
9. ibid.
10. ibid.
11. Pulcipher, The Pioneer Western Bank; First of Denver 1860-1980, pg. 4.
12. McGrath, The Real Pioneers of Colorado.
13. Perkins, The First Hundred Years, pg. 199.
14. Parkhill, Pioneer Denver Mint Robbery, Denver Westerner's Monthly Roundup, Vol. XIII, August, 1957.
15. Today, the Denver Mint continues to produce half of America's coins, with the Philadelphia Mint producing the remainder. The facility utilizes 400,000 pounds of metals annually to create over forty million coins every twenty-four hours.
16. Tour guides at the Denver Mint state that the institution has never been robbed, a misstatement because this current building was the site of Harrington's robbery in 1920.
17. Casey, Lee, (editor) Denver Murders.
18. Barker & Lewin, Denver.
19. Rocky Mountain News, November 29, 1928.
20. ibid.
21. ibid.
22. Rocky Mountain News, March 9, 1929.
23. Rocky Mountain News, November 30, 1928.
24. Denver Post, February 14, 1934.
25. Records of the Colorado Supreme Court - O'Loughlin v People opinion delivered February 8, 1932.
26. Humphreys, Denver Murders.
27. ibid.
28. ibid.
29. ibid.
30. ibid.
31. Humphreys, Denver Murders.
32. ibid.
33. ibid.
34. ibid
35. ibid.
36. Humphreys, Denver Murders.
37. Denver Post, December 18, 1930.
38. ibid.
39. Records of the Colorado Supreme Court - O'Loughlin v People opinion delivered February 8, 1932.
40. The Denver Post, May 26, 1951.
41. The Denver Post, May 30, 1951.

42. *Cervi's Rocky Mountain Journal*, May 31, 1951.
43. ibid.
44. Prendergast, *Denver Love Crazy*, pg. 2.
45. *The Denver Post*, November 23, 1928.
46. Prendergast, *Denver Love Crazy*, pg. 2.
47. People v. Ives, case #278 P. 792.798.
48. Colorado State Penitentiary Archives.
49. ibid.
50. Patterson and Alt, *Slaughter in Cell House 3*, pg. 20.
51. The prison riot of 1929 left twelve dead, including seven guards. The first to be killed in the uprising was Jack Eeles, 77, who had served as the prison's hangman for thirty years.
52. This was the same method of hanging used by the state of Colorado since the hanging of Andrew Green in 1886.
53. Colorado State Penitentiary Archives.
54. Wommack, *From the Grave*, pg. 358.
55. *The Rocky Mountain News*, July 6, 1965, What About Executions Before 1890?
56. King, *Going to Meet a Man*.
57. *The Denver Post*, May 9, 1933.
58. Radelet, University of Colorado.
59. *The Denver Post*, February 2, 1933, and *The Rocky Mountain News*, March 31, 1933.
60. The state of Colorado never adopted the use of the electric chair, or "Old Sparky."
61. Kreck, Smaldone:*The Untold Story of an American Crime Family*.
62. Van Cise, *Fighting the Underworld*.
63. Stevenson, *In the High Country: Settlers on the Land of Golden Gate State Park*.
64. Kreck, Smaldone:*The Untold Story of an American Crime Family*, pg. 2
65. ibid.
66. Wommack, *From the Grave*.
67. *The Denver Post*, February 19, 1933.
68. Kreck, Smaldone:*The Untold Story of an American Crime Family*, pg. 11.
69. *The Denver Post*, May 6, 1933.
70. As of this writing, the Denver police and the Colorado State Patrol have the highest number of peace officer deaths in the nation.

Denver's Larimer Street, circa 1960s.

Part V

1940 -1961

While Denver mob violence and murder continued, it soon became overshadowed with America's impending involvement in World War II. Obviously crime and murder still occurred on the streets of Denver, yet it was rarely reported in the Denver newspapers. That is, until the sensational story of murder in a normal suburban Denver home. The media would dub it "The Spiderman Murder."

* * *

The Spiderman Murder
"The itsy bitsy spider climbed up the..."

The quaint two-story bungalow-style house with a sharply gabled roof in North Denver was locked from the inside. No doors or windows showed any sign of tampering. Yet the homeowner, Philip Peters, lay dead in the house, brutally beaten. There was no one else in the home. The police were baffled, and for months they had not one clue as to who had killed the successful and well-liked elderly gentleman.

His wife of half a century, Helen, was temporarily confined in a local hospital recovering from a fractured hip so she was not a suspect. While she was recovering, a neighbor, Mrs. Jennie Ross, had offered to prepare meals for Peters, and when the punctual, kindly man failed to arrive on time for supper on the evening of October 17, 1941, Mrs. Ross, along with other concerned neighbors, gathered at the Peters' house. The doors were locked. One woman eventually found one screen not securely hooked from the inside. She loosened it, pried it off, broke the window, climbed in— and screamed.

Sirens wailed in the otherwise quiet neighborhood that evening as police squad cars raced to the scene, 3335 West Moncrieff Place. James Childers, captain of detectives in 1941, who would later become the Denver chief of police, was one of the first to arrive. As he bent over the dead body of Philip Peters, he noticed, among the horrific wounds to the body, that the right arm was stretched over the forehead in an obvious attempt to shield a blow. Childers also noticed that the index fingernail of the right hand had been pulled out.

About that time, the deputy's coroner arrived. After a preliminary examination, the coroner counted over a dozen severe blows to the body. Philip Peters was a powerful and healthy seventy-three-year-old man weighing more than two hundred pounds, but there were also multiple strikes to his head, any one of which could have killed him, according to the deputy coroner. He also surmised that Peters had been dead for at least four hours.

Childers quickly discovered the murder weapon — the cast iron shaker from the stove. Although it had been washed, a bit of Peter's blood remained. Childers then ordered the detectives to search the house.

The condition of the house revealed the story of the confrontation. Police surmised the fight had begun when Peters was startled, possibly awakened from a nap on the living room couch, as one slipper lay at the foot of the couch. He may have gone through the dining room, through a narrow hallway, as a chair and lamp had been overturned. In the rumpled throw rug the other slipper was found, as well as a set of false teeth. Blood was spattered on the walls. The police theorized that from there, Peters and his assailant had progressed throughout the first floor before ending in the bedroom, where the body was found. A valuable vintage pistol, found broken into pieces, suggested an attempt by Peters to protect himself. Peters had apparently also used one of his antique canes from his collection, as one was laying near his body.

The Denver newspapers ran bold headlines of the mysterious and ghastly murder, such as "Slain Man's Wife Learns of Death in Hospital," and "Killer Nameless as Inquest Ends." The accompanying articles had very little information regarding the baffling murder.

Not long after the murder of her husband, Helen Peters was released from the hospital and returned to her home of fifty years, a brave act for a semi-invalid. The next-door neighbor rigged a buzzer system between the two houses allowing Helen to summon help if needed. It was. Helen fell and refractured her hip. She insisted that this time she be treated at home, despite the fact she was in a cast and bedridden. A nurse was hired, Mrs. Hattie Johnson, but she hastily quit after hearing noises and "seeing a spook." Another domestic was hired; she also saw "a ghost" at the foot of the stairs. It was a filthy, wraith-like thing. "It vanished when I screamed," Mrs. Edith Clark later recalled. Relatives insisted that Helen leave the house, and she went to the home of her son on the Western Slope.[1]

Denver Public Library Western History Dept.
Theodore Coneys lived in the tiny attic of this house, biding his time until he murdered the home owner.

With no suspects, no motive and no witness, the brutal crime was soon eclipsed by headlines of World War II. But Captain Childers began keeping notes of the "ghost stories" that the neighbors whispered about the house on Moncrieff Place, stories about housewives and children occasionally seeing a tiny light under the roof or a "ghost face" that appeared for an instant behind one of the shadowy curtains of the deserted house.

Because of his suspicions, in the summer of 1942, Childers ordered a round-the-clock watch on the house at 3335 West Moncrieff Place. It wasn't long before the police got their first break in the case. On a particularly hot summer afternoon, July 30, 1942, two Denver policemen, assigned to surveillance of the area, stood across the street from the home, screened by a lilac bush. The policemen watched a mail carrier as he made his deliveries along the North Denver residential street. As the postman came to the Peters home, one of the Denver policemen spotted a ghostly face behind a sheer curtain. Not sure of what he saw, he nudged his partner and pointed toward the window. Sure enough, that policeman also saw the same image.

As the two policemen ran across the street, one of officers blew his whistle as hard as he could for backup. The image vanished from the window. As the two officers barged into the empty home, using their shoulders to break open the door, they noticed the house in complete disarray. The furniture was covered with sheets, old magazines lay on tables and the floor, and the kitchen had a nasty odor.

The policemen must have entered the house just as the figure they saw in the window disappeared through a hole above the closet in one of the two second-floor bedrooms, a hole only the size of three cigar box lids. At the time of the original investigation, nearly ten months ago, the police had noticed the tiny opening but dismissed it as too small for a human to climb through.

When investigators finally arrived to search the residence, the specter, undetected, had climbed into the attic. If an officer hadn't grabbed his ankles, the creature could not have been easily caught because the hole was too small for any of the detectives. Later the police enlarged the tiny entrance, and the smallest lawman on the force climbed through and investigated the minuscule space under the roof.

The place where the suspected murderer had hidden for more than nine months was only the size of a coffin, and it was an oven in the July heat. An old ironing board served as a bed. Spider webs hung everywhere. Open jars and tin cans brimmed with excrement. As police detective Fred Zarnow gagged at the sight, he gasped, "A man would have to be a spider to stand it long up there!"

William "Bill" Peery, a photographer for the *Rocky Mountain News*, gave the brutal murder a nickname : "The Spiderman Murder."[2]

As Captain Childers and his detectives pieced together the puzzle of the murder, they learned of the victim's passion for music, which had brought him into contact with a man of like interests decades before. This man would become their prime suspect.

The mandolin had been the rage in 1907, and Philip Peters and his North Denver neighbors formed the West Moncrieff Mandolin Club. Peters had invited a new acquaintance, Theodore Edward Coneys, to teach mandolin to the group at meetings in his home. At the time, Peters was enjoying a successful career as an auditor for the Denver & Rio Grande Railroad.

Coneys, on the other hand, was a misfit from early on. Theodore Coneys was born November 10, 1882 in Petersburg, Illinois. His father, T. H. Coneys, was a Canadian immigrant who owned a hardware store in Petersburg. Following the death of T. H. Coneys in 1888, Mrs. Coneys and young Theodore moved to a farm near Beloit, Wisconsin. Theodore Coneys suffered from poor health his entire childhood. He had been told by doctors that he would most likely not live to see his eighteenth birthday. As a result, Theodore seemed to have lost interest in life, as he failed to graduate from high school. In 1907, Mrs. Coneys relocated to Denver, where she found employment as a housekeeper at the Denver Democratic Club. Twenty-five-year-old Theodore made the move to Denver, where he lived with his mother. Here, Theodore also found work, for a time, as a bookkeeper at the Denver Brass Works.

Denver Public Library, Western History Dept.
Theodore Coneys was convicted of first degree murder on November 18, 1942. He was sentenced to life in prison with no possibility of parole.

Following the death of his mother in 1911, Coneys found odd jobs in sales and advertising. As time went on he was unable to hold a job and spent much of his adult life homeless. Coneys later said that he resented the way people treated him, due to his frail condition, expressing that he wanted a place where he could be alone and free from the judgment of others.[3]

As a homeless drifter, Coneys did manage to earn money from time to time, primarily by conning people. By this method he found his way into the Peters home, as a "musician."

Although music was their only common interest, Peters and Coneys saw each other only occasionally before the music teacher left Denver in 1917. The mandolin teacher wandered the country as a hobo, sometimes working in advertising or newspaper work, usually not. For whatever reason, Coneys never forgot his time with the wealthy

Philip Peters. Sometime in 1941, Coneys, now a fifty-nine-year-old homeless drifter, made his way back to Denver, to find Peters.

On a cool fall evening in September 1941, Coneys found his prey. Philip Peters was walking home when Coneys approached him. He introduced himself, as it had been over twenty years since the two had seen each other. After a brief conversation, Coneys explained how he was down on his luck and asked Peters for a loan. Peters respectfully declined and went on his way. However, Coneys was not to be denied.

Theodore Coneys had followed Peters to his house. For some time Coneys watched the comings and goings of Peters, thereby having an idea of his schedule. When Peters would leave for a significant portion of the day, Coneys would sneak into the yard and check the locks on the door. One day he got lucky. Peters had neglected to lock one of the doors and Coneys simply let himself in. Knowing Peters would not be returning for quite some time, Coneys helped himself to food from the icebox and even had time to explore the house. Inside a closet Coneys found a small opening leading into the attic. Coneys looked around, and although it was a small space, he realized that he could stay in the attic, safe, warm and hidden from Philip Peters.

Then, approximately a month later, Peters caught Coneys as the recluse was helping himself to food from the kitchen. Startled that Peters was there, Coneys must have attacked the homeowner and after a struggle, Coneys managed to grab the cast iron shaker and beat the seventy-year-old Peters to a bloody pulp.

And so it was that for the next nine months the "Spiderman" continued to hide in the attic in the gable of the empty house.

The winter after the murder was one of Denver's coldest, yet Coneys stayed in the unheated house. His diet that winter was canned fruit from the cellar and twenty pints of grape jelly. In March he began eating the strawberry jam. His only water in the hot summer was from the water heater, which no one had thought to drain. He weighed only seventy-five pounds when the police caught him, a fifty-nine-year-old scarecrow wearing clothing in tatters, incredibly filthy, with tangled hair.

The police summoned a doctor, who declared Coneys would live, despite being "the most amazing case of malnutrition I have ever seen that still breathed." The police could not believe this pale, weak wraith could possibly have killed the stronger Peters.

After a few days of recuperation in the hospital, Theodore Coneys was brought to the Denver police station for questioning. Gene Lowall, crime reporter for the *Rocky Mountain News*, along with the paper's photographer, William "Bill" Peery, were allowed to view the interrogation from a glass-partitioned room. Lowall later described the scene:

> *The smaller of the two dicks* [police officers] *folded a couple of sticks of gum in his ample jaws. The larger dick in an uncomfortable chair swiveled a lack-luster eye...* [and] *with a curt clearing of his throat from the command position behind the desk* [came] *the down-focused lights beat pitilessly.*[4]

After heavy police interrogation, headed by Captain James Childers, Theodore Coneys eventually broke and confessed to the murder of Philip Peters. Gene Lowall wrote:

> *The two men re-entered [sic] the room where the lights beat down upon the [suspect] and the sweating face of Captain Childers. The police stenographer hauled fourth another freshly sharped pencil. The reedy, sepulchral voice resumed beneath the down-focused lights. The nimble fingers of the police stenographer darted on and on across his notebook.* [5]

What followed was an 8,000-word confession to murder by Theodore Coneys. When the stenographer finished, the document was passed to Coneys, along with a pen for his signature. Lowall described the scene:

> *It was handed to the spidery hand, a hand without a tremor, reached out. Despite its filthy, broken fingernails, the hand almost daintily took the pen from Childers.*

Then in a calm voice Coneys said:

> *"Everything would have been all right and Phil Peters would have been alive today if he hadn't caught me robbing the ice box. It was him or me. I thought he had gone out but he was taking a nap. I hit him with the stove shaker when he tried to run for help. I don't know if he recognized me. It was nearly thirty years since he'd seen me last. I don't know why I hit him so many times. I guess it was just the hatred I'd been storing*

up for years against everyone who had the things I'd always
wanted and never could get. When it was all over, I picked up
the the broken gun and ran to my attic after I'd washed up and
dried the shaker." [6]

Theodore Coneys was tried and convicted of first-degree murder
on November 18, 1942. He was sentenced to life in prison with no
possibility of parole.

Years later, Gene Lowall, then city editor for the *Rocky Mountain*
News, interviewed Coneys at the Colorado State Penitentiary. Perhaps
confinement in a prison cell offered Coneys time to reflect. He finally
explained his peculiar actions which ultimately drove him to murder:

I was in the neighborhood in September, 1941 and found
the house unlocked and no one home. I went in and stole some
food. I was in bad shape, my lungs were giving me a lot of
trouble and I was at the end of my rope. Fall was coming on
and I couldn't face another winter on the road, I had to have
a place to stay. I found the hole in the closet, climbed through
and slept and slept. Whenever I heard him [Peters] *downstairs,*
I kept real still. Then I got bolder and used to shadow him from
room to room. It was sort of a game. It gave me a thrill. It was
the first time in my life I'd ever had anyone at my mercy, but I
didn't want to hurt him. It was miserable hot in the summer and
my feet froze in the dead of winter in that attic, but it was all
part of the price I was willing to pay. I can't tell you why I stuck
it out. I guess it was mostly because it was a world all my own.
I used to go down and look out the windows, and watch the
postman come by. Nobody's written to me in twenty-five years.
Whenever I saw people on the street, I hated them and would
go back to my attic.

Theodore Coneys, the "Spiderman Murderer" never had to see
"people on the street again." He died alone, in the prison hospital on
May 16, 1967.

Murder Most Foul
Suffer Not the Children

Perhaps the most gruesome case of child murder in America occurred undetected in Denver over a two-year period. When the multiple murders were discovered in the spring of 1943, not only were citizens of Denver horrified, so was the entire country, as newspapers from coast to coast splashed the hideous details on their pages.

Unwed Mother Tells How She Murdered Her Three Babies

This shocking headline appeared in the *Denver Post* on April 2, 1943, and was syndicated through the United Press, to newpaper affiliates across the country.

With diligent police work and interrogation, the story of premeditated, methodical murder of three innocent infants became known to all of America.

It began when the Denver apartment manager, Noah Layton, was in the basement of the apartment complex, attempting to trace a disagreeable odor. In his search, Layton discovered the bodies of three infants hidden in a green wooden chest. Knowing the chest belonged to one of his tenants, Layton immediately notified the police, giving them all the information he knew.

Denver police were immediately dispatched to the scene, as was Deputy Coroner Gus Economy. After a complete forensic examination by law enforcement, and a preliminary examination of the deceased infants by the coroner, it was decided that Coroner Economy contact the mother of the dead children for questioning. It must have been a difficult task, as everyone concerned was trying to withhold judgment. Yet the evidence clearly pointed to multiple murder.

Through information supplied by Layton, the coroner telephoned the suspect at her place of employment and asked her to come to her apartment for police questioning. When she arrived, before investigators were able to utter a word, the young woman quickly declared: "I know what you're here for."

Bernice Williams was a young, attractive twenty-three-year-old woman. Syndicated newspapers referred to her as a "statuesque blond career girl." Bernice was raised in a normal working-class home. At the age of sixteen, she graduated from high school as an honor student, in 1936. A gifted student, Bernice was awarded a college scholarship but chose to develop her own career path. She soon found work at a local department store. In time, ironically enough, as it would turn out, Bernice was promoted to the position of buyer of infants' wear. Over the next few years, as Bernice received increases in salary, she was able to move to nicer apartment complexes. She was even able to afford the luxury of hiring movers, rather than makeing the move herself.

All the while, Bernice Williams was hoarding a deep, dark secret in her personal life, and the movers she hired were innocently moving the evidence from apartment to apartment.

On that otherwise glorious spring day in April 1943, Denver police were stunned when after just a few questions, Williams, in a calm and direct manner, not only confessed to the murders of her three children, but detailed the manner in which they were killed as if she was in a routine business meeting. Following the confession and very little interrogation, Bernice Williams was arrested for three counts of first-degree murder. The police detectives were so taken aback by the confession, they asked for a psychiatrist to interview her upon her arrest.

Both local and national newspapers ran the story, including the *Denver Post*, with this April 2, 1943, headline: "Unwed Mother Tells How She Murdered Her Three Babies." The article described the morose confession of the mother murderess:

> *A statuesque blond career girl admitted in an emotionless monotone Friday; she gave birth to three illegitimate babies in the past three years, drowned each of them in a bathtub and hid their tiny bodies in a linen chest because, they 'were children of sin.'*

The *Waterloo Daily Courier*, dated April 2, 1943, carried the syndicated national coverage with the headline:

> *Infants' Wear Clerk Has 3 Killings on Conscience*

The article went on to further describe the confession and sub sequential arrest:

> *Arrested after the manager of her apartment found the bodies in the basement, Bernice Williams, 23, told authorities*

she thought the babies should die 'because I didn't want anyone else to have them and I didn't believe I could raise them.'

Then, she said, she placed each baby in a small cardboard box and put each box in the linen chest. She knew, she said, that some day she would be discovered, so the presence of the bodies in the basement did not disturb her. She could not explain why she made no attempt to dispose of the bodies permanently.

Bernice Williams was swiftly brought to trial on the charge of murder just two months later. The trial began on June 7, 1943. The prosecution based their case on Williams' confession given during the police interrogation handled by Detective Capt. James E. Childers. It was in this confession that Williams admitted to drowning her baby in the bathtub on February 11, 1943, after giving birth to the child alone.

Childers' testimony revealed many of the details of the interrogation as well as William's calm demeanor during the confession. Detective Capt. James E. Childers said that at one point following the confession, the detectives discussed the possibility of asking a psychiatrist to examine Williams. This unusual request by law enforcement and even the district attorney was subsequently done. Equally unusual was the fact that the defense attorney, Harry G. Saunders, did not contest the results of the examination, which declared Bernice Williams sane, nor did they order their own psychiatric examination.

Childers was asked if the defendant had an explanation for killing her three children. He said Williams did and that she replied: *"I couldn't help it because they were born, I'm just constituted that way. I'm over-sexed."*

Detective Childers' testimony went on to describe what the defendant said about the children. The first child, a girl, was born in April, 1941. The second, also a girl, was born in February, 1942, and the third child, a boy, was born February 11, 1943, just two months before the murders were discovered.

In her confession, Williams said that during each pregnancy, she continued to work until a day or two before the birth. Following the birth (and death) of each child, she asked her employer for three days off. Williams would not identify the father or fathers of the children, but did say that two of the children were by the same father. She also said in her confession that she never told the fathers she was pregnant. A curious revelation in the confession was that during the third pregnancy, her mother had moved in with her and had no idea her daughter was pregnant, nor did any of her friends or co-workers.

The prosecution ended their presentation before the jury by reading this damning excerpt from the confession of Bernice Williams:

> *I performed what surgery was needed with a pair of scissors. Each baby cried, but I choked off their cries with my hands so that no one could hear. Then I knelt beside the bathtub and held the baby under water twenty minutes until I was sure it had drowned.*

With very little to work with, given the confession by his client, defense attorney Harry G. Saunders called no witnesses. In his closing arguments, he did ask for leniency for his client.

Newspaper reporters from across the country came to Denver to cover the trial. A Texas newspaper, the *Corsica Daily Sun*, ran an article in the June 10, 1943 issue, which reported in part:

> *Miss Williams, who dresses modishly and is employed by a large department store as a buyer of infants' wear, described the slayings in detail. Each birth, she said, was unattended.*

Following closing arguments by the prosecution and defense, the jury received the multiple murder case for deliberations at approximately 10:45 p.m. on June 10, 1943. After a long night, the verdict was reached the following morning: Guilty...but not as charged.

Incredibly, all twelve men on the jury returned the second option available to them under the law: second degree murder, on only one count, not three counts, of murder. However, the jury also returned a second verdict against the defendant: concealing the birth of an illegitimate child. Bernice Williams, who had maintained a stoic calm throughout the three-day trial, displayed no emotion when the verdict was announced.

After the jury had announced its verdict, defense attorney Harry G. Saunders requested a jury poll. Each juror affirmed the conviction. Saunders then asked the court, and was granted thirty days to file a motion for retrial.

The *Denver Post* ran an article dated that same day, which read:

> *A district court jury, after deliberating nearly 13 hours,*

today found 23- year-old Bernice Williams guilty of second degree murder in the drowning of one of three infants born to her out of wedlock.

The verdict was returned at 11:37 a. m. (Mountain War time) by the jury of 11 married men and a bachelor, who had deliberated since 9:46 o'clock last night.

The Denver woman, a buyer of infants' wear for a department store, also was convicted on a second charge-concealing the birth of an illegitimate child.

Conviction on a second degree murder charge in Colorado carries a sentence of from 10 years to life imprisonment, at the discretion of the sentencing judge. District Judge Joseph E. Cook did not say at once when sentence would be imposed.

In the end, defense attorney Harry G. Saunders chose neither to appeal the guilty verdict, or file for retrial. Bernice Williams was transported to the Colorado State Penitentiary at Canon City, where she served a life sentence for second degree murder in the women's correctional facility.

Murder For Hire
"A Fiendish Plot"

It was shortly after midnight, December 1, 1953, when Denver police responded to a robbery and possible kidnapping attempt in a common Denver neighborhood. Officers found a bloody crime scene. It may have been a robbery gone bad, but it wasn't kidnapping.

The newspaper reporters working the crime beat didn't know that fact in the early morning hours, and they had a deadline to meet. The front page of the morning *Rocky Mountain News* of December 2, 1953, read:

Denver Woman Kidnapped and Murdered!

As the citizens of Denver were waking up to the tragedy reported in the paper, the police were diligently working the crime scene. So were the crime reporters. The home had been broken into and showed signs of an attempted robbery. By that time, the police had developed a theory of what happened in that home the previous night.

When the police first arrived, they found two women severely beaten. One woman was barely alive and was immediately transported to a local hospital. The other woman was dead. Not only was she beaten, there were signs of strangulation. There was a third victim, Leroy Adolph Leick, the homeowner. He also appeared to have been beaten. He managed to answer the initial questions the police had for him. He told the police there were at least two burglars. He also identified the women. The dead woman was his wife, Mrs. Evelyn Leick. The other woman was her sister. He didn't know if anything had been taken from the house.

The police had a nagging question. Why would a robbery attempt end with a strangulation? While they continued their investigation of the robbery-turned murder event, their focus also included Mr. Leick. At first glance, his background check didn't seem to raise any cause for concern. The thirty-six-year-old man was employed as a business executive for a Denver appliance firm. By all appearances, he and his wife enjoyed a typical middle-class lifestyle. However, when the criminal background check came in, the detectives raised an eyebrow or two. It seems Leick had been arrested, convicted, and spent jail time for the theft of a diamond ring, estimated to be worth approximately eight hundred dollars. As the police were set to question Leick again, the crime reporter for the *Rocky Mountain News*, Bill Brenneman, broke the story in the December 3, 1953 issue. The page-five story ran the headline:

Theft of $800 Diamond Ring Blots Leick's Record

When the police questioned Leick a second time, they had additional information they had kept close to the vest. The day following the murder, two men, independent of the other, had come forward to report that Leick had approached them with a proposition: to kill his wife. Each man gave details of the encounter, and both men turned down the offer. The police interrogation of Leick the second time around was relentless. However, an obviously nervous Leick revealed nothing.

Again, the reporters at the *Rocky Mountain News* were the first to break the page-one headline story:

Was Slain Denver Woman Victim of Fiendish Plot?[7]

Almost as soon as this story hit the streets of Denver, another man came into the Denver police department headquarters with his version of the murder-for-hire story. He told the police that nearly two years previous to this incident, Leick had tried to hire him to murder his wife. He further stated that he had reported the encounter to the police, but never heard anything further from them. The *Rocky Mountain News* again was the first to report the story, on December 6, 1953, this time with the sensational headline:

Police Were Told of Plot, Mrs. Leick Wasn't, Why Not?

As the press put the pressure on the police department, they in turn put the pressure on Leick. It didn't take long. Just days after the murder, Leick confessed to the murder of his wife and the robbery cover-up.

Denver Public Library, Western History, Dept. The *Rocky Mountain News* printed this photo of a smiling Leroy Leick, in handcuffs, led to the police station following his arrest on murder charges.

He explained the botched murder-for-hire ordeal and even named his accomplice, a man by the name of Gene Dukes. The *Rocky Mountain News* heralded the news with a banner headline on the front page of the December 4, 1953, issue,

Wife Killer Confesses!

The police brought in Gene Dukes for questioning. He too confessed to his part in the murder plot. He said Leick had hired him to stage the robbery, but that he was not at the home when the violence resulting in murder occurred. He emphatically said he took no part in the beating of the women or the murder of Mrs. Evelyn Leick. He said Leick told him he wanted to collect on the insurance policy. It was only after the newspapers reported the murder that Dukes realized that Leick meant a life insurance policy, not a homeowner's insurance policy. Or so he said.

Nevertheless, while the Denver district attorney filed a charge of first degree murder as well as a charge of attempted murder against Leroy Adolph Leick, he also charged Gene Dukes as an accomplice to murder.

Defense attorneys for Leick immediately entered a plea of insanity. As Leick underwent several state-ordered mental examinations, as well as examinations at the request of the defense attorneys, his eventual murder trial was delayed by nearly two years.

Meanwhile, the trial of Gene Dukes went forward. The prosecution presented Dukes' confession before the jury, admitting his involvement in the subsequent murder of Mrs. Leick. The jury returned with a guilty verdict, and Dukes was sentenced to life in prison.

As the mental examinations of Leroy Adolph Leick had proven the man sane, his murder trial finally began in 1955. Following a lengthy trial where the insanity issue was repeatedly raised and refuted, Leick was found guilty of first-degree murder and sentenced to death.

His defense attorneys filed a series of appeals which eventually went before the Colorado Supreme Court. The court reversed the murder conviction, and Leick was retried for the murder in 1958.[8]

Again the evidence was presented before a jury, and again Leick was found guilty by the jury. The defense team filed another set of appeals, but the Colorado Supreme Court affirmed the jury's conviction.

While Leick spent the next year of his life on death row at the Colorado State Penitentiary, his attorneys filed more appeals, including efforts to challenge his mental competency for impending execution. This effort also failed, as the court upheld the second jury conviction.[9]

After six years of litigation, primarily concerning the mental status of Leroy Leick, his attorneys had exhausted all of their appeal options. The state of Colorado set the date for his execution by asphyxiation for January 22, 1960.

Leick, now a "dead man walking," may have had some redeeming qualities after all. But it was too little too late. He sent a letter to the prison board and the media stating that Gene Dukes, currently serving a life term in the state prison, "should be absolved of any responsibility for the murder." Evidently, the letter carried no weight, as Dukes remained incarcerated. And it seemed the media had little interest in Leick's act of kindness, as well. The story was covered on page five of the *Rocky Mountain News* under the headline:

Leick Absolves Dukes As Slay Accomplice

Leick was placed in the gas chamber and his life ended on January 22, 1960.

Murder and a Swiss Watch
Just a Matter of Time

A young trombonist for the Denver Symphony Orchestra, Hubert Hahn had a bright future ahead of him when he was murdered in cold blood on the streets of Denver in 1955.

The building in which both Hubert Hahn and Joyce Danielson.,his twenty-three-year-old girlfriend, lived had a storied past, one that became etched in Denver history. An enormous mansion, complete with several embossed crosses in the molding and woodwork, was built at 1410 High Street in 1897, for Reverend Richard E. Sykes of the First Universalist Church. The good reverend became embroiled in a financial dispute with the church. In 1899, Sykes was forced to sell the mansion.

The new owner was a budding novelist from Indiana, Meredith Nicholson. His wife, the former Eugenie Kountze, was the daughter of Herman Kountze, one of the four Kountze brothers responsible for Denver's first banking institution, and the first president of the subsequent First National Bank.[12] Nicholson's day job was treasurer for his in-law's various enterprises, including their banking and coal interests, particularly the Northern Coal Company of Denver. Following a hard day at work, Nicholson used pen and paper to create best-selling novels such as *The Hoosiers, The Warriors, The Port of Missing Men,* and *The House of a Thousand Candles.* This later work was based on the peculiar and unexplained incidents in a rural mansion. Nicholson later said the inspiration for the novel came from his Denver home at 1410 High Street, incorporating the names of Denver streets into the narrative, such as "Uncle Gaylord," and "Grandfather Glenarm." Nicholson often referred to the mansion as the "House of

Inspiration," which was said to be full of secret passageways and an underground tunnel between the house and carriage house. Following the release of the novel, it was forever known in Denver as the "The House of a Thousand Candles."

The Nicholsons moved back to Indiana in 1905, selling the mansion to Harold Moore, owner of the H. W. Moore Equipment Company. After the death of Moore in 1926, the mansion went through several owners and vacancies. Allen Dearhammer, a retired building contractor, bought the home in 1938, living there until his death in 1946. His wife later died in the home in 1949, as did their daughter, in 1952. After the deaths of the Dearhammer family, the property was converted into an apartment complex.

It was at this storied location that the kidnapping and brutal murder of Hubert Hahn occurred.

On the night of September 22, 1955, Hubert Hahn performed with the Denver Symphony Orchestra at the illustrious Phipps Mansion. As was their custom, Joyce Danielson, a lab technician at St. Luke's Hospital, joined him for the evening. Following the performance, the couple left the mansion and stopped for a quick meal at the Holiday Drive-In located at the corner of Cherry Street and Colfax Avenue. From there, Hahn drove back to the tenant house at 1410 High Street. And, as was their dating custom, the two remained in the car for a period of time. On this particular night, they lingered too long.

Suddenly, and with no warning, a young man opened the passenger door of the car, pointed a gun at Hahn as he slid in next to Joyce Danielson. Closing the door, he ordered Hahn to drive through the Cheesman Park area to 12th Avenue. Then the man then told Hahn to drive north. Near the entrance to the Rocky Mountain Arsenal, the gunman ordered Hahn and Danielson out of the vehicle, demanding they leave their wallet and purse. The couple did as instructed and walked away from the parked car.

As the couple were walking away, their backs to the gunman, the man shouted at Hahn. When Hahn turned to respond, he was hit with six bullets fired from the .22 pistol the man had been holding on the couple during the entire joyride which had now turned to cold-blooded murder.

The kidnapper, now turned murderer, ordered Joyce Danielson to help him carry Hahn's dead body into the nearby ditch. After this gruesome task for Danielson, she was forced back into the car. The murderer then drove the car away from the scene. After some time, he stopped the car and attempted to rape Danielson, who put up a fight and was shot in the shoulder. The man then pistol-whipped her, threw her out of the vehicle and ran over her as he sped away.

Remarkably, Danielson's injuries were minor. A railroad train crew discovered her walking along the railroad tracks near East 52nd Avenue and Dahlia Street the following morning. They notified the Adams County Police Department.

Joyce Danielson was taken to the local hospital where she was questioned by the police detectives. Based on her information, Adams County policemen spent five hours searching for the body of Hubert Hahn. The body was found, along with a key piece of evidence.

The object the policemen found was an elaborate gold Swiss watch. The police were able to trace the watch to the American Academy of Horology, located at 1901 East Colfax Avenue. Officials at the school provided the police department with the information regarding the watch. It belonged to Robert Dearmin, an apprentice watchmaker.

When the police contacted Dearmin, he denied any knowledge of the kidnapping and subsequent murder. After further interrogation, and more denials, Dearmin's wife finally told the police the truth. She said that her husband had come home that night and told her of a simple robbery that had gone horribly wrong. He told her that during the robbery, he had lost his expensive Swiss watch, and asked her to buy an identical watch, which she did. However, she had no idea that the robbery her husband confessed to her had included murder.

Following this revelation by Mrs. Dearmin, Robert Dearmin confessed to the kidnapping of Hubert Hahn and Joyce Danielson, as well as the murder of Hahn and the attempted rape of Danielson.

In his written confession, Dearmin said that after leaving Joyce Danielson for dead, he dismantled his gun, throwing pieces of it into ponds, ditches, and storm sewers. He said he left Hahn's car at the corner of 14th Avenue, where his own vehicle was parked nearby. From there, he drove to his home.

Dearmin said that he burned the clothes he had been wearing and during the process he realized he must have lost his watch. In a panic, he told his wife of the "botched robbery" story and asked her to buy the same type of Swiss watch, so that he would never have to say he lost it, should the original ever turn up.

The police arrested Robert Dearmin, charging him with kidnapping, attempted murder and first degree murder. Under Colorado state law, because he confessed to the crimes, the death penalty was not an option for the prosecuting attorneys. However, Dearmin did face a life sentence in prison.

The sensational trial began in December of 1955 and was covered in newspapers across the country. Robert Dearmin pleaded innocent to the charges of kidnapping, attempted murder and first-degree murder by "reason of insanity."

The prosecution calmly and methodically laid out their case against Robert Dearmin, calling Joyce Danielson, Dearmin's final victim of crime, to the stand. After compelling testimony, the prosecution rested, The defense argued the insanity plea, bringing in several doctors. On cross-examination, prosecution attorneys were able to rebut much of the testimony.

In the end, the jury didn't buy the "insanity" plea. Robert Dearmin was convicted of murder and sent to the Colorado State Penitentiary to serve out a life sentence for the death of Hubert Hahn.

America's First Airline Bomber
Murder in the Skies

The year 1955 was one of prosperity for Coloradans. Businesses were booming, downtown Denver was growing, and urban sprawl was beginning. It was a time, a decade after World War II, of contentment and security. Families had outdoor barbecues with neighbors, and children walked safely to school. It was a time when family entertainment was a drive-in movie, or the newest rage, the black-and-white television.

It must have seemed somewhat surreal when an explosion in the skies of Colorado turned out to be intentional.

On the cold, clear night of November 1, 1955, United Airlines Flight 629, just eighteen minutes out of Denver's Stapleton Airport, exploded in flight and the flaming wreckage fell over the fields of farm land near Longmont, Colorado. All forty-four passengers and crew members were killed.

Colorado, as well as all of America, woke up to the shocking news the following day. The *Rocky Mountain News* headline blazed:

No Survivors.[13]

The *Denver Post* ran the story under the headline:

44 Die in Plane Crash[14]

The plane's departure from the Denver airport was fifteen minutes late. Had it departed on time, the explosion would have occurred as the plane ascended over the Rocky Mountains, thus making the identification of the cause of the crash a difficult, if not impossible, task.[15]

The FAA and the FBI were dispatched to the Colorado crash scene, where they fingerprinted the bodies, which sadly included a tiny infant. The prints were then sent to Quantico, Virginia. Meanwhile, a complete analysis of the gathered plane wreckage led to the determination by the FBI, as well as the FAA, that the airplane had been blown apart by explosives. The intentional bombing was the first such act in American history. The FBI was now on the hunt for a mass murderer.

In a time before baggage inspection, body wands, or X-ray machines were used at airports, the investigation was difficult. The investigators now moved to establish motive, intent. It would take authorities two weeks to piece together evidence and interviews that eventually led to a confession.

The FBI checked to see if any flight insurance policies had been taken out on any of the passengers aboard the flight — a common practice at that time. They found a rather curious set of transactions occurring within two hours of the flight leaving Denver's airport. Not one, but three insurance policies totaling $37,500 were bought in the name of passenger Daisie Walker King. The beneficiary on all three policies was her son, John Gilbert Graham. (In the 1950s, flight insurance could be purchased at convenient vending machines located in the terminals of nearly all airports.) With a possible suspect and motive, the detectives next checked into the background of John "Jack" Gilbert Graham.

Born January 23, 1932, Graham was raised in an orphanage until the age of eight. His mother later remarried, to wealthy Colorado cattle rancher, John Earl King. In 1940, Daisie King reclaimed her son, and by all accounts raised young John and his half sister Helen in a good home atmosphere. Following his first year in high school, John Graham dropped out of school and went to Alaska to stay with Helen. He joined the Coast Guard, going AWOL after seven months of service. The Coast Guard discharged Graham for disobedient action as well as the discovery that he was under age.

Returning to the Denver area in 1951, while living with his mother, he got a job as a time-keeper, where he forged $4,200 in company checks, fleeing to Texas when his theft was discovered. After a spree of petty crimes, including bootlegging, carrying a concealed weapon, and evading officers, he returned to Denver where his mother, Daisie King, paid all the fines and the criminal charges were dropped. Graham seemed to settle down, even marrying Gloria Elson, a student at the University of Denver.

Graham returned to his criminal ways when a series of planned mishaps occurred. Graham's automobile service station, financed by his mother, mysteriously blew up. Following investigations, the insurance claims were reluctantly paid. Then, Graham's new pickup truck stalled, conveniently in front of an oncoming train. Demolished, his auto insurance also paid that claim. Graham also was beneficiary to Mrs. King's $100,000 life insurance policy.

Unknowingly, Graham's wife gave a statement to the authorities that brought her husband in for questioning. Following the explosion of the airliner, when Graham returned home from Stapleton Airport, he learned of the explosion and his mother's death. Mrs. Graham recalled to the authorities that her husband had told her he had placed a Christmas-wrapped gift of shotgun shells in his mother's suitcase for hunting with her daughter. She said when Graham learned of the crash he said:

> *Can't you just see Mother when all those shotgun shells in her suitcase began to go off in the plane?*

With the flight insurance purchases, the insurance fraud, and evidence of Graham at the airport, the FBI brought twenty-four year old Graham in for questioning. After his initial interview with FBI agent Webb Burke, Graham was advised he was a suspect in the

On November 1, 1955, United Airlines Flight 629 exploded just north of Denver.
It was the first airline bombing in American history. This is a portion of the plane
discovered in a field.

murder of his mother, as well as the other fourty-three people on
the fateful flight. He was also advised that while he was under no
obligation to make a formal statement, he was not to leave the area.
An angry Graham nearly shouted:

> *Of course I'll make a statement! Why shouldn't I? And I'll
> do a lot more. I'll take a lie detector test if you wish. What's
> more you have my permission to search my house, my car, or
> anything else. I haven't done anything wrong.*[16]

He was released, at least for a time.

However, with this interview, the investigators gained a great deal
of information from Graham's statements. For instance, when asked
about the "wrapped gift" he first said it was a gift of craft tools. Then
he denied giving his mother any sort of gift. Still later he said that
his mother had packed the box of shotgun shells for hunting with

Denver Public Library, Western History Dept.
John Gilbert Graham was arrested and charged with forty-four counts of first-degree murder. His motive was to collect on his mother's insurance policy.

her daughter. FBI agent Webb Burke raised an eyebrow, given the previous statement of Graham's wife. The FBI not only had conflicting accounts by their suspect, they also had assembled a complete timeline of Graham's movements during the period both before the explosion and of his actions following the explosion, including his statement upon hearing of his mother's death. The investigators decided to take Graham up on his previous offer.

Following up on every detail of Graham's statement, FBI agents obtained a search warrant for Graham's home. During the search, the investigators found much evidence, including a roll of copper wire specifically used to detonate charges.

On November 13, Graham was again interrogated by FBI agents. Confronted with further evidence, and the statements made by witnesses, Graham denied his wife's claim that he told her of placing the Christmas-wrapped gift in his mother's suitcase, stating "She's wrong about that." The heated confrontation continued for hours. Finally Graham broke.

The clean-shaven, six-foot, 190-pound Graham broke into a sweat when Agent Burke said, "Let's have the truth." Graham replied, "Where do I start?" Throughout the long afternoon, Graham admitted that he had set off the explosion of his gas station and admitted to driving his truck onto the railroad crossing, all for the insurance payoff.

Graham then detailed the events that caused the explosion on United Airlines Flight 629. He assembled a bomb consisting of twenty-six sticks of dynamite wired together with two electric primer caps, a six-volt battery, and a timer set for ninety minutes. Graham said he had wrapped the device in Christmas paper to look like a present. He then snuck the package into his mother's suitcase just before the two left the house for Stapleton Airport.

Graham's mother, Daisie King, was flying to Portland, Oregon where a connecting flight would take her to Alaska, where she would visit her daughter, Graham's half-sister. When the plane was in the air, Graham calmly went to the coffee shop and waited. The matter-of-fact, detailed and unemotional confession shocked the FBI investigators. On November 14, 1955, Jack Gilbert Graham was arrested and formally charged with forty-four counts of murder.

Plane Dynamiting Is Confessed!
Denver Youth Gives Details on Killing Mother
and 43 Others for Her Insurance

This was the headline of the *Rocky Mountain News* of November 15, 1955. Colorado and all of America breathed a heavy sigh of relief. However it would be months before the federal case against Graham would go to trial, as Graham's attorneys entered a plea of insanity.

Because of the insanity plea, Graham spent a brief stint at the Colorado Psychopathic Hospital for examination. After a complete evaluation by no less than six psychiatrists, Graham was found to be sane, thus the insanity plea was withdrawn. In a statement released by the FBI, Graham said that he made up the confession when he saw a World War II photograph on the wall. "It showed FBI men digging up dynamite after capturing Nazi men in Florida, which gave me the idea. But really, I didn't do it." It was a ridiculous statement, one that no one believed, including the jury.

The murder trial of T*he People v. Graham* began in May 1956. On May 5, following a relatively short trial, given the evidence and horrific sense of the crime, Jack Gilbert Graham was convicted on all forty-four counts of first-degree murder and sentenced to death. After his conviction, Graham's attorneys filed several appeals. After four months of legal battles, all appeals failed, as the Colorado Supreme Court affirmed the conviction.

Sent to the Colorado State Penitentiary at Canon City, Graham, inmate #29625, was a dead man walking.

In one of the shortest prison terms to end by execution, Graham's date with death was set for January 11, 1957, just eight months after his murder conviction. As was the practice at the time, a select group of witnesses, including reporters, were allowed to view the proceedings. One of those reporters was Zeke Scher, of the *Denver Post*. According to Scher, who had covered the entire story for his paper, Graham had invited him to "sit on his lap while the execution was taking place." Scher declined that invitation, but did attend the execution.[17]

On that cold January evening, a silent Jack Gilbert Graham was escorted on the long walk to death to the penitentiary's gas chamber. Prison Warden Harry Tinsley stood guard as the prison staff prepared the prisoner. Placed into the chair inside the chamber, Graham's arms, legs and chest were then strapped with the cardiograph connecting points.

The gas chamber, Colorado's method of execution adopted by law in 1934, proved not to be a perfect method of execution in the case of Jack Gilbert Graham. During the execution, Graham, who was visible to witnesses in the room, strained against the straps that tied him to the chair inside the gas chamber. Soon, Graham began to gasp, and then scream. The scene must have been horrific, prompting Warden Tinsley to later comment that this was not "normal procedure.[18]

A commentary in the *Rocky Mountain News*, the day following the execution, under the headline, "Solution to the Air Crash," contained the following:

> *We doubt that the general public ever would stand for the opening or inspection of luggage. And anything short of that would hardly detect any sort of explosives...Fortunately this tragedy has been solved. We find it difficult to believe that it could-or would likely be repeated.*

Obviously, the unnamed writer could not know what the future would have in store.

Child Murder
The Death of Innocence

In the summer of 1958, then as now, Denver's children were enjoying their vacation from school with fun, sun and frolic. Many were looking forward to attending what was perhaps the highlight of their summer; the circus was in town.

On a glorious summer day, August 27, 1958, one of those eager children, eleven-year-old Lester Gordon Brown, Jr., made his way to the Denver Coliseum where the circus was performing. Young Lester was enamored as he watched the many tricks and antics of the circus animals.

Walter J. Hammil, a circus animal trainer, noticed the young boy's enthusiasm. Hammil approached the boy and suggested that Lester return after the circus events ended for the day and he would give Lester a ride on an elephant. The excited youngster returned at the given time, in the company of an equally excited friend. Hammil greeted the boys, and soon directed Lester's companion to a site where he could pet the circus animals. Hammil then engaged Lester in conversation and suggested they take a walk. At some distance away from the circus area, Hammil sexually assaulted the child. Young Lester pleaded to be left alone, saying he "just wanted to go home."[19] When Hammil continued his unwanted advances, Lester, who must have been terrified, screamed out for help. At this point, Hammil began choking the boy. Lester slumped to the ground.

Incredibly, Hammil left the scene and went to a neighboring restaurant where he enjoyed a fine dinner. Following his epicurean delight, Hammil then returned to the scene of his despicable crime. Finding the innocent defenseless youth quite dead, Hammil carried the body to a nearby sand pile and buried it.

Lester's parents were alarmed when their young son did not return home from the circus that day. Lester and Edna Brown lived in a small home at 4612 Brighton Boulevard, just a few short blocks from the Denver Coliseum. By nightfall, they contacted the police. With good police work and poor judgment on Hammil's part, Hammil was arrested the next day.

During police interrogations, Hammil eventually confessed to the murder of eleven-year-old Lester Gordon Brown, Jr. In his signed confession, Hammil said that he would "...probably have to die..."[20]

Hammil then led the officers to the shallow grave of his child victim.

Walter J. Hammil was formally charged with first degree murder. The Denver District Attorney's Office immediately announced they would ask for the death penalty. The *Denver Post* quickly picked up on the story. In the August 30, 1958, issue, the paper advanced the tragic story with the headline, *"Hammill* [sic] *Has Long Record".*

The paper reported that Hammil had an extensive record of juvenile delinquencies and prior convictions, dating back to when he was nine years old.

In the meantime, the grieving parents of eleven-year-old Lester Gordon Brown, Jr. buried their son in a quiet ceremony at Riverside Cemetery.

The accused murderer faced two trials. The first was limited to the defendant's plea of not guilty by "reason of insanity." At this time in Colorado law, the "insanity" plea required a separate trial. The prosecution called Dr. James A. Galvin, Medical Director of the Colorado Psychopathic Hospital, and Dr. John MacDonald, a member of the staff of the Colorado General Hospital. Both doctors had examined Hammil and testified that the defendant was indeed sane. The jury concluded that Walter J. Hammil was sane at the time of the murder, and was bound over to stand trial for murder in the first degree. The *Denver Post* ran the story which included in part, "Physicians described Hammill [sic] as mentally retarded but legally sane."

During the murder trial, the prosecution systematically presented their case against the defendant, including Hammil's long criminal record. Evidence was introduced, including pieces of the deceased boy's clothing and police photographs of the crime scene, and most shocking, photos of the boy's dead body.

The defense council relied on Hammil's mental condition, introducing testimony by several doctors, but the testimony was limited by the judge. Dr. Jack Hilton testified, stating that in his opinion the defendant was insane at the time of the "alleged murder."

The prosecution countered by calling their own experts, including

Dr. James A. Galvin, an associate of Dr. Doris Gilbert, a clinical psychologist, who had conducted a number of psychological tests on Hammil. He testified that in his expert opinion, Hammil, through his methodical actions, was indeed sane.

The defense made one more attempt. In closing arguments, the attorneys introduced to the jury the idea as to whether the defendant had sufficient time in his capacity to deliberate his actions. With the prosecution's objection, the judge ruled: *"No particular time need intervene between the formation of the intent to kill and the act of killing."*

In the end, on March 3, 1961, the jury rejected the contention of "insanity" and pronounced Walter J. Hammil guilty of first-degree murder. The sentence was the district attorney's desire; the death penalty. Walter J. Hammil was immediately transported to the Colorado State Penitentiary at Canon City.

The defense attorneys immediately filed a motion for retrial. The motion was denied and the attorneys took the case to the Colorado Supreme Court. The original motion was denied by the Colorado Supreme Court, on March 13, 1961. Attorneys Harold A. MacArthur and Walter F. Scherer refiled a motion, dated May 1, 1961; *Walter J. Hammill*[sic] *Plaintiff in Error, v. People of the State of Colorado, Defendant in Error.*[21]

The request for appeal read in part:

> *Plaintiff in error, who will be here referred to as defendant, was convicted of first degree murder and sentenced to death. It will be sufficient for the purpose of this review to merely outline the essential facts surrounding the happenings which furnish the basis for the charge and it will be unnecessary to detail all of the shocking and sordid facts which appear in the record.*

With that side-stepping, the provable facts of murder, by a jury of Hammil's peers, were conveniently left out of the appeal. The motion went on to address the "insanity" plea.

> *The present review applies to both the sanity trial and the trial on the charge contained in the information. On the sanity issue, error is assigned in connection with the refusal of the trial court to allow defendant to cross examine Dr. James A.*

Galvin regarding the use by the latter of a certain psychological report prepared by Dr. Doris C. Gilbert (who was not in court). The alleged error is based upon the contention of the defendant that the witness Galvin was shown to have read the report and, according to the defendant, to have used it in a limited way for the purpose of furnishing suggestions incident to his own investigation. The court's ruling sustaining the objection of the prosecution and striking all of the cross examination having to do with the contents of this report, was, it is argued, prejudicial error.

With regard to the murderous act, the attorneys wrote:

Defendant admitted that he was afraid that the boy would inform his parents and that on a sudden impulse he started to choke Brown.

The only issue relating to sufficiency of the evidence to establish the charge of murder has to do with the element of premeditation. A question is raised concerning the length of time essential to existence of such element.

Apart from this one point dealing with the merits, the assigned errors pertain to the alleged insanity of the accused.

Judge Doyle of the Colorado Supreme Court issued the dissenting opinion, writing in part:

Both [jury instructions] sought to define 'willfully, deliberately and with premeditation.' The court's instruction also included the statement [upheld by the presiding judge] *that: 'It matters not how short a time interval, if it were sufficient for one thought to follow another.'*

Therefore, we perceive no merit in questioning the giving of instructions...

Being of the opinion that the trial was carefully conducted by a highly competent trial judge and that the defendant was very adequately represented by most capable appointed counsel, and that no error resulted, the judgment should be and is hereby affirmed, and it is ordered that the same be executed during the week beginning May 8, 1961.

Walter F. Scherer, attorney for Hammil, then filed a petition in the

U. S. District Court on a writ of habeas corpus, against the Colorado State Penitentiary, and the warden, Harry C. Tinsley. The petition, dated November 21, 1961, came to a quick resolution by the court. Chief Judge J. Arra signed the dissenting opinion, dated the same day, which read in part:

> *This matter comes before the Court on a petition for a writ of habeas corpus; the Court having previously granted petitioner leave to proceed in forma pauperis.*
>
> *The files and records in this case reveal that the petitioner was convicted in the District Court of the City and County of Denver, State of Colorado, of the crime of first degree murder and was sentenced to be executed.*
>
> *This conviction was affirmed by the Colorado Supreme Court, Hammil v. People, Colo. 1961, 361 P.2d 117.*
>
> *Petition for a writ of certiorari was denied by the United States Supreme Court.*
>
> *The original judgment has been stayed by the Colorado Supreme Court.*
>
> *Petitioner alleges that no state remedy is available to him. Respondent does not deny this allegation and does not raise the question of exhaustion of state remedies in his answer. The questions here raised were presented to the highest court of the State; therefore, it is not necessary to again present these here.*

Exhausting all legal means available, the date of Hammil's execution was set by the warden at the Colorado State Penitentiary. On the night of May 25, 1962, thirty-one-year-old Walter J. Hammil was escorted by prison guards to the gas chamber where he was asphyxiated for his horrific murder of an innocent child.

Colorado Rocked by Coors Murder
In Cold Blood

Every so often in history, major events in life, and history, for that matter, make their way full circle. Such is the case of a horrific murder that occurred over fifty years ago. It was the morning of February 10, 1960, when Coloradans woke to the headline in the *Rocky Mountain News*:

Adolph Coors III Feared Kidnapped!
Blood Stains Found Near Abandoned Auto

The heir to the famous Coors fortune was missing. It seemed as if it was a high-profile kidnapping for ransom. Not unusual for the era. For seven months the manhunt gripped Colorado and all the nation. It would end in murder. Fast forward to the headline in the *Denver Post* of August 26, 2009:

Coors Killer Corbett Takes His Own Life

The circle of events began on the morning of February 9, 1960, when forty-four-year-old Adolph (Ad) Coors III, one of the heirs to the Coors brewery fortune, was reported missing. When he failed to show up for an important 10 a.m. board meeting at the Coors facilities, his brothers, William and Joseph, called his wife, Mary. She said he left the house at 8 a.m. Both brothers and the wife were now worried. Bill Moomey, the company's advertising executive and Ad's close friend, was sent to backtrack Ad's route.

As Moomey turned off from US Highway 285 in Turkey Creek Canyon and onto Turkey Creek Road toward Ad's house, he was blocked by a milk truck stopped on the narrow road. The driver of the milk truck was obviously annoyed, constantly honking the horn. Moomey got out of his car to investigate. The milk truck driver pointed to the car ahead of him which was blocking his path. The car, with the motor still running, was Ad's green and white International Travelall.[22] The driver's door was open and the radio was blaring. Moomey walked to the vehicle, turned off the engine, and in the sudden silence, called out for Ad. He wandered around and then approached the small wooden bridge just ahead of Ad's car. Leaning over the rail, he peered into the shallow creek below. He saw a pair of glasses with flesh-colored rims, the style of glasses worn by Ad. He also noticed a tan-colored baseball cap, a favorite of Ad's, and near the bank was a dark brown fedora hat. Moomey backed away from the bridge in horror and bewilderment. As he did so, he nearly fell as his foot slipped from under him. Looking down, he realized he was standing in a pool of blood. Gaining his foothold, he also noticed blood stains smeared along the rail of the bridge.

Moomey hollered to the milk man to back up his truck and go for help.[23]

296

Denver Public Library, Western History Dept.
This was the last photograph taken of Adolph Coors III.

The local sheriff's department recovered Ad Coors' glasses and ball cap from the creek, as well as a brown fedora hat. The next day, the *Rocky Mountain News* reported that it appeared Coors had been kidnapped:

Adolph (Ad) Coors III, millionaire head of the Adolph Coors Co. in Golden disappeared mysteriously Tuesday while en route to work. Coors' car, its motor still running, was found abandoned on a tiny wooden bridge across Turkey Creek, just two miles north of the missing man's home near Morrison. Blood stains were found on the side of the road near the car and splattered on the bridge railing.

Ad's brothers immediately phoned their father. Adolph Coors II was vacationing in Honolulu, Hawaii, with his wife. As he and his wife waited to board a plane bound for Stapleton International Airport, a horde of reporters had gathered to get Mr. Coors' statement. The *Rocky Mountain News* issue of February 10, 1960, contained the headline all of Denver and Colorado, for that matter, were wondering about:

Coors offers Ransom for Son

The article included a quote from Mr. Coors: *"They have something I want to buy, my son."*

It did indeed seem to be a kidnapping for ransom, for the very next day, as Ad's parents arrived back in Denver, Ad's wife received a communication from the alleged yet unknown kidnapper. The first was the ransom demand mailed to the Coors' home. The postmark was dated the previous day from Denver, and there was no return address.

Inside the envelope was a single sheet of paper containing the type-written message:

> *Mrs. Coors: Your husband has been kidnaped.* [sic] *His car is by Turkey Creek. Call the police or the F.B.I: he dies. Cooperate: he lives. Ransom: $200,000 in tens and $300,000 in twenties.*
>
> *There will be no negotiating.*
>
> *Bills: used/non-consecutive/unrecorded/unmarked.*
>
> *Warning: we will know if you call the police or record the serial numbers.*
>
> *Directions: Place money & this letter & envelope in one suitcase or bag.*
>
> *Have two men with a car ready to make delivery.*
>
> *When all set, advertise a tractor for sale in Denver Post section 69. Sign ad King Ranch, Fort Lupton.*
>
> *Wait at NA 9 4455 for instructions after ad appears.*
>
> *Deliver immediately after receiving call. Any delay will be regarded as a stall to set up a stake out.*
>
> *Understand this: Adolph's life is in your hands. We have no desire to commit murder. All we want is the money. If you follow the instructions, he will be released unharmed within 48 hours after the money is received.*[24]

Mary Coors was nearly beside herself. She did her best to conceal the severity of the situation from her four children, ranging in ages from ten to eighteen. She appealed to her father-in-law for help in obtaining the ransom money. While Adolph Coors II worked to secure the money, very quietly behind the scenes, Sheriff Art Wermuth was working the case, with the assistance of local police departments, including Denver, and had called in the FBI.

Meanwhile, Mary placed the classified tractor ad in the *Denver Post* issue of February 11, 1960, as instructed. She kept the phone line open, also as instructed. No call came. She ran the ad for two weeks. Again, no call came. Fear and apprehension gripped the entire Coors family.

Working behind the scenes, the investigators soon made great strides in following several leads. Two neighbors who lived near the bridge in Turkey Creek Canyon reported seeing an old yellow car in the area. They further stated that on the morning of the alleged kidnapping, they heard loud voices in an argumentative manner. One of the neighbors said she heard what sounded like lightning, not once but twice, and close together. They even supplied a partial Colorado license plate number: AT 62. Ad's daughter, Cecily, also corroborated the neighbor's statement by stating she had also seen a yellow vehicle in the area over the past few weeks. She also had noticed, on many separate occasions, a stranger standing by the bridge. He held a rifle and wore a dark brown fedora hat.

With the solid lead of a partial license plate number, the FBI obtained information that four registered vehicles in

The ransom note.

the state of Colorado began with AT 62. One of those was a 1951 canary yellow Mercury. It was the crack in the case the investigators were looking for, but it had a few snags along the way.

The registered owner of the vehicle was one Walter Osborne, with an address of 1435 Pearl Street in Denver. The FBI searched the empty third-floor apartment. While there were no clues as to Osborne's movements, they did manage to lift several good sets of fingerprints. They also found a stash of receipts from recent purchases, including a mail-order pistol, four pairs of leg irons, and three sets of handcuffs. They also found a copy of the vehicle registration and purchase order from the car dealer of the 1951 Mercury, dated January 8, 1960. However, outside of the apartment, there was no sign of a yellow Mercury. The landlord told them Osborne had lived there for four years, moving in on April 1, 1956, and that he worked at the Benjamin Moore paint plant north of Denver. She also said that he had just moved out the previous Wednesday. That just so happened to be the day after Adolph Coors III was reported missing. The FBI questioned Osborne's co-workers at the Benjamin Moore Paint plant. Several of them claimed that Osborne had boasted that he was about to receive a half-million dollars or more.

Another interesting lead came into the FBI offices the following week. This one would crack the case for the investigators. Among the police reports regarding the vehicle license plate number, came one from the police department in Atlantic City, New Jersey. The report contained the information that a yellow 1951 four-door Mercury had been located in a dump on the west side of Atlantic City, on February 17, 1960. It been burned, apparently deliberately. However, the police were able to match the vehicle identification number with the Colorado registration to Osborne. The FBI were able to get fingerprints from the burned vehicle.

The fingerprints from the burned vehicle matched those taken from Osborne's Denver apartment. The FBI now had their suspect, but there was another snag in their case. The fingerprints also matched another set in the FBI database, belonging to one Joseph Corbett, Jr. The FBI immediately requested the file on Corbett. FBI Director J. Edgar Hoover went on national television to bring attention to this "most wanted" killer.

As it turned out, thirty-one-year-old Corbett was indeed a wanted man, having escaped from a minimum security prison in Chino, California, in 1955 while incarcerated for a murder conviction. The FBI learned he was wanted in California for "unlawful flight."

In 1950, Corbett was a student at the University of California at Berkeley, when he was arrested for the alleged murder of an Air Force sergeant. Police reports indicated that Corbett had picked up the hitchhiking sergeant near Hamilton Air Force Base north of San Francisco. The sergeant was later found dead from two gun shots to the head. The district attorney filed a charge of first-degree murder. Corbett pled self-defense, stating that the sergeant pulled a gun on him. There was a scuffle he said, and Corbett got the gun. He shot the man in self-defense, he said. However, the evidence collected at the crime scene, along with the autopsy report, did not comport to

Denver Public Library, Western History Department
FBI sent this wanted poster to enforcement agencies across the country.

Corbett's statement. The Air Force sergeant had been shot behind the left ear, and shot again behind the right ear.

A clear case of murder, yet astonishingly enough, the district attorney agreed to a plea of second-degree murder. Joseph Corbett, Jr. was sentenced to a prison term of five years to life at California's San Quentin Prison. Once incarcerated at San Quentin, Corbett underwent a series of evaluations, including psychiatric. The prison psychiatrist concluded that Corbett was "schizoid," and recommended he be sent to the local psychiatric hospital, where he spent the next three years.

In 1953, Corbett, no longer deemed a threat to humanity, was transferred to a minimum-security prison in Chino, California. After being incarcerated in an actual prison for two years, evidently the former "schizoid" murderer had had enough. In 1955, Corbett simply went over the wall and disappeared for the next five years.

The FBI had a solid case against Corbett. They had his previous criminal record and proof of his alias of "Walter Osborne." They had his vehicle registration, under the alias, of the canary-yellow 1951 Mercury with the license plate beginning with AT 62, seen in the area of Coors' disappearance. They even discovered through local police records that Corbett, under the name "Osborne" and the vehicle registration, had received a ticket for speeding in that yellow Mercury, just two weeks before the disappearance of Coors. The ticket noted the location of the violation as approximately three miles north of Morrison, the vicinity of the Coors' home.

They also had his fingerprints from both the Pearl Street apartment in Denver, where he had been living quietly ever since, and the burned vehicle recovered in New Jersey. What they didn't have was the criminal or the victim.

The detectives worked the Coors kidnapping case for nine long months with little progress. The Coors family coped as best they could. But it wasn't easy.

On September 14, 1960, thirty-year-old Edward Greene was out hiking in the hills south of Sedalia in Douglas County. He stumbled upon some rumpled clothing. First kicking at the bundle, a curious Greene picked up the filthy pants and reached into the pockets, retrieving some change and a pocket knife. Examining the knife, he noticed the engraved initials of AC III. He rummaged more. He found a pocket watch, also inscribed with AC III.[25] As Greene looked around the area, he came across a human skeleton. Greene alerted the sheriff of Douglas County, and the FBI immediately took over the crime scene. The remains of the blood-soaked clothing, the skull, and personal items were all taken to the FBI lab. Through forensics, the remains were identified as that of Adolph Coors III. The coroner concluded that Coors had been shot twice in the back. The kidnapping that had gripped the country was now a murder. As the Coors family planned a funeral, the FBI began an international manhunt.

They eventually got a tip that Corbett had fled to Canada. With the assistance of the Royal Canadian Mounted Police, the FBI stormed an apartment he had rented in Toronto, only to find it recently vacated. Obviously, Corbett knew they were on to him. Among the

Denver Public Library, Western History Dept. Joseph Corbett Jr. was convicted of the murder of Adolph Coors III. Following his release from prison, Corbett lived out his life in a small Denver area apartment.

few items left behind were a set of chains and padlocks and a copy of Robert Traver's book *Anatomy of a Murder*. Was he planning another kidnapping or murder?

The Corbett trail was soon picked up again, and the authorities went to Vancouver, British Columbia, where they interviewed an employee of the Maxine Hotel. She stated that a man matching Corbett's description had rented a room under the name Thomas C. Wainwright.

On October 29, 1960, a Saturday, two members of the Royal Canadian Mounted Police, along with FBI agents, knocked on the hotel room door, and announced themselves. Corbett opened the door, saying simply, "Okay, you got me." It was all he said and all he would ever say in the ensuing months and even years. Nearly seven weeks after the discovery of the remains of Adolph Coors III, the FBI had their man.

Following extradition back to Colorado, Corbett was formally booked into the Jefferson County Jail on a charge of first-degree murder. Corbett stayed silent, refusing to talk to the investigators.

The murder trial finally began on March 13, 1961. The jury heard the horrific details of the kidnapping of Adolph Coors III, and the subsequent finding of his remains and skull. The prosecution team put into evidence the receipts found in the Pearl Street apartment, receipts for leg irons and handcuffs and guns. The jury also learned a great deal about the life of Joseph Corbett aka Walter Osborne, including his previous criminal history as well as the sightings of that yellow 1951 Mercury in the foothills north of Morrison, near the home of Adolph Coors III. The defense team had little to work with. Corbett never provided an alibi, and did not testify in his own defense. After two

This *Rocky Mountain News* photo shows detectives collecting evidence from the Coors murder scene. The detective on the right carries the box which contained the skull of Adolph Coors III.

days of deliberation, on March 29, 1961, the jury convicted Corbett of first degree murder. Because the prosecution team did not seek the death penalty, Joseph Corbett was sentenced to life in prison at the Colorado State Penitentiary.

In 1964, Corbett granted a rare interview to the *Denver Post*. Printed in the January 5 issue, Corbett said:

> *"I grant you if one believed all the testimony, it would arouse suspicion, but the case was purely circumstantial. The*

evidence was not sufficient to sustain a verdict. No man should
be incarcerated for a crime he did not commit. I am innocent. "

The kidnapping and murder of the heir to the Coors fortune does not end with Corbett's life sentence in prison.

During his time in prison, Corbett's case came up for early parole on several occasions. The first was in June 1978. The prison parole board heard the case and granted an early parole on June 15, 1978. When the newspapers printed the story, the public outcry caused the parole board to reverse the decision.

However, just over a year later, on July 5, 1979, fifty-year-old Corbett was granted parole. Released from the state penitentiary, after serving nearly nineteen years for the Coors murder, instead of reporting to his parole officer, Corbett boarded a flight to California. It was a violation of his parole under Colorado law. On July 15, just ten days after his release from prison, authorities arrested Corbett in California for violating his parole, and he was returned to Colorado.

Incredibly, in just under a year and a half of his parole violation, Corbett was again before the parole board. Sitting before the board members that would decide his chance at freedom, he said: *"I see myself as a pretty commonplace man who through sheer, bizarre circumstances got involved in something notorious."* [26]

Not exactly a confession, nor was it a denial; however, the citizens of Colorado objected to his possible release from prison. Even Governor Dick Lamm weighed in on the debate, questioning the wisdom of allowing a two-time convicted murderer back into society. The parole board had its way. Just a year and half after his first parole and the violation, Corbett was again released from prison on Friday, December 12, 1980. Conditions of the parole were five years of regular supervised parole visits and monitoring.

Corbett returned to Denver where he was able to gain employment at a local manufacturing company. That same month he rented an apartment at 2801 South Federal Boulevard. He would live in that one bedroom apartment on the third floor for the rest of his life.

His neighbors at the apartment complex knew almost nothing about him. He kept to himself and seldom spoke to anyone. Corbett never again owned a car. He walked everywhere he needed to go. He seldom, if ever, used the bus. He eventually got a job driving a truck for the Salvation Army, a job he held until he retired.

He complied dutifully with his supervised parole condition and was released from mandatory supervision on December 12, 1985. In an interview with the *Denver Post*, his parole officer Ron Olson said, "I knew him as intellectually very, very sharp. Emotionally, very immature. High strung. Excitable."

As the years went on, Corbett became more and more like a hermit in a reclusive world he alone created. A cousin, Gordon Myers, told the *Denver Post* that he had offered to help Corbett, but nothing ever came of it. "I would like to have, but he didn't seem very interested," Myers said.

Very few people knew of Corbett's criminal past. For the most part, those that did kept it to themselves. There were those, however, who loved a good story and leaked it to the media. For years, reporters would try to obtain an interview. At first, Corbett refused. Then he simply quit answering the door. Then, for whatever reason, on a cold February day in 1996, he agreed to an interview with *Denver Post* reporters Paul Hutchinson and Marilyn Robinson.

During the interview, which appeared in the February 7, 1996 issue of the paper he said he was "haunted" by bystander's comments of, "There goes the guy who killed Adolph Coors." He further stated, "I don't want to stir things up again, because it just gets me all wrought up." His final comment to the reporters clarified for all his thoughts on the brutal murder of Adolph Coors III. *"It would be futile to retry the case now. What's the point? It just goes against all my instincts, all my conditioning, to say anything at all now that would add to my notoriety."*

For the next thirteen years, Corbett got his wish. The media left him alone, the neighbors left him alone, and Corbett went into a solitary existence.

On a warm August morning, Monday, August 24, 2009, the apartment manager of the Royal Chateau Apartment complex on South Federal Boulevard became concerned when he had not seen Corbett for two days. The newspaper lay outside the door of his apartment, unit #307. The manager received no answer to his repeated knocks on the door.

Entering the apartment, he discovered the body of eighty-year-old Joseph Corbett, on the bed of the one-room apartment. Corbett's lifeless body had a single gunshot wound to the head. The pistol was laying on the floor. The paramedics were called to the scene. At approximately 8:30 that morning, Joseph Corbett was pronounced dead. There was no note, no final goodbye, and no one to claim his body.

The headline in the *Denver Post* the following day, summed up the tragic events of nearly thirty years ago:

Coors Killer Corbett Takes His Own Life
Notorious Killer's Quiet End

Domestic Violence & Murder
The Case of Luis Monge

Denver policemen arrived on a domestic violence call at an average home in an average Denver neighborhood. It was an unusually hot summer night, June 29, 1963, when officers entered that home and discovered a horrific scene.

Inside the walls of that average Denver home, the police found four dead bodies: two children, an infant, and a pregnant woman.

The investigation was an open and shut case; the murderer not only confessed, but was the one who called the police to his residence.

Luis Jose Monge, a native of Puerto Rico, grew up in New York. He married and started a family and seemed to do well. However, he soon wandered off for a time, abandoning his family. In 1961, he served a jail sentence in the state of Louisiana for vagrancy. Sometime following his release from the Louisiana jail cell, he reunited with his family and moved to Denver.

In Denver, Monge found stable employment as an insurance salesman. Apparently, Monge was doing well, as his family eventually grew to include ten children, with one on the way, when his comfortable lifestyle suddenly came crashing down.

Leonarda Monge confronted her husband with allegations of the unspeakable act of incest. Mrs. Monge had learned of the act from her tearful daughter.

What went through Luis Monge's mind is anyone's guess. What we do know through Denver police reports and autopsies, is that on that fateful night, as his wife and children slept, forty-four-year-old Luis Monge took a steel bar and beat his pregnant wife, Leonarda, to death in her bed. Six-year-old Alan was found dead in a similar manner, while four-year-old Vincent was choked to death. Baby Teresa, not yet a year old, was stabbed to death. The other children were unharmed.

The *Denver Post* splashed the horrific story on the front page of their June 29, 1963, issue:

Father of Ten Kills His Wife, 3 of Children

The same paper also went on to describe Monge and his life leading up to the murders under this bizarre headline:

Slayer's Disappearance Recalled; Described as Good Father

The public had no sympathy for Monge. It was a horrible senseless murder of four innocent people, three of which were children. As the community outrage intensified, the *Denver Post* reported on June 30, 1963, that security at the Denver County Jail was increased.

Police Guard Slayer of Expectant Wife, Three Children

The state of Colorado filed *Monge v. People*, charging Luis Jose Monge with first-degree murder and asked for the death penalty. In the filing, the alleged motive was revealed. Monge, confessing to the murders, offered his reason. The filing read in part, that the motive was "to prevent exposure of sex crimes committed by defendant with his own children."[27]

The trial of Luis Jose Monge for quadruple murder, held in 1965, was anything but routine. The defense attorneys did not have much to work with on Monge's behalf. Under the advice of his attorneys, Monge pleaded not guilty by reason of insanity. Psychiatrists, approved by both the defense and prosecuting attorneys, evaluated Monge extensively and found him to be sane.

As the murder trial moved forward, the prosecution dropped the bombshell confession on the jury that was included in their original filing. When it was revealed to the jury by the prosecuting attorneys that Monge had not only confessed to the murders, but said it was "to prevent exposure of sex crimes," the defense team did their best to have the confession thrown out. The judge overruled. The local newspapers, reporting on the activities of the courtroom drama, splashed the confession on their front pages.

At some point during the exchange between the defense attorneys and the judge regarding the confession, Monge changed his mind. He told his attorneys that he wanted to change his plea to guilty. The defense team had nothing left.

The jury convicted Luis Jose Monge of first-degree murder for the murders of his pregnant wife and three children. A second jury was then convened for the penalty phase of the convicted murderer. This jury recommended the death sentence, and Monge was sent to the Colorado State Penitentiary in Canon City.

The attorneys for Monge immediately filed an appeal. The appellate court affirmed the conviction of first-degree murder, as well as the death sentence.

As Monge spent his last days on earth safely ensconced behind bars on death row in the state penitentiary, the national debate over the death penalty once again became a hot issue, particularly during the summer of 1965. It was a summer of protesters who raged, sometimes violently, against a variety of issues, from the Vietnam War, to college students' protests following the Kent State shootings, to the death penalty.

With the fall elections looming, in an effort to stem the growing political unrest, Governor John A. Love took executive action. In January 1966, Governor Love suspended all pending executions in Colorado until the death penalty referendum on the November ballot would be decided by the voters. During the interim, a few more murders occurred, including the rape and brutal murder of Elaura Jaquette, a student attending the Colorado University at Boulder. On November 8, 1966, the voters of Colorado decided to retain the death penalty, at a three-to-one margin. In the end, Governor Love's action proved to be correct, both in calming the social unrest, and by letting the vote of the people be heard. Reflecting on that tumultuous time, Governor Love later said:

> *I feel pretty proud of the fact that in a period that nationwide the country was filled a good deal of upset and violence that we did manage Colorado, I think partly through my efforts to maintain an equilibrium.* [28]

Just as the social unrest seemed to be quelled by the recent vote by the citizens of Colorado, Luis Jose Monge managed to stir things up. In March 1967, Monge gained the attention of the local media when he petitioned the Denver courts to allow him to be hanged at "high noon," on the front steps of the Denver City and County Building. This request was denied.[29]

In what appeared to be a sign of defeat on the part of Monge, he eventually fired his attorneys and stipulated that there would be no further attempts to save his life, voluntarily relinquishing all of his appeals and requesting his execution.

In another turn of events, Monge's surviving children (who stood by their father during the trial) disagreed with their father's recent actions and appealed to the state for clemency. Incredibly, Colorado state officials accepted the clemency plea. State-approved doctors again evaluated Monge's mental capacity, and again, found him mentally competent for execution. The headline in the *Rocky Mountain News* of June 1, 1967, read:

Monge Ruled Sane: Execution Slated Friday

Friday was June 2, 1967, the day after the newspapers hit the streets. It wasn't much of a lead time, but the protesters against capital punishment marched in front of the state capitol building. More than seventy members of a group who called themselves the "Colorado Council to Abolish Capital Punishment" gathered on the west side of the state capitol building where they held a rally to protest the execution.

On the afternoon of that fateful day, preparations were underway at the state prison for the execution of Luis Jose Monge, inmate #35563. Warden Wayne K. Patterson had inspected and was assured that the execution chamber would function properly, having been tested for any leaks. A crew of ten men would then perform the execution.

As the crew prepared the acid mixture that would eventually be released into the chamber, Warden Patterson was reading the Colorado state-issued death warrant to Monge. He then escorted the condemned man to the holding cell, where his clothing was removed except for his underwear and socks. The prison doctor and an assistant strapped bands with electronical contact points around Monge's legs, arms, and chest. These bands would be connected to a cardiograph inside the gas chamber. According to records held by the Colorado State Penitentiary, Monge inquired, "Will that gas bother my asthma?" Monge was led to the gas chamber by the warden and the prison chaplain. He was placed in the chair inside the chamber and the electronical contact points were attached. The door clanked shut and the crank locked. The lever was then pulled which released the cyanide mixture into the chamber. At 8 p.m., June 2, 1967, forty-eight -year-old Luis Jose Monge was executed by lethal gas.

Following his death, and in accordance with his wishes, one of Monge's corneas was successfully transplanted to a teenaged reformatory inmate upon his death.[30]

Monge's body was buried unceremoniously on the hill above the penitentiary, known as Woodpecker Hill. The grave was marked by a license plate, with his name carved in. Not quite a week later, the makeshift marker was shot through with seven bullet holes. The marker, bullet holes and all, still stands at the cemetery on Woodpecker Hill.[31]

Meanwhile, the story of Monge's death lived on in the local papers and sparked again the national debate on capital punishment. The *Denver Post* headline of June 3,1967, read:

Silent Vigil Protests 'Shame' of Execution.

Across the country the cry to abolish the death penalty grew louder. Through a series of legal maneuvers resulting in litigation moving through several state courts, the issue of capital punishment was placed before the United States Supreme Court. As the Supreme Court reviewed the issue and heard oral arguments on both sides, the lower courts in all states which had the death penalty law stayed all pending executions.

In Colorado, Governor Love issued a moratorium on pending executions until the decision of the Supreme Court was announced. In effect, the execution of Luis Jose Monge became the last legal execution in the state of Colorado, (a total of seventy-seven) pending a decision on capital punishment that would affect the entire country. It would take years before this very controversial issue would be decided, and even then, it would remain controversial and even negated by many states, including Colorado.

At the core of the issue before the Supreme Court was the

constitutionality of the death penalty. It was argued on the grounds that it violated the Eighth Amendment of the Constitution: "cruel and unusual punishment." The decision before the Court relied on the 1972 case of *Furman v. Georgia, 408 U.S. 238*. In this case, the Georgia court had ruled that by imposing the death penalty, the very act was indeed unconstitutional on the very grounds of "cruel and unusual punishment" and a direct violation of the Eighth Amendment to the United States Constitution.

In 1972, when the Supreme Court handed down its decision, there were thirty-two states in the country which had a death penalty law, including Colorado. The Supreme Court voted five-to-four to abolish the death penalty. As a result of that decision, over six hundred prisoners, spanning those thirty-two states, immediately found their death sentences commuted to life.

In today's politically charged atmosphere, it is hard to imagine that when this lightning-rod decision was announced forty years ago, the five justices in the majority of the decision did not offer their written opinions to the public for dissemination of their reasoning, but issued a simple public statement. However, the short statement did include opinions expressed by both Justice Potter Stewart and Justice Byron R. White, that while the decision was based on concerns about the "inconsistent application" of the death penalty, it did not preclude the possibility of a constitutional death penalty law.

This open-ended opinion gave way to a new wave of legislation that would eventually lead to thirty-seven states enacting new death penalty statutes by 1976, an increase of five states before the 1972 Supreme Court decision. It would be ten years before any of these states would carry out a legal execution, and nearly thirty years before the state of Colorado would do so. In 1988, Colorado state law instituted lethal injection as the method of execution, thereby replacing the infamous gas chamber.[32]

Thus, the 1967 execution of quadruple murderer Luis Jose Monge has the dubious historic distinction of not only being the last execution in the nation pending the Supreme Court ruling of 1972, Monge was also the last convicted murderer to be executed in the gas chamber in Colorado.[33]

1940 - 1961

Notes to Part V

1. Denver Public Library Western History Collection, Clippings - Denver Murders.
2. Melrose, Rocky Mountain Memories.
3. The Rocky Mountain News, "Spider Man Murder Made Attics A Spooky Place To Be," September 9, 1999.
4. Denver Murders.
5. ibid.
6. ibid.
7. The Rocky Mountain News, December 3, 1953.
8. The People v. Leick, 281 P.2d 806, 813, 1955.
9. The People v. Leick, 322 P.2d 674, 688, denied, 357 U.S. 922, 1958.
10. The People v. Leick, 345 P.2d 1054, 1057, 1959.
11. The Denver Post, January 23, 1960.
12. The Rocky Mountain News, January 23, 1960.
13. Smiley, History of Denver, and Pulcipher, The Pioneer Western Bank; First of Denver 1860-1980.
14. The Rocky Mountain News, November 2, 1955.
15. The Denver Post, November 2, 1955.
16. The Rocky Mountain News, November 2, 1955.
17. Nash, Bloodletters and Bad Men, pg. 149.
18. People v. Graham, 302 P.2d 737
19. The Denver Post, June 12, 1957.
20. Colorado State Penitentiary Archives.
21. Confession of Walter J. Hammil. Court trial transcript.
22. ibid.
23. Colorado Supreme Court case #19377.
24. Baum, Citizen Coors, pg. 55.
25. ibid.
26. ibid, pages 57 and 58.
27. ibid.
28. Colorado State Penitentiary Archives.
29. The Denver Post investigative reporter, Kevin Vaughan, wrote extensively on the life of Joseph Corbett and his subsequent suicide in the August 30, 2009 issue of the paper.
30. ibid.
31. Monge v. People, 406 P. 674, 676 (Colorado filing, 1965).
32. Lamm and Smith, Pioneers & Politicians, pg. 164.
33. The Congressional Quarterly Researcher, March 10, 1995 Volume 5, No. 9.
34. The Denver Post, June 3, 1967.
35. Wommack, From the Grave, pg. 359.
36. Gary Davis was executed at the Colorado State Penitentiary in October of 1997 for the murder of Virginia May.
37. That very gas chamber is on exhibit at the Museum of Colorado Prisons in Cañon City with a brief description of the history and Monge's death.

ADDENDUM

Murder and Capital Punishment in Colorado
A Chronology of the First Century

•**1859:** The citizens of Denver City assembled and adopted The People's Court of law, later agreed to by the Kansas Territory officials. Judge Seymour became the first judge of the court, declaring, "...we the people are the power here."

•**1859:** The hanging of convicted murderer, John Stuffle, is the first recorded incident of The People's Court carrying out the legally mandated execution in Colorado. He became the first person to die by legally mandated execution in Colorado.

•**1860:** The last trial conducted by The People's Court resulting in an execution was that of Patrick Waters. Convicted of murder, he was hanged on December 21, 1860.

•**1861**: The Colorado Territory is established and The People's Court is abolished. Civil and criminal laws, including a formal death-penalty law are adopted by Governor William Gilpin and the Territorial Congress.

•**1876:** Colorado achieves statehood. The Centennial State's first legislature adopts both the 1868 death penalty statute as well as the 1870 provision amending it. The form of execution is death by hanging.

•**1887:** Colorado lawmakers introduce legislation to abolish public hangings after the horrific execution of Andrew Green in 1886. Governor Benjamin H. Eaton declared: "The public execution of criminals sentenced to death should be expressly prohibited by law. It is not the intention of the law to make the agonizing atonement of the condemned furnish forth an entertainment for the depraved. The execution should take place in seclusion, attended only by the executioner and a regularly inpanelled jury." The bill dies in committee.

•**1889:** Colorado lawmakers pass legislation remanding all executions to be carried out under the jurisdiction of the warden at the Colorado State Penitentiary, in Canon City. Governor Job A. Cooper signs the bill into law. Thus, the execution of Andrew Green is the last public hanging in Denver.

•**1897:** Legislation is introduced and passed by both the House and the Senate, abolishing the death penalty. Signed into law by Governor Alva Adams, the law reduced the previous penalty to life imprisonment at hard labor for defendants convicted of first-degree murder. Governor Adams said the repeal of the death penalty was "The most forward step in criminal legislation that has yet been taken in Colorado."

•**1901:** Following the sensational and very public lynching of Thomas Reynolds in 1900, public outcry caused the state legislature to once again debate the issue of capital punishment. On March 29, 1901, a bill to reinstate capital punishment in the state of Colorado passed with bipartisan support. Governor James B. Orman did not sign the bill, nor did he veto it. Thus, on July 31, 1901, capital punishment was once again reinstated in Colorado.

•**1934:** The decade of the 1930s became Colorado's busiest decade for executions — twenty-five hangings took place, seven in 1930 alone. With the hanging of Eddie Ives in January 1930, the Colorado legislature voiced their displeasure of the state's method of carrying out the death penalty. The two-year debate included testimony on both sides of the issue. Thomas J. Tynan, prison warden from 1909 to 1927, said, "Colorado has one of the most ghastly hanging machines possible. More than half of the men executed at Canon City have not been hanged at all. They have strangled." In March 1933, the Colorado Senate passed a bill abolishing the death penalty by a vote of twenty to twelve, however, the bill later died in the House of Representatives. That same year, President Franklin D. Roosevelt called for a national end of the death penalty. While this action failed, several states, including Colorado (the second state to do so) did pass legislation formally changing the state's method of execution from "hanging to asphyxiation." -Radelet, University of Colorado.

•**1934:** During the year of 1934, there were sixty-nine hangings and thirty-two executions by gas in the country.

•**1972:** The U.S. Supreme Court agreed to hear arguments regarding the constitutionality of capital punishment. The case was argued on the grounds that it violated the Eighth Amendment of the Constitution: "cruel and unusual punishment." As the Supreme Court reviewed the issue and heard oral arguments on both sides, the lower courts in all states which had the death penalty law stayed all pending executions.

In Colorado, Governor John Love issued a moratorium on pending executions until the decision of the Supreme Court was announced. The decision before the Court relied on the 1972 case of *Furman v. Georgia, 408 U.S. 238.* In this case, the Georgia court had ruled that by imposing the death penalty, the act was indeed unconstitutional on the very grounds of "cruel and unusual punishment" and a direct violation of the Eighth Amendment to the United States Constitution. In 1972, when the Supreme Court handed down their decision abolishing the death penalty, in a five-to-four decision, there were thirty-two states in the country which had a death penalty law, including Colorado. As a result of that decision, over six hundred prisoners, spanning those thirty-two states, immediately found their death sentences commuted to life in prison.

317

BIBLIOGRAPHY

Primary Sources
Arapahoe County District Court Records.
Colorado State Archives Correction Records.
Colorado State Division of Vital Statistics
Colorado State Penitentiary Index 1871 - 1973.
Colorado Supreme Court Archives
Denver County District Court Records.
Local History Center, Canon City Public Library. Canon City, Colorado.
Witness statements to Warden Clarence P. Hoyt:
   Frank "Kid" Wallace, and Anton Woode Statement, January 1900, pages 1-9.
   Anton Woode Statement Given To C. P. Hoyt. January, 1900: pages 1-9.
   Lawrence, W. E. Statement Given To C. P. Hoyt. January, 1900: pages 1-9.
   Starke, Fred. Statement Given To C. P. Hoyt. January, 1900: page 1-9. Local
   History Center, Canon City Colorado.

State and Federal Documental Archives and Sources
The National Archives and Records Administration. Denver Federal Center.
Report on Indian Affairs by the Acting Commissioner, including the years of 1865,
   1866, 1867, and 1868. Washington D. C.
U. S. Congress, House of Representatives, Massacre of Cheyenne Indians. Report of
   the Joint Committee on the Conduct of War, 38th Congress, 2nd Session.
Report of the Joint Special Committee. "The Chivington Massacre." Appointed Under
   Resolution of March 3, 1865. "The Chivington Massacre."
U. S. Department of the Interior; Bureau of Indian Affairs. Annual Report, 1865.
U. S. Senate."Sand Creek Massacre" Report of the Secretary of War. Senate Document
   26, 39th Congress, 2nd Session, 1867.
U. S. War Department, War of the Rebellion. Official Records of the Union and
   Confederate Armies. Four series, 128 volumes.

Archival Sources and unpublished works
Chavez History Library, Palace of the Governors, Santa Fe, New Mexico. Angelico
   Fray Collection
Colorado History Center
Cherry Creek Settlements, MSS 194, Box 5.
Crimes in Denver, 1859-1864, Owen, Elizabeth.
Diary of William Larimer Jr.
   Fred Mazzulla Collection
Howe, Sam, Sam Howe Murder Book, 1883-1920
Howe, Sam, Sam Howe Scrapbooks, 1883- 1915
Indian Affairs Ledger Book, John Evans Collection
Kehler John H. Collection, MSS 721.

Soule Silas S. Papers, MSS 982.
United States Military Commission reports of Camp Weld.
Wynkoop, Edward W. Unfinished Colorado History, 1876, MSS 695.
Denver Public Library Western History Department
    Denver Red Book: A Reliable Directory of the Pleasure Resorts of Denver, 1892.
    Silas Soule Papers
    William Wise scrapbook
Memorial Booklet for Father Leo Heinrichs.
Hemphill, Anne E. Collection, Silas Soule and Hersa Coberly Soule Letters, Byron Strom, custodian.

Newspapers
The various local newspaper archives accessed for this work are foot-noted or cited in the exact quotes used throughout the text.

Books
Abbott, Carl, Leonard, Stephen and Noel, Thomas J. *Colorado; A History of the Centennial State*. Fifth Edition, University Press of Colorado, 2013. Barker, Bill and Lewin, Jackie. Denver. Doubleday & Co., 1972.
Baum, Dan. *Citizen Coors; A Grand Family Saga of Business, Politics, and Beer*. Harper Collins Publishers, 2000.
Buchanan, Joseph R. *The Story of a Labor Agitator*. Outlook Publishing, 1903.
Casey, Lee (editor). *Denver Murders*. Duell, Sloan and Pearce, 1946.
Cook, David J. *Hands Up*. Originally published in 1882, republished by The Narrative Press, 2001.
Denver Police Department. *The Denver Police Department Pictorial Review and History, 1859-1985.*
Dial, Scott. *The Saloons of Denver*. Old Army Press, 1973.
Dorsett, Lyle. *The Queen City; A History of Denver*. Pruett Publishing, 1977.
Dunn, William R., Lt. Colonel. *I Stand By Sand Creek: A Defense of Colonel John M. Chivington and the Third Colorado Cavalry*. The Old Army Press, 1985.
Fowler, Gene. *Timber Line: Denver — The Rip Roaring Years*. Ballantine Books, 1933.
Goodstein, Phil. *The Seamy Side of Denver*. New Social Publications, 1993.
Greene, Jerome A. and Scott, Douglas D. F*inding Sand Creek: History, Archeology, and the 1864 Massacre Site*. University of Oklahoma Press, 2004.
Hoig, Stan. *The Sand Creek Massacre*. University of Oklahoma Press, 1980.
Hollister, Ovando J. *Boldly They Rode: A History of the First Colorado Regiment of Volunteers*. Golden Press, 1949.
Hollister, Ovando J. *History of the First Regiment of Colorado Volunteers in New Mexico*, 1862. R.R. Donnelley & Sons, 1962.
King, William M. *Going to Meet A Man: Denver's Last Legal Public Execution, 27 July 1886.* University Press of Colorado, 1990.
Kraft, Louis. *Ned Wynkoop and the Lonely Road From Sand Creek*. University of Oklahoma Press, 2011.
Kreck, Dick. *Anton Woode: Boy Murderer.* Fulcrum Publishing, 2006.
Kreck, Dick. *Murder at the Brown Palace: A True Story of Seduction & Betrayal.*

BIBLIOGRAPHY

Fulcrum Publishing, 2003.

Kreck, Dick. *Smaldone, The Untold Story of an American Crime Family*. Fulcrum Publishing, 2009.

Lamm, Richard D. and Smith, Duane A. *Pioneers & Politicians, 10 Colorado Governors in Profile*. Pruett Publishing, 1984.

Leonard, Stephen J. *Lynching in Colorado: 1859-1919*. University Press of Colorado, 2002.

McGinn, Elinor M. *Female Felons: Colorado's Nineteenth Century Inmates*. Fremont-Custer County Historical Society, 2001.

Marr, Josephine Lowell. *Douglas County: A Historical Journey*. B & B Printers, 1983.

Melrose, Frances. *Rocky Mountain Memories*, Denver Publishing Company, 1986.

Miller, Max. *Holladay Street*. Signet Publishers, 1962.

Nash, Jay Robert. *Bloodletters and Bad Men*. Warner Books, 1973.

Noel, Thomas J. *The City and the Saloon*. University of Nebraska Press, 1982.

Noel, Thomas J. *Colorado Catholicism*. University Press of Colorado, 1989.

Ortiz, Lenny. *Denver Behind Bars: The History of the Denver Sheriff Department & Denver's Jail System, 1858-1956*. Aventine Press, 2004.

Owens, *Sister Lilliana*. St. Mary's. Self-published, 1940.

Pikes Peak Gold Rush Guidebooks of 1859. Edited and republished, Arthur H. Clark & Company, 1941.

Parkhill, Forbes. *Wildest of the West*. Henry Holt and Company, 1951.

Roberts, Gary L. *Sand Creek, Tragedy and Symbol*. University of Oklahoma Press, 1984.

Patterson, Wayne K, and Alt, Betty L. *Slaughter in Cell House 3*. VanderGeest Publishing, 1997.

Pulcipher, Robert S. *The Pioneer Western Bank: First of Denver 1860-1980*. First Interstate Bank of Denver and Robert S. Pulcipher, publishers, 1984.

Roberts, Gary L. and Halass, David F. *Written in Blood: The Soule-Cramer Sand Creek Massacre Letters*. Reprinted by Fulcrum Press, 2004.

Secrest, Clark. *Hell's Belles: Prostitution, Vice, and Crime in Early Denver*. University Press of Colorado, 2002.

Smiley, Jerome C. *History of Denver*. Times-Sun Publishing Company, 1901.

Smith, Duane A. *Rocky Mountain Mining Camps*. University Press of Colorado, 1992.

Smith, Duane A. *The Birth of Colorado: A Civil War Perspective*. University of Oklahoma Press, 1989.

Smith, Jeff. *Alias Soapy Smith: The Life and Death of a Scoundrel*. Klondike Research, 2009.

Smiley, Jerome. *History of Denver*. The Denver Times, 1901.

Stevenson, Malcolm. *In the High Country: Settlers on the Land of Golden Gate State Park*. Reprinted by Birdwood Press, 2009.

Student, Annette L. *Denver's Riverside Cemetery: Where History Lies*. CSN Books, 2006.

Turner, Carol. *Notorious Jefferson County: Frontier Murder and Mayhem*. The History Press, 2010.

Ubbelohde, Carl, Benson, Maxine, and Smith, Duane. *A Colorado History*. Pruett Publishing, 1976.

Van Cise, Philip. *Fighting the Underworld*. Houghton Mifflin Company, 1936.

Washburn, Josie. *The Underworld Sewer: A Prostitute Reflects on Life in the Trade, 1871-1909*. University of Nebraska Press, 1997.

Whitmore, Julie. *A History of Colorado State Penitentiary, 1871-1980*. Self-published, 1983.

Wommack, Linda. *From the Grave: A Roadside Guide to Colorado's Pioneer Cemeteries*. Caxton Press, 1998.

Wommack, Linda. *Our Ladies of the Tenderloin: Colorado's Legends in Lace*. Caxton Press, 2005.

Wynkoop, Edward W. *The Tall Chief: The Autobiography of Edward W. Wynkoop*. Edited by Christopher B. Gerboth, Colorado Historical Society, 1993.

Zamonski, Stanley W. and Keller, Teddy. *The '59er's Roaring Denver in the Gold Rush Days: The First Three Years*. Platte 'N Press, 1961.

Magazines, Periodicals and Historical Journal Articles

Cobb, Frank. M. The Lawrence Part of Pike's Peakers and the Founding of St. Charles, *Colorado Magazine*, September, 1933, pg. 194-97.

Gower, Calvin W. Vigilantes, *Colorado Magazine*, Spring, 1964, pg. 93-104.

Isern, Tom. Dueling in Denver, *Denver Post Empire*, November 28, 1976, pg. 10.

Kraft, Louis. When Wynkoop Was Sheriff, *Wild West Magazine*, April 2011.

Milavec, Pam. Alias Emma S. Soule: Corrected Historical Fictions Surrounding Silas Soule and the Sand Creek Massacre. *Denver Westerners Roundup*, July-August, 2005.

Parkhill, Forbes. Scarlet Sister Mattie. *Denver Westerners Brand Book*, 1948.

Parkhill, Forbes. Pioneer Denver Mint Robbery. *Denver Westerner's Monthly Roundup*, Vol. XIII, August, 1957.

Perkins, LaVonne. Silas Soule, His Widow Heresa [sic], and the Rest of the Story. *Denver Westerners Roundup*, Mar-Apr, 1999.

Prentice, C. A., Captain Silas S. Soule, a Pioneer Martyr. *Colorado Magazine*, Nov-Dec, 1935.

Radelet, Michael L. *CU-Boulder Law Review*, 2009.

Romero, Tom I. II, Western Legal Studies Fellow, Last Night Was the End of the World: Prohibition in Colorado, *University of Colorado-Boulder*, 2008.

Williams, Francis S. Trials and Judgments of the People's Court of Denver, *Colorado Magazine*, October 1950.

Wommack, Linda. Tragedy at Sand Creek, *True West Magazine*, September, 2003.

Wommack, Linda. In The Eye of the Storm; The Sand Creek Massacre, *True West Magazine*, November, 2003.

Wommack, Linda. Mo-chi: The First Female Cheyenne Warrior, *Wild West Magazine*, 2008.

Wommack, Linda. Assassination: Silas Soule, *Wild West History Journal*, August 2012.

Wortman, Roy T. Denver's Anti-Chinese Riot, 1880. *Colorado Magazine*, Fall 1962.

Wunder, John R. Anti-Chinese Violence in the American West, 1850-1910.

THE AUTHOR

A Colorado native, Linda Wommack, is a Colorado historian and historical consultant. Her books include *From the Grave: Colorado's Pioneer Cemeteries, Our Ladies of the Tenderloin: Colorado's Legends in Lace, Colorado History for Kids, Colorado's Landmark Hotels*, and *Colorado's Historic Mansions and Castles, Colorado Gambling, A History of the Early Days* and *Cripple Creek Tailings.*

Linda has been a contributing editor for *True West Magazine* since 1995. She has also been a staff writer, contributing a monthly article for *Wild West Magazine* since 2004. She has also writes for *The Tombstone Epitaph*, the nation's oldest continuously published newspaper, since 1993. Linda also writes for several publications throughout her state.

Linda's research has been used in several documentary accounts for the national Wild West History Association, historical treatises of the Sand Creek Massacre, as well as critical historic aspects for the new Lawman & Outlaw Museum in Cripple Creek, Colorado.

Linda feeds her passion for history with activities in many local, state, and national preservation projects, participating in historical venues, including speaking engagements, hosting tours, and is involved in historical reenactments across the state.

As a longtime member of the national Western Writers of America, she has served as a judge for the acclaimed national Spur Awards in Western Americana literature for eight years. She is a member of both the state and national Cemetery Preservation Associations, the Gilpin County Historical Society, the national

Wild West History Association and an honorary lifetime member of the Pikes Peak Heritage Society. As a member of Women Writing the West, Linda has organized quarterly meetings for the Colorado members of WWW for the past seven years and served on the 2014 WWW Convention Steering Committee. Linda is currently serving as a member of WWW Board.

INDEX

325

For a free catalog of Caxton titles write to:

CAXTON PRESS
312 Main Street
Caldwell, Idaho 83605-3299

or

Visit our Internet web site:

www.caxtonpress.com

Caxton Press is a division of THE CAXTON PRINTERS, Ltd.